READER RESPONSE
IN THE
CLASSROOM

READER RESPONSE
IN THE
CLASSROOM

EVOKING AND INTERPRETING MEANING IN LITERATURE

NICHOLAS J. KAROLIDES
EDITOR

University of Wisconsin, River Falls

Longman
New York & London

READER RESPONSE IN THE CLASSROOM:
EVOKING AND INTERPRETING MEANING IN LITERATURE

Longman, 95 Church Street, White Plains, N.Y. 10601

Associated companies:
Longman Group Ltd., London
Longman Cheshire Pty., Melbourne
Longman Paul Pty., Auckland
Copp Clark Pitman, Toronto

Senior editor: Naomi Silverman
Production editor: Marcy Gray
Cover design: Renée Edelman
Production supervisor: Joanne Jay

Library of Congress Cataloging-in-Publication Data

Karolides, Nicholas J.
    Reader Response in the Classroom: Evoking
and Interpreting Meaning in Literature / by Nicholas J.
Karolides.
        p.   .cm.
    Includes bibliographical references and index.
    ISBN 0-8013-0792-9
    1. Reader-response criticism.   2. Literature—Study and teaching.
I. Title.
PN98.R38K37   1991
801'.95—dc20   91-20137
                                                            CIP

1 2 3 4 5 6 7 8 9 10-MA-9594939291

CREDITS

To Louise M. Rosenblatt
Teacher, Mentor, Friend

Contents

Preface

The upsurge of reader-response criticism has caught the attention of many teachers at all levels of instruction. This consciousness has been fomented by an array of books on response-centered critical theory as well as numerous journal articles and conference presentations. Thus the words *reader response* (which are generally applied to a range of theoretical positions) have moved into the mainstream, in effect rocking the boat of traditional literary thinking and instruction. Yet, practice and, perhaps, full understanding of the pedagogical implications of reader-response theory, have not followed principle.

The focus of these writers has been primarily theory—deciphering and clarifying the reading process, determining the role of the reader in relation to the text, exploring how meaning is made, defining the nature of the interpretive act, and assessing the influence of reading communities and literature conventions. In these analyses, there is evident a continuum of reader-response thinking, a range of attitudes with considerable disagreement among theorists (see Mailloux, Suleiman and Crosman, and Tompkins). However, each acknowledges the significant and active role of the reader, an assumption that runs counter to the premises of traditional theories.

This volume is based on the transactional model of literature asserted by Louise M. Rosenblatt. Soundly expressive of each aspect of response-centered critical theory, it is pedagogically the most meaningful for teachers. As detailed within this text, her approach insists on the reader's role in conjunction with the text, the reader's individuality affecting and being affected by the text. In contrast, other theoretical positions give prominence to the reader or to the text. However, this volume is not specifically concerned with close scrutiny of these variations and emphases. Rather, it focuses on the application of the transactional theory of literature, activating it in the classroom, expressing theory as background.

Frequent requests for teaching suggestions—how to put theory into practice—establish the need for this book. Furthermore, some teachers seem to believe that reader response somehow refers to helping students relate to the texts they have been assigned to read—a motivational lesson, perhaps, to hook them. Once accomplished, the next step is to revert to a traditional analysis of structure and techniques or a search for the author's presumed meaning. Teachers and prospective teachers seem ready to learn more about the transactional reader-response approach in the classroom.

Thus, this group of original chapters is proposed not simply as a what-should-I-do-on-Monday cookbook but as an expression of the practice of theory. The chapters portray a spectrum of strategies, using as examples individual works from the several genres. Although a chapter may focus on a particular technique, other procedures or processes are often conjoined with it to illustrate developmental patterns in a lesson or sequence of lessons.

The authors of these chapters are cognizant that teachers, who may have been trained in other theories and methodologies, may not be ready for their quite different role and expectations in the reader-centered classroom. The spontaneity and unpredictability may be discomforting, indeed, unnerving, at the outset. Students, too, may not be ready to take on primary reactive roles. They may already have been trained that literature study is recall of data, definition of forms and techniques, and learning of codified interpretations prescribed by their teachers. Recognizing these attributes, the authors have provided stepping stones to develop readiness and confidence, suggestions and insights to ease the passage into the transactional model of teaching and learning.

In order to facilitate understanding of classroom processes, the chapters are arranged in four sections. The first section establishes the transactional theory of literature—its significant features and understandings. The two sections that follow draw attention to the initiation of readers' responses to literature but also to developing those responses, that is, exploring, expanding, reconsidering, and refining these responses in relation to the text. The concluding section focuses on the exploration of differences among readers in responding to texts. (An explanatory introduction precedes each section.)

The genesis of this book may be traced back to my undergraduate and graduate study at New York University. I am particularly indebted to Louise M. Rosenblatt who imbued me with the essence of the transactional theory of literature both in the discussion and modeling of it. She inspired me to create this book. Moreover, her criticism of and suggestions for the theory chapter were most valuable.

I wish to extend appreciation to the chapter authors for their contribution of meaningful chapters and for their cooperative willingness to undertake revisions; the strength of the book in large measure results from this joint effort. My sincere thanks also go to my colleagues, David Furniss and Marshall Toman, for their readiness to react to chapters or passages as potential readers and critics; their comments were direct, honest, and helpful. In this vein, I also thank Jeffrey T. Rissman, graduate student and high school teacher, whose thoughtful reading of the theory chapter gave me special audience insights, and James C. Anderson, who reacted to the glossary from the same perspective with comparably meaningful insights. I acknowledge with professional respect my editor, Naomi Silverman, of Longman Publishing Group for her insightful advice and editing, and her enthusiastic belief in this book.

I am also deeply grateful to my family for their consistent support: to Inga Karolides, especially, for her sensitive sense of language nuances and meaning.

Nicholas J. Karolides
University of Wisconsin, River Falls

Contributors

Deborah Appleman is assistant professor of Educational Studies at Carleton College, Minnesota. She has published articles and book chapters on adolescent response to literature, adolescent alienation, and teaching poetry. She was a high school English teacher for nine years.

Marilyn Hanf Buckley, formerly a teacher in the public schools of California, is active in the writing and literature programs in California and Alaska. Her PhD dissertation on language and thought was recognized by the National Council of Teachers of English (NCTE) for the Promising Research Award. Presently, she is an associate professor at the University of Alaska at Anchorage.

Jean E. Brown, professor at Saginaw Valley State University, Michigan, is a past president of the Michigan Council of Teachers of English and currently edits the Council's newsletter. She is the co-author of *Toward Literacy: Theory and Practice in Teaching Writing in the Content Areas.*

Leila Christenbury is associate professor of English Education at Virginia Commonwealth University. She directs the Capital Writing Project and currently is serving on the executive board of the Conference on English Education and as the co-editor of *The ALAN Review.* She has co-authored *Questioning: A Path to Critical Thinking.*

Frank C. Cronin, professor of English, Ohio University, has published over sixty articles on rhetoric and the teaching of English in such journals as *Research in the Teaching of English* and *Written Communication.* He has been president of the Southeastern Ohio Council of Teachers of English and a high school principal and teacher for four years.

James E. Davis is professor of English at Ohio University. He is president-elect of the National Council of Teachers of English. He has served as chair of the executive board of the Conference on English Education. His publications include *Dealing with Censorship, Your Reading* (a bibliography), and numerous articles, published in a wide range of journals.

Ogle Burks Duff, an associate professor of English Education at the University of Pittsburgh, has served as the university's director of the Race Desegregation Assistance Center. She has spoken and consulted nationally and internationally on issues related to school desegregation and multicultural education. Dr. Duff has taught high school English.

David Furniss is an assistant professor of English at the University of Wisconsin, River Falls, and serves as director of Freshman English. Prior to this, he taught high school English in Connecticut and Minnesota. His courses include Literature for Adolescents, Composition Theory, and Freshman English. He has written about Vietnam War literature, baseball literature, and composition teaching.

Louise Garcia Harrison, a finalist in 1990 for Michigan Teacher of the Year, teaches in the Saginaw (Michigan) Public Schools, 9th grade at South Intermediate and grades nine through twelve at the Center for the Arts and Sciences, a school for gifted students. Currently, she serves as secondary section chair for the Michigan Council of Teachers of English.

Nicholas J. Karolides, professor of English and associate dean, College of Arts and Sciences, at the University of Wisconsin-River Falls, has served on the Conference of English Education executive board and as editor of the *Wisconsin English Journal.* He frequently consults with school districts about curriculum development. His major publications include: *The Pioneer in the American Novel, Celebrating Censored Books* (editor), and *Focus on Physical Impairments.*

Patricia P. Kelly, formerly a high school English teacher, is an associate professor at Virginia Tech. She directs the Southwest Virginia Writing Project, is editor of *SIGNAL,* the young adult literature publication of the International Reading Association (IRA), and is co-editor of the *Virginia English Bulletin.* She co-authored *Questioning: A Path to Critical Thinking.*

Ron Luce is teaching at Hocking Technical College in Nelsonville, Ohio. He has published poems, articles on innovative teaching techniques and the teaching of writing, and in-house texts for the technical college. He is president-elect of the Southeastern Ohio Council of Teachers of English.

Elizabeth Ann Poe, a high school English teacher for 13 years, is assistant professor of English education at the University of Wisconsin-Eau Claire. She is president of the Assembly on Literature for Adolescents (ALAN), Book Review Editor for *The ALAN Review,* and author of *Focus on Sexuality: A Reference Handbook.*

Robert E. Probst is professor of English education at Georgia State University. A former secondary school teacher and supervisor of English, he is the author of *Response and Analysis: Teaching Literature in Junior and Senior High School* as well as numerous articles on the teaching of literature and composition. He has served on the National Council of Teachers of English Committee on Research, the Commission on Reading and on the board of directors of the Adolescent Literature Assembly.

Laura Quinn is visiting associate professor of English at Allegheny College, Pennsylvania. She has published articles and reviews on Victorian popular fiction, feminist issues, ethnic women writers, and censorship.

Duane Roen, associate professor of English at the University of Arizona, has co-edited *Richness in Writing: Empowering ESL Students* and *A Sense of Audience in Written Communication,* and has co-authored *Becoming Expert: Writing and Learning in the Disciplines.* He has also published nearly forty chapters and articles.

Mary Jo Schaars teaches at Stevens Point Area Senior High School in Wisconsin. Her professional publications include articles on teaching *My Antonia, Thoreau,* and the writing of poetry to high school students.

Anne Sherrill is professor of English at East Tennessee State University. Publications include *Voices of Readers: How We Come to Love Books* and *Four Elements: A*

Creative Approach to the Short Story, both co-authored. She is a reviewer for *The ALAN Review* and has had articles published in various professional journals.

Robert Small is past chair of both the Assembly on Literature for Adolescents of the National Council of Teachers of English and the Conference on English Education. He is currently co-editor of *The ALAN Review* and chair of the Intellectual Freedom Committee of the International Reading Association. He is dean of the College of Education, Radford University, Virginia.

Marshall Toman, an assistant professor of English and coordinator of the Ethnic Studies Program at the University of Wisconsin, River Falls, has completed a book-length manuscript, "Nonsense and Sensibility," a study of Joseph Heller's novels. He has previously published in *Studies in Contemporary Satire, The Explicator,* and *Literature and Belief.*

PART I

The Transactional Theory of Literature

The theoretical base for the teaching strategies exhibited in this book is represented in this section. The active, central role of the reader in concert with the text is expressed; in conjunction, the role of the teacher in the instructional setting is clarified. The authors provide discussion of theory and explanation of methodological principles. They also provide transcripts of class discussions and excerpts of journals to illustrate and validate their points.

The first chapter provides an experience of response-based instruction in contrast to traditional teaching methodology. The essay invites comparative analysis. The other chapters are direct in their explanation of reader-response theory but the authors also include appropriate illustrations to entice the pedagogical imagination. Embedded in the presentations are examples of teaching approaches and suggestions that may be usefully applied to other learning situations.

What role does the teacher play in the response-oriented classroom? What goals are sought? In Chapter 1, Robert C. Small, Jr. compares the attitudes and questioning procedures of two teachers, one with a traditional, the other with a response orientation. A transcript of both classes discussing "A Bird Came Down the Walk" by Emily Dickinson provides a meaningful contrast of processes and learnings. He clarifies the goals implicit in these strategies, and in the planning conducted by the teachers. Small establishes the active, experiences of the readers—in contrast to the carefully orchestrated hunt for the traditional teacher's predetermined answers.

In Chapter 2, Nicholas J. Karolides expresses the dynamics of the reading act as a transactional process. He discusses the reader's active, central role and the factors that influence the preliminary and ongoing responses to the text.

The concept of selective attention and the impact of the stance—aesthetic or efferent—a reader takes toward the reading are among the factors examined. The possibility of more than one valid response to a text is asserted and illustrated, this resulting both from the differences among readers and the dynamic nature of the text itself. Karolides concludes by describing the classroom processing of transactional theory as well as its impact on teacher attitudes and classroom activities.

Leila Christenbury builds her discussion in Chapter 3 of reader-response methodology on the dual premises that selected literature must have some connection with students' lives and the teaching approach must be inductive. She identifies five guiding principles: encouraging extensive student talk; making a community of meaning; asking not telling; linking to personal experience; and affirming students' responses. These are illustrated in the teaching of three poems in two classrooms. The apparent understandings generated in these discussions affirm that students can make meaning out of their responses. Moreover, they affirm that student discussion need not be limited to a question-short answer format with the teacher spoon-feeding the "correct" interpretation.

The central questions raised by Marilyn Hanf Buckley in Chapter 4 are directed at teachers: How do you read? How might you read? These lead to parallel questions about students' reading that are pedagogical in nature. In this chapter she concentrates on strategies for teachers to discover how they read and to examine conditions for effecting curricular change. She demonstrates the process of teachers reflecting on their own reading processes with extended excerpts from teachers' reading journals and self-analyses. Buckley outlines stages in the procedure of such research leading to curriculum change.

CHAPTER 1

Connecting Students and Literature:

What Do Teachers Do and Why Do They Do It?

Robert C. Small, Jr.

HELEN JOHNSON'S CLASS

It is a Monday in late February, 10:45 in the morning. Helen Johnson is ready to begin her poetry unit with her third-period, seventh-grade class. She has taught this unit a number of times, and she always looks forward to it, especially because it begins with several poems by Emily Dickinson, one of her favorite poets. Her knowledge of the life, poems, and critical material on Dickinson is rich and extensive, and she enjoys sharing it with her students.

"Today," she begins, "we're going to start our poetry unit with a couple of poems by Emily Dickinson. Does anyone know anything about her?"

The students look at her. Nobody moves.

"Well," Ms. Johnson continues, "has anyone ever read any of her poems?"

After a pause, Martha raises her hand. "Did she write a poem about two toy animals waiting for the dead little boy who owned them? I remember reading that back in elementary school."

"No, Martha, I don't think so." Helen Johnson smiles at her, "But I'm glad you remember that poem." She pauses, "Anyway, because none of you have read any of Emily Dickinson's poems, this'll be a good chance to get to know her. So, first, I'm going to tell you a little bit about her. Then we'll study those poems. She's one of America's finest writers, and, you know, one of my favorites." She smiles at them while sharing this personal insight.

Her students watch her as she stands behind the speaker's stand. A few take notes. Most sit quietly, waiting. Joe and Susan, in the back row, watch each other. Sam, near the back by the window, has his eyes closed.

After a pause, Ms. Johnson begins her lecture on the life of Dickinson. She emphasizes Dickinson's educated family background, the fact that she published almost none of her poems, that she became a recluse, the individuality of her style. "She chose every word very carefully, as I've urged you to do when you write compositions for me. But she also chose unusual words at times, words that make us stop and think about what she means. And sometimes she gives us an example and then leaves it up to us to see what it is an example of."

Having finished the formal part of her lecture, Helen moves to the teacher's desk at the side of the room and leans back against it. "So, I've got to admit her poetry isn't the easiest in the world to read. But I know you can handle it. After all, you're in the seventh grade now. And the ideas are so fresh, the language so perfectly right, you'll find it worth the effort."

The lecture and the period conclude with an assignment: "For tomorrow," she says, "I want you to read the poem on page 23 in your books, 'A Bird Came Down the Walk.' It's one of her easier poems, so you shouldn't have any trouble with it."

She pauses for the class to write the assignment in their notebooks. "Before you read it, be sure to read the biographical sketch of Dickinson in the back of the book on page 403. And don't forget to read what the textbook tells you about the poem in the headnote. It seems to me like a very good introduction to the poem.

"And remember how we read poetry. Robin, can you remind us how we read poetry?"

Robin frowns with the effort to remember. "Uh, we read through it all the way without trying to stop to figure things out." She stops. "Is that right?"

"Right. And then?"

Robin smiles. "Then we read through it again, stopping to worry . . ."

"Think about."

"Think about the ideas and words."

"Very good, Robin. And don't forget to use the notes in the margin. They'll help you understand hard words and some references you might not know. And watch for the metaphors that Dickinson uses at the end of this poem. Like most poets, she's writing about something more than the poem may seem to be about." The bell rings.

A day has passed, and it is third period again.

"Today," says Helen Johnson, "we're going to discuss the Emily Dickinson poem you were assigned to read last night, 'A Bird Came Down the Walk.' Open your books to page 23."

There is rustle as the students pull their books out from their desks. Sam raises his hand.

"Yes, Sam."

"I forgot my book, Miss Johnson."

"Again. Well, don't forget, that's two points off. Now, look on with Dana. And no talking, either one of you."

Sam smirks. Dana looks annoyed.

"Now, is everyone looking at 'A Bird Came Down the Walk'? Okay. It's a poem about something that all of us have seen, so all of you should be able to say what it means. Dana, will you read it to us first so we can all hear how it sounds and what it says?"

Dana, pale, blond, hunches over her anthology and reads smoothly but nervously:

A bird came down the walk:
He did not know I saw;
He bit an angleworm in halves
And ate the fellow, raw.

And then he drank a dew
From a convenient grass,
And then hopped sidewise to the wall
To let a beetle pass.

He glanced with rapid eyes
That hurried all abroad—
They looked like frightened beads, I thought.
He stirred his velvet head

Like one in danger. Cautious
I offered him a crumb,
And he unrolled his feathers
And rowed him softer home

Than oars divide the ocean,
Too silver for a seam,
Or butterflies, off banks of noon,
Leap, plashless, as they swim.

"Thank you, Dana. Very nice." Ms. Johnson looks around the room. "Mark," she asks, "why do you think the poet included the second line?"

Mark studies the text. "Well, the bird doesn't know he's being watched."

"That's right, of course."

Mark sighs.

"But why is that important?"

Mark has not escaped. He re-reads the line. "Well," he stalls.

The class is silent.

"Well, think of it this way: Where does a writer usually tell us the topic of a paragraph? Think of the poem as a theme you're writing for class. Where would you tell me the topic of each paragraph? Mark, do you know?"

Mark has been reading through the poem and doesn't seem to have heard. "Well," he says again. "Well, the bird flies away later when he does know that he's being watched."

"So?" Ms. Johnson prompts.

"And, well, the bird wouldn't act natural if it knows the poet's there, right?" He looks at her hopefully.

"Maybe," she says. Her tone of voice and the expression on her face are not encouraging. "So, Michelle, do you think the poem is about flying birds?"

Michelle understands that it isn't. "No, Miss Johnson."

Michelle has also learned to wait.

"Then what might the poem be about?"

"Being afraid?"

"So where in the poem does Dickinson tell us about being afraid?"

"Well," Michelle continues, encouraged by Ms. Johnson's expression, "I'd guess that the worm was afraid of the bird. And the bird's certainly afraid of the poet."

"Let's look at what she says about the bird being afraid." Ms. Johnson reads, "'He glanced with rapid eyes / That hurried all abroad— / They looked like frightened beads, I thought. / He stirred his velvet head / Like one in danger.'" She pauses. "Notice how she describes him. What do you think 'rapid eyes that hurried all abroad' means? Harry?"

Harry is a small, plump boy, who answers in a thin, high voice, "The eyes are moving back and forth rapidly."

"Right, and what does that mean?"

"It's scared it'll miss something."

"Very good, Harry. And isn't the phrase 'rapid eyes that hurried all abroad' a wonderful picture of just how the eyes of a frightened animal look." She pauses. "But now let me ask you, is the poet afraid? Gale?"

"I don't think so. She admires how the bird flies."

"So, what did the poet do when she saw the bird? Henry?"

"Watched it."

"And what else?" Helen Johnson prompts.

"Offered it food," Henry suggests. "At least I guess that's what she means by 'a crumb.'"

"So how did she feel as she offered it the crumb?"

"Cautious," several students shout.

"One at a time, please. Now, Gale, you told us she wasn't afraid of the bird. What does 'cautious' tell us?"

"I just think she didn't want to scare it away. You know, by moving too fast or something."

"Good, and what did the bird do when he came across the worm? Henry?"

Henry is silent.

"He ate it," Karen shouts out.

"Right," Ms. Johnson says. "But please wait to be called on, Karen."

"Now," she continues after a pause, "What is the poet trying to tell us by describing her encounter with the bird? Karen?"

"That poets and birds are different?"

The class laughs.

"Quiet," Ms. Johnson scolds. "And what is the difference between the poet and the bird?" With a frown, she looks at the class. "Sam, you seemed to think Karen's answer was so funny. Can you answer my question?"

"Could you repeat the question," Sam stalls.

"Certainly. What is the difference between the poet and the bird?"

Sam proposes tentatively, "She can see the bird as beautiful, the way it flew especially."

"Yes, we already said that."

"But the bird only saw the worm as something to eat, right?"

"Right."

"So that's the difference." Sam is clearly frustrated.

"But how did she feel about the bird?"

Dana offers, "She saw it was beautiful, like we've said. And she tried to feed it, so she must have cared about it, or why feed it."

"Right," Ms. Johnson says. "And what does that tell us?"

The class is silent.

"Well, how did the bird feel about her?" Ms. Johnson asks.

"It was afraid of her," several students shout.

"One at a time, please. So we know the poet is sensitive to and aware of the bird, but the bird is self-centered."

Several students write down what Ms. Johnson has just said. Dana raises her hand.

"Yes, Dana?"

"So does the poet look down on the bird because it ate the worm instead of admiring it?"

"No, of course not. Because the poet is sensitive to nature, she knows that the bird is what it is. Notice how she compares the bird's flight to butterflies."

The class is quiet. Martha raises her hand.

"Yes, Martha?"

"Does that mean the bird is like a butterfly?"

"How might they be alike, Martha?"

"They fly"

"And what else?"

Martha shakes her head.

"Does anyone know? Richy?"

Richy, a tall, thin boy who looks older than the other students, speaks in a deep, loud voice. "They're both beautiful too."

"Good. Anything else?"

There are no volunteers. "Well, they're also both a part of nature, aren't they? But what happens then?"

"The bird flies away," several students say.

"And look at how she describes his flying." Helen reads, " 'he unrolled his feathers / And rowed him softer home.' Can't you just see the bird rolling out its wings and moving itself into the air. And then she says the bird rowed itself 'softer home / Than oars divide the ocean, / Too silver for a seam.' What do you think she's comparing the bird's flying to?"

After a delay, Martha raises her hand. "Well, she uses the words 'oars' and 'rowed' and 'ocean' so I'd guess she sees the bird as like somebody rowing a boat in the ocean."

"Excellent, Martha. And what do we call that kind of comparison? Anyone remember?"

No one does.

Helen Johnson moves the blackboard and writes "metaphor." "When a poet—or anyone else, even you or me—compares one thing or action to another without saying so, we call it a metaphor. You might write that in your notebooks. And if the poet tells us that she's made a comparison and uses 'like' or 'as' then we call the comparison a 'simile.' " She writes the word *simile* on the board.

"So, what other comparisons does she make the bird's flying to?"

"Butterflies," Mark offers.

"And what about those butterflies?"

"They're swimming."

"And what else? Michelle?"

"Leaping."

"And the word 'plashless,' as your book tells you, means 'without making splashes.' So these butterflies are swimming and leaping without making splashes. How is that like the rowing of the boat?"

No one answers. "Well, look back at line 18. Notice that the oars don't make a seam in the ocean. And the butterflies don't make splashes. Now what does that tell us about the way the bird's wings move through the air?"

Dana raises her hand. "I guess the bird's wings don't disturb the air either."

"Very good. So the bird flies off softly, as softly as oars that don't even leave a mark on the ocean or butterflies move in the air and don't disturb it either as if they were swimming and diving in water. Isn't it wonderful the way she uses water to compare the bird's flying to and then compares its flying to butterflies in the air and describes the butterflies as if they were also in water. Only a great poet can effortlessly build one metaphor on top of another like that."

She pauses to let them think about that. "But let's go back and think about what the poem's about. Let me ask you a question: Who did we say was watching whom?"

Puzzled at this sudden shift, the students look back at the poem. After a moment, several hands go up.

"Sara?"

"We said the bird was watching the worm. And it also says the bird watched a beetle go by."

"Why do you think it just watched the beetle?"

"Oh," Sara says, "it probably wasn't hungry."

"Does anyone have a different answer? Tom?"

"Well, of course, I don't know. But I bet it would have eaten another worm if it'd found one."

"So?" Helen Johnson prompts.

"So, I'd guess the beetle wasn't something the bird ate. I mean it didn't taste good or was too hard or something like that."

"Anyway, it didn't want to eat it, but it did watch it. OK, so who else was watching whom? Sara?"

"The poet watched the bird."

"Right. And."

"The bird watched the poet before it flew away," several students shout out.

"Okay, one at a time. Now, let me ask one last question: Was anyone else watching anyone else?"

The students looked surprised. "But, Miss Johnson, there isn't anyone else in the poem," Michelle says.

Helen Johnson walks to the blackboard at the front of the room. "Okay, lets make a list." She writes "Bird," "Worm," "Beetle," "Bird," and "Poet." "Now, let's draw an arrow from each watcher to each watchee." She laughs. "If there is such a word."

When they have finished, she asks, "Let's see. Did we get them all?"

Sam speaks up, "Well, the beetle may have been watching the bird. Maybe even the poet."

"But we don't know that, do we, Sam. The poet doesn't tell us."

"No," Sam says sullenly.

"We have to be careful to stick with what the poet actually says. So did we miss any?"

"No," several students call out.

"But we did," Ms. Johnson says. "We forgot that the poet was watching herself."

"How do you know that, Miss Johnson?" Sam asks.

"Well, look at that second line I tried to get Mark to study. What does the poet say?"

Sam mumbles, " 'He did not know I saw.' "

"But she knows that she saw the bird; so she must have been watching herself, not just the bird. And look at line 11. She says, 'They looked like frightened beads, I thought.' So she's still watching herself watching the bird. And then in line 14 she watches herself try to give the bird a crumb. So I'd say she was watching herself as well as the bird, the beetle, and the worm. Does that make sense?"

They watch her.

"And what did we say earlier about the difference between the bird and the poet? Dana?"

"The poet was sensitive but the bird was self-centered."

"And now we know that the poet was the only character in the poem who watched everyone else and also watched herself. What does that tell you?"

"I know," Tony says. "She's human. The others aren't."

"Very good, Tony. And why is that important?"

"Well, the Bible says God made man after His own image, right? And gave man control over the animals. I guess that includes birds and bugs."

"Well, I'm not sure she was thinking of the Bible; but that's close. It seems clear that the poet realizes that only she, the one with intelligence, is able to watch with sensitivity to beauty, to care, and to be aware of her own actions and feelings."

Closing her textbook, Helen Johnson walks back to the speaker's stand. "So much in so few words and such simple words! That's why she's considered one of America's greatest poets. Now, for tomorrow, I want you to read the poem on page 24, "Success Is Counted Sweetest." It's a harder poem in some ways, but I'm sure you can deal with it. Just remember what we did today and you won't have any trouble."

The bell rings.

Later, in the teachers' lounge, when we asked Helen Johnson, "How'd it go today?" she told us, "We had a really good discussion of the poem. It took them awhile, but they finally saw the contrast between the poet's sensitivity for nature and the bird's natural self-centeredness."

JANE GRAHAM'S CLASS

Was Helen Johnson right? Well, consider the following episode in which Jane Graham asks her class to consider the same Emily Dickinson poem that Helen taught her class.

It's that same gray February day. The lights are on and the windows firmly closed in room 202. A sleepy group of seventh-graders sit looking at Ms. Graham, her chair drawn up to their circle.

"Have you ever seen a robin hopping around in your yard?" Ms. Graham asks. She laughs. "They're supposed to be a sign of spring."

Several hands go up.

"You've seen a robin already?" she asks.

"Well, not this year," Karla says. "But we usually have one hoppin' around in March. Sometimes even at the end of February."

"Don't mean a thing around here, does it. I remember a time when we had a dozen robins and then it snowed for two days," Joey says.

The class laughs.

"I remember that year, too, Joey," Ms. Graham says, laughing. "But have you ever watched a robin when he finally did get to your yard?"

"Sure," several students say.

"Well, then, what was that robin doing hopping around?"

"Gettin' worms," the students call out.

"Why, sure," Ms. Graham says. "Did you ever try to save a worm from a bird?" The class is silent. Ms. Graham waits.

"Why do that, Mrs. Graham?" Salley asks. "I mean a worm's a worm. Who cares!"

"Well," Ms. Graham says, "and a bird's a bird and a person's a person. So?"

They wait. She waits.

"You mean worms are important too?" Jerry asks.

"I don't know, are they?"

"The Bible says God created all living things," Jack says. "I guess that makes worms important too."

"And," Greg says, "my dad told me that some people buy worms to put them in their yards because, well, those worms make the ground better, make the grass grow better."

"Is that right?" Ms. Graham exclaims. "I didn't know that. So suppose you watched a robin looking for worms. What do you think you'd see?"

"A bird hoppin' on the grass," John says.

"Sure, and what do you think the robin would see when he saw you were watching him?"

"Me," Alan says.

"True, but what do you think you look like to a robin?"

"Big, I guess," Alan says.

"Real big, I bet," Ms. Graham agrees. "Most of us said we'd watched a robin. Why do you think we did that?"

"Cause it was there?" Jack answers doubtfully. "I don't know."

Ms. Graham looks at the class. "What d'ya think? Is that why?"

"Maybe," Salley says.

"We watch lots of things just cause they're there," Alan says in a rush. "Lots of things like . . ." He stops.

"Like?"

"Cars."

"TV."

"People."

"Girls," Jack adds with a snicker.

"Well, I'd never watch a boy," Salley adds.

"Sure," Ms. Graham intercedes. "And we look at clouds and rainbows and water running by."

"I'd rather watch a football game," Joe adds.

"So what can you say about us?"

They think about the question. "We like to watch different things?" Salley answers tentatively.

Ms. Graham waits.

"And we watch things for different reasons?" Joe suggests.

"But what do we all do?" Ms. Graham prompts.

"Watch!" the class answers.

"Okay. Now, there's a poem in our book by someone who watched a bird and thought about it just as we've been doing and then wrote down what she thought. It's on page 23. Have you all got your books?"

Harry raises his hand, "I don't, Mrs. Graham."

"Just as I thought. Anyone else?"

Several hands go up.

"Well, just for those of us who are so forgetful, I made some copies of the poem. Here, Jack, you pass them out."

When everyone has a copy, Ms. Graham says, "Okay, let's read it silently all the way through without stopping. Raise your hand when you finish, then read it again. Okay, go."

The class is quiet, heads bent over their books. Ms. Graham watches until the last student has finished. "Great, now I'm going to read it aloud. Follow along in your book if you want or just listen."

When she has finished reading the poem, she pauses, then asks, "So, who'd like to tell us how you felt about what Emily Dickinson said?"

Several hands go up. "Frank, why don't you start us off."

Frank takes a deep breath and speaks in a rush, "Well, she told about what happened okay, I guess. I mean about the bird and it being afraid and flying away and all. But I didn't get that stuff with the beetle and that last part with the butterflies and ocean, well, I just don't see where the ocean came from." He finishes with a gasp.

"That beetle part gave me problems, too, the first time I read it. Anyone have an idea what it means. Salley?"

"Well, I'm not sure, of course," she says cautiously, "but when you were reading it to us, I thought maybe—well, this may sound silly—but maybe the beetle wasn't something the bird would eat, so he just watched it go by."

"But, but, but . . ." Tom is anxiously waving his raised hand in the air.

"Tom," Ms. Graham says quietly.

"But birds eat beetles. I've seen 'em do it."

"So have I," Ms. Graham nods. "What about that?"

"Maybe some beetles, but not all beetles," Harry joins in. "It didn't eat this one."

"Maybe it wasn't hungry," Tom insists.

"Both seem like good reasons to me," Jane Graham says.

"So, if he wasn't gonna eat the beetle, what's it doing in the poem?" Jack asks. "I still don't understand."

"Good question. Anyone got any ideas?"

"Maybe it just really happened, so she put it in," Anne suggests shyly.

"Oh, a poet wouldn't do that," Jack says.

"Could be. Why not," Salley comes to the defense of her friend Anne. "I bet Anne's right."

"Maybe we can find out later, or maybe we'll never know," Ms. Graham intervenes. "Anyway, who else wants to tell us what you thought of the poem? Anyone?"

More hands go in the air. "Anne."

"Well, even if I'm not right about the beetle—and I still think I am—" she says, looking at Jack, "I could see myself watching that bird, you know, to see what it did, just wondering, how did it feel eating a worm. Ugh! I'd rather eat a beetle!"

The class laughs. Jack adds, "I once saw a can of fried ants for sale in the store."

"Oh, Jack, you did not," Karla says.

"I did so. Mrs. Graham haven't you seen 'em?"

"Well, I'm sorry to have to say I have. Chocolate-covered ants, too," she agrees. "But I wanted to ask Anne about what she said."

The class looks at Anne, who blushes.

"You said you wondered how the bird felt eating a worm, didn't you?"

Anne nods.

"So how did you decide the bird felt?"

"Oh, I'd die before I'd eat a worm, but I guess the bird felt good, maybe like I'd feel with a hamburger."

"So maybe it wasn't hungry after eating that worm," Tom insists, going back to defend his earlier contribution.

"Nah," Harry says, "we read in science that animals like birds and mice, little things, have to eat all the time or they die. It's called metabolism."

"So maybe it was an untasty beetle after all," Ms. Graham intervenes again. "Suppose it was, what do you think the bird thought when it 'hopped sideways to the wall / To let a beetle pass'?"

"I'll bet it was thinking 'no food there,' " Jack agrees.

"But mostly it was afraid," Karla said, "hungry and afraid."

"What does Dickinson say, Karla?"

Karla takes a deep breath and reads, " 'He glanced with rapid eyes / That hurried all abroad— / They looked like frightened beads, I thought. / He stirred his velvet head / Like one in danger.' See, he was afraid."

"What do you think he was afraid of?" Ms. Graham prompts.

Several hands go up.

"Tom."

"Not getting enough to eat, maybe."

"Maybe a cat," Salley adds. "Our cat catches birds all the time and puts them on the porch. I hate it."

"Maybe that somebody was watching it," Henry says. "After all, somebody was."

They think about that idea for a moment.

"Sure," Tom concludes, "and when she tries to feed it, it flies away, pouff."

"Just what a bird would do," Henry says.

"But she was trying to feed it," Ms. Graham points out. "Why didn't it take the crumb?"

"Oh, it didn't know that," several students say. Then Anne adds, "No, it didn't.

Maybe it thought she was going to catch it and eat it like Salley's cat. Remember what we said about how we'd look to a bird."

"Big," several students say.

"If you look big to a bird, then, how does a bird look to you?" Ms. Graham prompts again.

"Small," several students say.

Ms. Graham waits.

"Well," Mike speaks up for the first time, "when we were talking about birds before we read the poem, I wondered if you were going to ask us that."

Ms. Graham laughs. "Saw right through me, did you. Well, I thought I'd wait on that question. So what's the answer, Mike?"

"I was thinking then that it would just look like a robin, you know, nothin' special. But here in the poem, see, she talks about its eyes moving around—'rapid eyes,' 'frightened beads'—that's how robins do look, nervous, jumpy. Like what my grandpaw calls 'a cat on a hot tin roof.' "

"And then the bird flies away and what does it look like?" she prompts.

"To me, or in the poem?" Mike asks.

"Either. Start with to you."

"Well, if it's a robin, a little clumsy, maybe, at first, and then quick. Wouldn't it be great to be able to fly!"

Ms. Graham nods, then waits.

The class waits. Finally, Jack says, "That's the part of the poem I didn't understand—other than the beetle, and I don't want to get into that again."

"How the flying bird looked to Emily Dickinson," Ms. Graham restates the idea.

"Yeah. All that stuff about oars and oceans and butterflies. How did that get in there?"

"It was my favorite part of the poem," Salley says. "I thought the first part was kinda dull, really. But that last part, it was so pretty."

"Would someone like to read it out loud again?" Ms. Graham asks.

After a long pause, Anne says, "I will" and reads,

"And he unrolled his feathers
And rowed him softer home

Than oars divide the ocean,
Too silver for a seam,
Or butterflies, off banks of noon,
Leap, plashless, as they swim."

The class is quiet for a moment; then Salley says, "See, isn't that beautiful."

"Beautiful, maybe," Jack insists, "but what does it mean?"

Ms. Graham waits. When no one volunteers, she says, "Let's take a minute to think about what a flying bird looks like. I'm going to make a list of as many things a flying bird looks like as I can in two minutes. Anyone else who wants to write down a list can, or just try to think of as many as you can."

The class is quiet as Ms. Graham writes. At first only a few seem to be making lists; then a few more start writing. After five minutes, Ms. Graham stops, looks up, and says,

"Well, I came up with, let's see . . ." She counts silently. "Eight. Did anyone get more than that?"

After a pause, Jack raises his hand. "I got twelve."

When other hands go up, Ms. Graham says, "Wonderful. I'm going to read my favorite one. Then I'd like to hear from anyone else who has a favorite one. Mine is 'A flying bird is like a quiet voice singing in the dark.' "

She waits. Finally, Georgie raises his hand.

"Georgie?"

In a shaking voice, Georgie reads, "A flying bird is like a horse running through a field."

"Ah," Ms. Graham says, "I like that. I really like that."

After a dozen others have read their favorite simile for a flying bird, there is a pause; and Ms. Graham says, "Well, I almost think I could fly. And, Mike, after hearing those comparisons, just like you, I think, Wouldn't it be wonderful to be able to fly!"

She pauses, then says, "Salley, you liked the way Emily Dickinson described flying, and so do I. Would you help us look at what she said?"

Salley sighs, then says, "Okay, but I liked a lot of what we said, too." She waits a minute, then continues, "Well, it seems to me she saw him as like somebody rowing a boat, but so smoothly he didn't even upset the water. And she saw the bird as like butterflies floating in the air so smoothly there aren't any—well—whatever 'plashless' means—I guess no waves in the air."

Ms. Graham says, "I can see that, Salley."

"But," Jack asks, "what's a seam in the ocean?"

"Oh, the boat doesn't leave any mark," Salley says. "Think of a lake with the sun shining on it. A boat moving but not leaving any mark. Can't you see that?"

Jack frowns.

"So," Ms. Graham says quickly, "that's how she saw the bird flying. What do you think of what she said?"

They are quiet. Ms. Graham waits. Then Mike says, "Well, I guess this is wrong, but I liked what I said about a horse better than her butterflies."

"Actually, Mike," Ms. Graham says, "so did I. But I liked the picture of those butterflies swimming in the noon sun, too."

The class murmurs some yeses.

"Okay," Jack asks, "so now I understand. But why write a poem about it?"

Salley, Anne, and some other students, mostly girls, make negative sounds. Ms. Graham says, "Anyone have an answer for Jack?"

Mike says, "Well, remember when we were talking about bird watching? Well, somebody said we might watch a bird because it was there. I guess she could write a poem about it because it was there."

"Why not?" Ms. Graham asks. "I guess I started a poem about a bird flying today. And Mike did. And Salley. Well, everybody did."

"But, Mrs. Graham," Salley insists, "this poem is in our textbook. There must be more to it than just a person watching a bird."

"Probably. Anybody got any ideas?"

There is a long silence. Then Anne says, "I don't know. Does there have to be another meaning?"

Ms. Graham waits. Finally Harry says, "Well, I guess she might just've written about something that happened to her. But I bet she thought it meant something more."

"So what more could it mean?" Jane Graham prompts.

"We talked about watching birds. She's watching the bird, right?" Harry says at last. "Okay."

"And we said the bird was watching the beetle, right?"

"And then the bird sees her. That's watching, right?"

Ms. Graham says, "Could be."

"Oh, I don't know," Harry says.

"Hey, don't stop."

"And then she watches the bird fly away. So is the poem about watching?"

Ms. Graham waits. The students wait. "Well," she says, finally, "is it?"

"Bird watching?" Salley says.

"No," Mike says, "people watching birds, birds watching people."

"And what about birds watching beetles?" Jack asks.

The class groans.

"Sure," Mike says, "and maybe, maybe even worms watching birds. Who knows?"

"Anyone else watching anyone else?" Ms. Graham asks.

They're silent.

"Well, I'm going to make a list of everyone in the poem who watched everyone else. Anyone else who wants to can."

There is a short pause while Ms. Graham and the students make their lists. Then, "Okay, who'll share a list with us?"

After a pause, Tom reads, "Bird watches worm. Worm watches bird, maybe. Bird watches beetle. Beetle watches bird, probably. Emily watches bird hop. Emily watches worm being eaten. Emily watches beetle walk by bird. Bird watches Emily. Emily watches bird fly away. That's it."

"Anyone have anybody else on the list?" Ms. Graham asks.

They look at their lists. "There isn't anyone else," Mike says at last.

Ms. Graham waits. Finally, Anne says, "Can you watch yourself, Mrs. Graham?"

"Well, I've heard of mirrors," Jane Graham says. "Can you?"

"Yes," Anne says, "I watch myself all the time."

Ms. Graham waits.

"Right," Salley says, "we all watch ourselves."

"And," Ms. Graham prompts.

There is silence. Then Mike says, "So, who in the poem was watching itself? The worm? Nah. The beetle? Nah. The bird? Nah. So who else is there?"

Several students shout out, "Emily."

"Ah," Ms. Graham says.

And the bell rings.

"See you tomorrow," Jane Graham says.

PLANNING

Later, both Helen Johnson and Jane Graham discussed how they planned for these classes. This was Ms. Johnson's reply:

"How did I prepare to teach that poem? Well, pretty much the same way I prepare to teach any piece of literature. In a very real way I feel my English major and master's in

English took care of that. Then, when I'm going to teach something I haven't taught before, I read it carefully several times. If I need to, I sometimes read about the author. And I always look in the library for any critical articles or analyses in books. I take notes, and then I decide what points I need to be sure my students understand. Then I work up a lecture and a set of questions to ask the class after they've read the work, or, in the case of a novel, after they've read chapters. If I think the students will have real problems with the work, I sometimes give them study questions to use while they're reading.

"The final thing I usually do is prepare a quiz for the work, or maybe for a long work some small quizzes and a longer test for the end. If I'm going to have the students do some kind of project with the work, I'll decide what that will be like and prepare some sample topics.

"Sometimes, if there is a movie or a record or something like that that's worthwhile, I'll arrange to get it and use it, though I believe that works of literature should be read and valued for themselves.

"Of course, I've taught these Emily Dickinson poems several times before, so all I had to do was reread them and my notes and think about the students in this class so I'd be prepared to help any of them who'd have special problems understanding."

Ms. Graham had a somewhat different reply:

"Well, I'm afraid preparation for me doesn't have much to do with scholarship. I guess traditionalists would say I'm wrong, but when I prepare, I'm looking for ways to help my students' efforts to understand for themselves. Oh, of course, I read the poem or short story or novel I'm going to teach even if I've taught it a dozen times before. I'm not the same each time, you see, and neither are my students. But I've found I need to read whatever I'm going to teach not just as a person reading it but as a teacher reading it.

"I've found, if you're preparing to help another reader be able to respond to the poem or story, then you have to read that work from the point of view of that other reader, my students, I mean. That's not easy, but it's important for me if I'm going to teach literature the way I want to."

Jane Graham explained that, as she read the poem, she tried to think of pre-reading activities that would be valuable to her students, ways to make the class interaction productive, and possible follow-up activities that would help her students rethink and deepen their insights. She saw it as her job to try to anticipate the areas where her students would be lacking in the knowledge and experience they'd need in order to begin responding immediately to Dickinson's poem they were about to read and discuss.

"I asked myself, Are they likely to have thought about what it's like to be a bird? Have they ever stopped to watch a bird hopping around on the lawn? Have they stopped to think about what they were seeing? I decided, probably they hadn't. So I asked myself, will they have seen how animals and people are similar and different? Again, probably not. But I was pretty sure they'd see the bird catching the worm. But they probably hadn't looked at it from either the perspective of the bird or the worm. So I decided to start with what they could see and work from there."

COMMENTARY

Jane Graham believes that a work of literature only comes to life when readers meet it half way, bring to it their unique experiences and insights. She believes that putting a class full of teenagers together in a room to listen to an adult talk about a work of literature is, for most of her students, the worst way to help them interact with that work. At best, they would interact with her lecture; in most cases, they would doze.

There are, of course, times when teachers have information that they want to give to their students. It may well be that the best way to get students interested in the life of Emily Dickinson is to deliver a lively, sensitive lecture on what her life must have been like—if the teacher can be lively and sensitive about that subject. It may be important for students to understand the special qualities of Dickinson's style before reading "A Bird Came Down the Walk." And maybe a lecture on her poetic style is the best way for the teacher to get them ready to understand that style and how to cope with its demands. Helen Johnson decided to take that approach.

But whenever she was tempted to lecture, Jane Graham reminded herself of two points she remembered reading some years ago: "Most people learn better when they are looking for answers to important questions than when someone is giving them those answers, and most people—and especially most teenagers—stop listening to someone else talking after about five minutes, at the most."

Also, works of literature like "A Bird Came Down the Walk" are creations that people read, respond to, and then, maybe, discuss with other people. So, a class discussion makes better sense than a lecture, if what happens really is a discussion. But consider Ms. Johnson's class. She believes that her class had discussed the poem, but what happened in Ms. Johnson's class—and very many other English classes—was probably more an oral quiz. As she said later, when she discussed how she planned to teach, she knows what the poem says. She had read the poem several times and thought through it using her training as an English teacher. She had read an analysis of it in the teacher's guide for the text. She had studied Emily Dickinson in more than one class in college. Also, she had taught the poem to more than one class. She had worked out the lesson plan for the poem in advance. She'd gone through it line by line and prepared questions for each phrase and sentence. Where she thought the students might have problems answering her questions, she had worked out simpler questions to lead them to the "big question." She knows what the poem means and what every word, phrase, line, and sentence in it means. She had questions to ask that would help her find out whether or not her students had gotten the correct meaning. If they still didn't get the point, she was prepared to tell them what it means.

But her class was not a discussion in the usual sense of that word. It is probably more accurate to say that Ms. Johnson was fishing for the answers that she had decided in advance are the correct ones. The students—at least those that care to please her or those that want to get the top grades—were trying to guess what she wanted them to say. Emily Dickinson's poem was lost in the game that teacher and students were playing, a game that resembles what Theodore Sizer has called "Horace's Compromise." Here's how Theodore Sizer describes that compromise:

> Finally, the students accept the system. As long as school is fun some of the time and rarely humiliating, they go along. They strike their bargains with teachers, and they value the rituals of going to school. For them, school is a rite of passage, and they accept it, even though they may be bored by much of it. The American adolescent is a remarkably tolerant animal. (211)

A discussion of a work of literature among people who have read it is a sharing of different insights. It may be led by someone like Helen Johnson or Jane Graham, but that leader cannot pretend to herself or to her students to have the right answers. In literature classes, we all have the same evidence: the text. As readers, we bring what we bring to it, and then we begin to discuss—not the right and wrong "discussion" that Ms. Johnson conducted, but a real sharing of possibilities.

If a teacher decides to have an entire class read the same selection and discuss that work, it is important to consider what Jane Graham did with "A Bird Came Down the Walk." She carried the discussion from experiences that her students had had with birds and bugs to the experience the poet had and from there to what they learned and what the poet learned. She accepted the students' ideas. She waited for them to decide how they wanted to answer her questions. Most important, her questions were open ones. That is, although she probably had her own answers to her questions, she understood that there were many answers, as many as there were students; and she was willing to look seriously with the class at any serious answer, however different from her own it was. Respect for ideas was the key to her class discussions. Using what they said, she guided her students in the direction of the poem. They shared their responses, but she drew from them elements that would help them understand Emily Dickinson's encounter with the bird.

It took them a while to get to the poem itself—but not more time than Helen Johnson took. When they got there, Jane Graham's students were almost ready to write their own poems and so were ready to consider the poem that Dickinson wrote. Ms. Graham was willing to accept the fact that some of her students might like the Dickinson poem and some might not, but she had created a situation where most of them could judge it from the perspective of informed readers, understanding what the poet was thinking and judging the poem on the basis of how well Dickinson put into words what she had seen and thought.

CONCLUSIONS

Far too many teachers of literature—and, therefore, readers of literature—believe that reading is a passive act. In that view, the one that Helen Johnson seems to hold, a reader opens a book as one might open a package, reaches down into it, and pulls out what the author put there. Some readers who are careful and perceptive get more from their response to the text. Less attentive and less able readers get less and get it less accurately. But all are mining for the gold that the author has deposited.

In 1938, Louise Rosenblatt published *Literature as Exploration* (4th ed., 1983) in which she presented to teachers of literature a concept that is still not understood by many of them. In that book, Rosenblatt urges teachers and readers not to think of the reading of literature as a passive act. Rather, she points out, when a piece of literature is successful for readers, that success comes from the fact that they bring to the selection all that they are and have experienced. A merger, a mingling of reader and work occurs. From that amalgam comes a new creation that never has been and never will be duplicated because it contains the unique quality of the single reader. As she puts it:

> The process of understanding a work implies a recreation of it, an attempt to grasp completely all the sensations and concepts through which the author seeks to convey the qualities of his sense of life. Each of us must make a new synthesis of these elements

with his own nature, but it is essential that he assimilate those elements of experience which the author has actually presented. (133)

When Ms. Graham's students read the Emily Dickinson poem, their responses were uniquely theirs. They brought to their reading everything that they know and everything that they had experienced. As they responded to the poet's words, they were continually creating their own poem. Many students probably had seen birds hopping on a lawn; so they were able to bring to the poem that experience. A few may have stopped to watch birds catch worms. Others may have frightened away the bird, intentionally or without meaning to. On the other hand, other students may have put out food for birds in the winter and watched them flutter around a bird feeder. They may have seen the birds fly away when they noticed a movement through a window. And so they created somewhat different works of their own as they read the poem. That individuality is the real glory of literature and probably the reason why so many people like to discuss literature, even if the only literature they have to discuss is soap operas and movies.

Teachers like Jane Graham, who accept this view of the reader as active creator, do not teach literature in order to give students the one true interpretation. They accept as fact that such singularity does not exist, although they know that many other teachers believe that it does. Instead of posing as authority, such teachers of literature try to make possible a sharing of their students' personal responses, be they valid, semivalid, and erroneous in relation to the text. In that sharing, their students can learn from each other; reconsider what they found in a poem; keep, modify, or reject parts of their own responses; and go away to rethink their reactions.

Such teachers do not consider it important or even desirable that their students agree with their own view of the work or with that of critics and scholars. It is important that those students share their responses, consider with respect the responses of other students and the teacher, and think seriously about the entire array of reactions they have encountered in the class.

As Rosenblatt cautions, the creation that results from the merger of reader and work should be true to the work, just as it should be true to the reader. The work of literature is not reduced to a trivial part of the interaction. Rosenblatt, for example, uses a musical score as an illustration of valid but individual readings or interpretations: no two violinists play a composition in exactly the same way, yet each of them plays it within the parameters of the score. Being true to the literary work, like being true to the score, is essential to response. Nevertheless, with young readers, although a teacher might help students to correct responses that are not true to the work, as Ms. Johnson did by pointing out those errors, many teachers agree with Jane Graham, who dismissed misreadings by saying, "Oh, now and then some of them never do get rid of what is pretty clearly a wrong idea. But, you know, I've found, if they liked what they did make of it, they'll probably go back to it later; and, as more mature readers, they'll discover new meanings."

After one's own discovery, the excitement of literature comes from the very diversity of valid responses. There may be a mild satisfaction in finding that a friend who has read a poem I have just finished agrees in every way with what I say about it; but much more interesting is a discussion with someone who has seen the poem differently.

The joy of Jane Graham's approach to teaching lies in the fact that she is not locked into a boring and repetitive telling of the one right way, an interpretation that she has told her students year after year. Rather, each reading of the work is a new discovery for her, partly because she has changed, but, more important, because this year's students are different from last year's students.

REFERENCES

Dickinson, Emily. "A bird came down the walk." In *Selected Poems of Emily Dickinson.* New York: Random House, 1948, 80–81.
Rosenblatt, Louise. *Literature as Exploration.* 4th ed. New York: Modern Language Association, 1983.
Sizer, Theodore. *Horace's Compromise.* Burlington, MA: Houghton Mifflin, 1984.

CHAPTER 2

The Transactional Theory of Literature

Nicholas J. Karolides

"What story are you reading anyway?" My teaching colleague flung that remark at me in the heat of a discussion of John Steinbeck's "The Chrysanthemums." The class of seniors and graduate students laughed, as did she, the tone of the class being relaxed as well as honest. However, despite the humor of the retort to something that I had said, it expressed emphatically the disparity between our interpretations.

We were team teaching a course focusing on literature by and about women. The discussion had moved from introductory responses about the character's behavior to the apparent alienation of Elissa Allen from her husband and her separation from his world of ranch management. Students had offered their perceptions of her feelings and of what had affected her. The view that Elissa is a victim of social attitudes that prevent her from realizing her full potential led to the idea that she is victimizing herself in response to these attitudes. Her childlessness as a key factor in her self-victimization was asserted.

Disagreement of interpretation bubbled up, with my colleague and me on different "sides" of the response; she had perceived Elissa as self-victimizing, blaming herself because she was childless while I sensed her frustration as resulting from the socially enforced limitations in her role and freedom, given her evident capability and power; thus, the earlier remark. Curiously, the factor of childlessness had not occurred to any of the several men in the class; those to whom it was evident were women, though a few of the younger ones hadn't considered this idea. Scrutiny of the text and class reflections about these responses found support for both interpretations. Proponents of the childlessness view pointed to Elissa's unfulfillment as expressed in her manner—her overeagerness in caring for her mums that were seen as child substitutes, in the fact that there were no children, and the story did not specifically place blame on her husband or society for her condition; they found further support in the several symbols of fertility and Elissa's subdued passion. Contrasting responses focused on the societal constraints on women alluded to in the text—what they can do, where they can go—and the noncommunicative relationship of wife and husband; childlessness is not mentioned in the text. Steinbeck does not state precisely the factors involved in the character's condition or conditioning.

How much each reader contributes is clearly signified in this class's exchange. All readers do not come away from reading a text with the same impressions. Even when those readers are trained and experienced, their felt emotions and ideas will vary from the subtle to the affectively and intellectually significant. Revelations of these differences expand the meaningful potential of the text and of the readers' transactions with it.

This classroom experience illustrates theoretical issues surrounding reading and interpreting of literature and the role readers play. In recent decades, theories of literature, termed *reader-response criticism* have signaled an important role for readers as active agents in the reading process, a role that had been minimized or rejected by previous theoretical approaches. (These are briefly discussed later in this chapter.) However, not all reader-response approaches are identical in their emphasis, though they underscore the role of the reader. Subjective criticism gives prominence to the reader over the text by focusing on the reader's identity and internal motives as well as the reader's developing self-understanding. In contrast, the transactional theory of literature acknowledges the "compenetration" of a reader and a text, each conditioning the other; meaning evolves from the fusion of the author's text and the reader's personality and experience. This latter theoretical focus, first promulgated by Louise M. Rosenblatt in *Literature as Exploration* and expounded in *The Reader, the Text, the Poem*, is the core of this book.

READING AS A TRANSACTIONAL PROCESS

Consider reading, the act of reading. It necessarily involves a reader and a text. (The word *text* signifies the marks—that is, the words as symbols—on the page, as differentiated from "literary work" or "poem" that, as I explain in more detail, evolves from the transaction of a reader with the "text.") Everyone would agree that a friend or teacher telling you about a book is not an act of reading for you. Others can no more read and experience a book for you than they can relieve your hunger pangs by eating your dinner. Similarly, reading a synopsis of a book does not substitute for reading it. You may learn something *about* the book, but you will not have experienced it.

This focus on the reader and the text grows out of an understanding of what happens during the process of reading; it recognizes how active readers are during this process, rather than assuming they are passive spectators of the text. According to the central premise, the literary work exists in the *transaction* between the reader and the text.

The term *transaction* denotes the special nature of the relationship between the reader and the text during the reading event: mutually acting on each other, affecting each other to evoke an experience, a meaning, for the particular reader of the text.

> In discussion of the reading process, as in other disciplines undergoing revision, we need to free ourselves from unscrutinized assumptions implicit in the usual terminology and in the very structure of our language. The usual phrasing makes it difficult to attempt to do justice to the nature of the actual reading event. The reader, we can say, interprets the text. (The reader acts on the text.) Or we can say, the text produces a response in the

reader. (The text acts on the reader.) Each of these phrasings, because it implies a single line of action by one separate element on another separate element, distorts the actual reading process. The relation between reader and text is not linear. It is a situation, an event at a particular time and place in which each element conditions the other. (Rosenblatt, *Reader* 16)

Several prerequisites are necessary before the reading transaction can take place. The reading act begins with the assumption that the marks on the page are decipherable as words. For more to occur, not only must the text be understandable, within the grasp of the reader, but also the reader must be an active participant. The former may be self-evident, but it merits comment as it applies to the selection of materials for classroom use.

The language of a text, the situation, characters, or the expressed issues can dissuade a reader from comprehension of the text and thus inhibit involvement with it. In effect, if the reader has insufficient linguistic or experiential background to allow participation, the reader cannot relate to the text, and the reading act will be short-circuited.

The reader's willingness to engage with the text is another necessary ingredient for the fulfillment of the reading act. Distraction or indifference can similarly cause a short circuit. The reader may read words, but inattention blocks response. Engagement with the text, both emotional and intellectual—though not necessarily immediate or concurrent—is necessary for the evolution of a literary work.

THE READER

What influences a reader's responses to a text? Given the text's understandability and the reader's active participation, what happens during the reading process? Presumably, the text is the same for all readers, that is, the marks on the page—the words, the structures—appear the same. Individual readers, however, approach these words and structures with a particular frame of mind formed by their own personal milieu. Indeed, readers' responses to individual words may well vary in connotation, expression, and interpretation. Over time and region, words may even vary in denotation. Readers, influenced by past experiences and current circumstances, regional origins and upbringing, gender, age, past and present readings, will vary in their responses from those of others. Even readers of the same age, similar background, and circle of relationships will express differences in general impression and nuances of feelings.

These differences are also influenced by the given moment—the situation, the mood, the pressures, and reasons (perhaps, teacher's directions) for reading, the *stance* taken toward the reading. Thus considering the breadth of experiences among readers at any one time and over time (as well as the same reader), the range of possible readings of a single text is potentially infinite. The reading event for each reader is unique.

Through the medium of words, the text brings into the reader's consciousness certain concepts, certain sensuous experiences, certain images of things, people, actions, scenes. The special meanings and, more particularly, the submerged associations that the words and images have for the individual reader will largely determine what the work communicates. . . . The reader brings to the work personality traits, memories of past events, present needs and preoccupations, a particular mood of the moment, and a particular physical condition. These and many other elements in a never-to-be-duplicated combination enter into the reader's relationship with the text. (Rosenblatt, *Literature* 30–31)

The *reading event* initiates the literary experience, the first formulation of the literary work. It should not be construed, however, that this constitutes an immediate flash of insight, of meaning, comparable to Athena emerging full grown from the head of Zeus. Rather, the process is more evolutionary. The reader reacts to words and situations and the interplay of one word or situation with another. Expectations of the text are projected, but later features can bring about a revision. The reading is not linear, but rather, recursive, a backward-and-forward exploration of what is being evoked in relation to the text. Clues of context are perceived and integrated. The reader constructs a constantly adjusted scaffold of understandings attempting to account for the text's many features. A second reading, if there is one, can reveal additional or revised nuances. Depending on the reader's involvement and reading maturity as well as the text itself, the reading process is reflective and demanding.

The reader makes choices, both conscious and subconscious; the concept of *selective attention* operates. One semantic nuance may be selected over another; one feeling state may be heightened in the interplay among the text, the individual's emotional attitudes, and the surrounding situation. From the array of meanings and feelings that are conjured up, the reader selects those that fit with what has already been evoked, or, if necessary, reviews and revises the choices or syntheses that have been made (Rosenblatt, *Writing* 11–12). A dominant perception or purpose in the reader may activate or emphasize certain features or language over others, may skew the reading event to conform to the current circumstances. Close identification with characters or events may intensify the response. Implicit in this situation is the continuous, dynamic interplay between reader and text during which meaning evolves. The created response is the realized experience of the reader.

Thus, a range of responses results from the dynamic relationship between readers and text, from differences among readers, and from aspects of the text that are ambiguous or undefined. And, each transaction by a reader, given different reading occasions—particular times and circumstances—will be unique as the reader's frame of mind, situation, and experiences change.

THE AUTHOR'S ROLE

Authors create the written text. They process the language and select the moments in time and the characters to convey feelings and sensations, concepts and attitudes to readers. In a meaningful way, they, too, live through the experience of the text in initiating and incubating it, processing and reading it until it reaches final form. Writers create out of their experience and imagination.

However, a text, once removed, once published, is no longer in the author's control. In a very real sense, the author is outside the immediate, intimate reading circle. A body of words exists, the author's intentions threaded within them, waiting for a reader to respond to them, to enliven them. The words, in effect, have no symbolic meaning—are only marks on the page—until the reading event occurs, until the literary work has been lived through by the reader. To what extent this is a replication of the author's intention cannot be established. Even if authors have identified their intention, we cannot be sure that the text fulfills it, that there are, further, no unbidden, unconscious elements reflected in the text.

In real terms, we can imagine the author's work as an intricately designed, multi-colored tapestry; the multilayered symbols, figured in the author's design, are perceived by readers through their individual consciousness. Under the stimulus of the author's text, through its guidance and direction, readers create (or recreate) out of their experience and imagination a literary work.

THE TEXT

The discussion up to this point has concentrated on the reader, who has long been the neglected performer of the reading act. But the transactional theory of literature by no means ignores the text. It is a necessary component of the reading transaction within which the literary work comes into being.

The transactional nature of the reading process demonstrates the dynamic nature of the text, as differentiated from the traditional view of the text as unchanging, static, with a single meaning. Though the words on the page appear the same, the text is variable. What the reader makes of the verbal signs reflects shifts in the denotation and connotation of words as well as differences in the images called forth and in the social and psychological attitudes and behaviors of readers. The effect of such language flexibility is to shift the pattern of response. Thus, though an author may have carefully chosen language and incident with quite specific references and impressions—perhaps readily understood by the author's immediate contemporaries (though this is unlikely to be universal)—responses of audiences with variant experiences, especially those of another time and place, are subject to other environmental forces.

The changing dynamics of a text's issues, characters, relationships, and structures are illustrated by some examples from my classes. During the late 1960s and 1970s when the civil rights movement was at its peak, student readers readily perceived the racial factor as critical to Othello's self-doubt and disintegrating self-control, and easily empathized with his psychological loss; before and after this period, however, this aspect of Othello's character has emerged less forcefully in discussion and is only minimally explored. During the height of the Vietnam War, some readers of Stephen Crane's *Red Badge of Courage*—particularly those with antiwar sentiments—acknowledged the possibility that the soldier's leaving the battle was his "red badge of courage"; such responses echoed support for Americans who resisted the call to arms. Readers of John Knowles's *A Separate Peace* tend to identify with either the protagonist Gene, who is a good student but personally uncertain, or with Finny, the carefree, exuberant athlete; this choice, a reflection of the reader's personal sense and maturity, alters the shape and sense of the novel. Responses to Charlotte Gilman's "The Yellow Wallpaper" have moved from seeing it as a horror story to seeing it as feminist protest, reflecting the late twentieth-century angles of vision, influenced by feminist criticism, and increased understanding of the situation of women.

STANCE

A critical factor that affects the reader's activity in responding to a text is the way the reader approaches the text, that is, the reader's focus of attention or purpose. Thus, a student in a biology class concentrating on a text, especially when preparing for an examination, reads with a quite different stance than one who is engrossed in Jack London's *The Call of the Wild.* When reading, Rosenblatt explains, readers adopt a *stance* toward the text. The stance taken may be "predominantly efferent" or "predominantly aesthetic," on a continuum of response possibilities somewhere between the two extremes. The same text may be read with one or the other focus depending on the occasion of the reading event. If the purpose is to evoke a literary work of art, the personal aesthetic stance is used. Rosenblatt notes:

> The term "efferent" (from the Latin *efferre,* to carry away) designates the kind of reading in which attention is centered predominantly on what is to be extracted and retained after the reading event. An extreme example is the man who has accidentally swallowed a poisonous liquid, and who is rapidly reading the label on the bottle to learn the antidote. Here, surely, we see an illustration of [William] James' point about "selective attention" and our capacity to push into the periphery of awareness those elements that do not serve our present interests. The man's attention is focused on learning what is to be done as soon as the reading ends. He concentrates on what the words point to, their barest public referents, and on constructing the directions for future action. Reading a newspaper, a textbook, or a legal brief would usually provide a similar, though less extreme, instance of the predominantly efferent stance.
>
> The predominantly aesthetic stance covers the other half of the continuum. The term "aesthetic" is used because its Greek source involved perception through the senses, feelings, and intuitions. In this kind of reading, the reader adopts an attitude of readiness to focus attention on what is being lived through *during* the reading event. Welcomed into the awareness are not only the public referents of the verbal signs but also the ideas that are the residue of past psychological events involving those words and their referents. Attention may include the sounds and rhythms of the words themselves, heard in "the inner ear." (Writing 12–13)

The usual explanation of these differences in reading stance is to cite differences in the texts themselves. Some are seen as basically informational whereas others are literary, suggesting that the differences in the reading of a text arise out of the nature of the content and/or the structure and style, leading to the reader's approach. For example, a psychology textbook is different from *Crime and Punishment,* often termed a psychological novel. There is some validity to this distinction. Some authors provide language and structural clues that invite or guide the reader to take a particular stance.

However, this explanation does not express what happens in a reading situation. It assumes the reader is passive and neutral; it assumes a given text is always read the same way. In fact, the reader determines, consciously or unconsciously, the purpose of the reading; the reader is influenced by many factors—the particular reading occasion, present needs, personal concerns—and decides what clues, what practical effects or feeling states to attend to, and what results to expect or desire.

The nature of the reader's activity—the stance taken before and during the processing of the text—determines how a response is generated and what response is evoked. Readers are more likely to adopt an aesthetic stance toward a novel that explores a character's reactions to a death, identifying with the loss and emotional travail. However, if the novel is read to ascertain and analyze coping strategies, perhaps because that is the basis of an assignment, then the reading may be limited to the gleaning of information parallel to a reading of the Elizabeth Kubler-Ross analysis of the stages of grief in *On Death and Dying.* Another example: The first question, "What is the color of the bride's dress?" asked in a college reader at the end of Stephen Crane's short story "The Bride Comes to Yellow Sky," certainly projects an efferent/informational stance for the reader. Similarly, despite the aesthetic stance suggested by the structure of a poem, the directions for a classroom assignment and the discussion questions, may induce an efferent reading. (Of course, the reader's aesthetic sensibilities may be engaged but the assignment would lead to their neglect.) In contrast, an essentially informative text—about, for example, destruction of the rain forests or child abuse—may well evoke feeling states during the reading that take precedence over the efferent stance for a reader. For example, Rachel Carson's *Silent Spring,* which discusses the destructive effects of chemicals on the environment, has engendered reactions across the stance continuum from efferent to aesthetic. As this suggests, different readers may approach the same text from a different stance; indeed, the same reader may do so from one reading to another.

The dynamics of the reader's stance are particularly significant in a classroom situation. Indirectly or directly, the teacher can markedly affect the stance that predominates in the transactions of student readers with texts through classroom atmosphere, questions, and assignments.

VALIDITY OF READERS' RESPONSES

You may well ask, if a range of responses is recognized as probable and acceptable, how can one response be more "valid" than another? How can validity be measured? Within the context of the transactional theory of the literary work, validity of a reading is identified in relation to a consistent set of criteria, implicit or explicit. Adequacy of interpretation can be measured against the constraints of the text: to what degree does the individual response include the various features of the text and the nuances of language; to what degree does it include aspects that do not reflect the text; to what degree has the reading evoked a coherent work? Thus, the out-of-context response—a memory or experience triggered by something in the text—takes the reader far afield or the strongly skewed response leads to the neglect of features of the text. These may be valuable responses for the reader but, given the criteria, invalid or less valid transactions with the text.

An example of such a valuable-but-invalid response can be seen in a college student's transaction with Robert Frost's poem, "Stopping by Woods on a Snowy Evening." She asserted that the poem is set on Christmas Eve, the coldest and stillest night of the year, and that the speaker is Santa Claus. She used several lines—"promises to keep, and miles to go before I sleep"—to support her view but ignored others that do not fit.

However, the concept of valid responses to a text is not the same as the belief that there is a single correct interpretation or meaning of a literary work. This notion of correctness is based on the belief that the text holds the answers—that a careful scrutiny of all the evidence within the text (aided by supporting data outside the text) will lead to a particular result. The classroom situation described at the beginning of this chapter, as do numerous other examples in this book, exemplify the fallacy of this position.

SHARED RESPONSES TO A TEXT

In discussion situations, readers will discern a range of responses to a text. Such interactive processes, encouraging personal review and revision, have the effect of building and developing the literary work, of clarifying the reader's "poem." Readers may discover and acknowledge more than one valid interpretation, each supported by the text. This will help them to understand their own interpretive experiences and strategies, as differentiated from those of others, and to understand themselves. Often, given the nature of human existence, the shared personal experiences and feelings of readers and the author's selected words and situations, there may emerge a core of common response, a convergence of feelings and understandings among readers. Such shared responses are accompanied by individual variations among readers. They may also occur within differentiated responses.

Examples from class discussions readily illustrate these concepts. Responses to Theodore Roethke's poem, "My Papa's Waltz" reflect two quite divergent perspectives, one embracing the good-time frolics between parent and child, the other projecting a vivid sense of child abuse. The disparate reactions to John Steinbeck's "The Chrysanthemums," illustrated at the beginning of this chapter, expose divergent reactions to the text, its clues leading readers to diverse understandings. Yet the readers generally understood the heroine's entrapment and victimization, diverging as to cause (personal or societal), and recognized her husband's "good guy" qualities, though his attempts to communicate are feeble and inept. Comprehension and empathy of Nora's plight in Henrik Ibsen's *A Doll's House* are fairly universally related to; readers' feelings—thus insights and valuation of her actions, particularly at the close of the drama—vary.

THEORIES AND CLASSROOM PRACTICE

The transactional theory of literature explored here differs markedly in its thesis and application from those of the "traditional" theories and instructional practice. Whereas the transactional approach concentrates on the reader's transaction with a text and evocation of a literary work, other approaches focus on literary content through emphasis on the author, the society, and/or the text. When these latter approaches inform instruction, the tendency is for teachers to teach *about* literature.

Traditional approaches are based on several underlying assumptions: (a) the author's intention is the key to ascertaining what the work means and this meaning can be identified; (b) the text is an object that has a determinate meaning of its own; (c) the text can be analyzed through objective, close scrutiny of its formal structure and techniques to establish the meaning. Furthermore, it is often assumed that there is but one meaning. In these approaches, the reader's role is neglected or omitted entirely.

Teaching of literature, from the biographical-historical vantage point, has focused on the life and times of the authors—including, perhaps, personal influences such as psychological and social factors, and literary relationships—literary periods and movements. Often, the author's identified themes and attitudes are used as a preliminary framework and applied to texts, sometimes within a literary history or a cultural-philosophical framework.

The study of the text in isolation of the author, in accordance with the tenets of the New Criticism, rejects biographical and social factors and focuses on form: the nature of genre; identifying structural patterns; exploring the language, symbols, and images. These elements are objectively analyzed in relation to their literary effects.

According to the literary-pedagogical basis for these approaches, such knowledge prepares or supports the readers so that they can more adequately read and understand. Presumably, with such background knowledge they can understand what the author is saying and what the text is doing. At times such visions are helpful. However, they tend to predispose or misdirect the specific reading, especially if introduced prior to reading or at the outset of discussion and are proposed directively; they have the effect of derailing the reader's transaction with the text and denying the opportunity to attend to and develop that experience. Furthermore, by focusing on content and form and on knowledge *about* literature, these approaches diminish the capacity of literature to portray and enliven the human experience for readers.

The transactional theory of literature does not reject the relevance of such biographical, historical, or formal considerations in the process of developing and enhancing insights to literature. The issue is *when* these should be introduced and *how* they should be projected. The central question: are such studies ends in themselves or are they used to enhance and develop the reader's transaction?

TRANSACTIONAL THEORY IN ACTION

The class sat in an uneven two-tiered semicircle with their teacher, Linda Larson. I, an observer, joined the circle at its outer edge. After glancing at me momentarily, the students turned their attention back to her; she had just introduced the book *Hiroshima* by John Hersey. Random mutterings about the difficulties of the assigned first chapter surfaced around the circle. These high school juniors (in the lowest level of the school's three achievement tracks) had found the shifting array of "characters" and the details of the text too complicated. Linda acknowledged their comments, indicating that she would be helping them with the reading.

Moving away from direct discussion of the text or their reaction to it, she asked them instead to imagine they had just heard that Minneapolis-St. Paul, a metropolis some forty miles away, had been targeted for a nuclear attack, expected in about an hour. They, in their windowless classroom, were relatively safe. She paused and asked, "How would you react? What would you do?"

Their reactions came slowly, but gradually a buzz of talk filled the room as the students exchanged reactions of surprise and fear, as they offered ideas about what they would try, what they would do: warn others, find their families, organize emergency stations, amass provisions. Then, a girl, previously silent, who, head down, had been filing her nails, interrupted the buzz. "Oh, you wouldn't do that!" she said abruptly. She glanced around the circle. "You wouldn't do that. I wouldn't do that. You know what I'd do? I'd run and run and run and run." Just as abruptly, she bent down her head again. The students were still for a few moments; when they took up the discussion again, it had taken a new turn.

On this initial day of her literature unit, Linda Larson had accomplished a great deal: She had created involvement among her students and, more important, had raised feelings and issues that could be applied to their primary text, *Hiroshima*. This introductory discussion had set the stage for bringing about their sense of relatedness to the text, helping to bring the work into being; and furthermore, for developing their thinking about the issues in the book and about themselves. Indeed, given the involvement she had established, she had probably created access into the text and had made it easier for them to engage and understand it.

Discussions of readers' transactions with the text—what they would make of it—would come in subsequent lessons. Linda, by invoking directly her students' transactions—experiences—with the text, would encourage them to relate to and reflect on those experiences with the events and people. She would draw from them their emotions and understandings, eliciting their attitudes and concerns. Thus, she would focus on helping her students understand the experience they were living through in the reading of *Hiroshima*, and understand the literary work they were evoking.

The students would not all respond with the same impressions. As in the introductory session, their felt emotions, their ideas and experiences would vary. She would help them to interact with each other to comprehend the varying responses; perhaps, they would modify or expand their impressions. Generally, they would find commonalities among their responses to the text. However, their developing interpretations of the text would also remain, at least in some measure, individualized.

The text was both springboard and resource; the readers' responses were stimuli for discussion. Through these discussions, along with a survival newsletter and projects, the students' interpretations would be honed, their attitudes clarified. Historical information, structural underpinnings, and language features would be introduced in the discussions, as appropriate, as catalysts for deeper understandings or explanations to help students comprehend a feature of the text. In addition, this reader-oriented process of building the literary work would help students to develop their interpretation ability. Furthermore, by reflecting on their thinking, the readers would come to understand what triggered their own responses, how these affected the developing impressions, and how they might be affected by the insights of others.

Embedded in this scenario are significant teaching principles and strategies. Cognizance of and developing the readers' transactions with the text is at the center of the classroom instruction. Class dialog starts where the student readers are (not where the teacher is), focusing on their initial reactions and understandings. This discussion functions as an initial expression, a comparative unfolding, of what they are making of the text, what feelings are induced, and what attitudes and ideas are emerging. Aspects of teacher assessment—recollection of data and analysis of text—are not considerations. By maintaining the reader orientation, students are disposed to acknowledge their own perceptions and their responsibilities as readers; they begin to recognize the role of their backgrounds, beliefs, and personalities in the reading act, that is, how each of them shapes their reaction and each is shaped by the text. By maintaining reference to the text, invoking it in relation to interpretive reactions, its role as stimulant and guide is acknowledged and processed; the students begin to recognize the need to support and validate a reading.

Teachers, focusing on the readers' experiences with the text, provide opportunities for them to identify and reflect on their reactions and invite them to compare reactions by questioning themselves and others. Such classroom discourse promotes cross-fertilization of ideas among students. In an atmosphere of acceptance and honesty, students will sense an appropriate, expressive reading or a limited or misdirected reading; they will measure and receive the ideas of others, incorporating them in their own, revising and building their interpretation of the literary work. There is internal growth of response to the text— not merely the noting and organizing of the teacher's knowledge. Through this process, they will have been led to support their statements by referring to the text, thus exploring their responses more deeply. Teachers will provide guidance—thoughtful questions, personal responses, and compelling information—so as to encourage a deeper consideration, a clarification, of the literary work being evoked by the students.

Various strategies may serve to clarify and enrich the readers' perceptions. Oral discussions of literary transactions are a mainstay of literature instruction—as a class but also in small groups of various numbers. Small groups can function as preliminary sounding boards or, all the way to the other end of the spectrum, as a culminating means of pulling together of ideas. Small-group activities have the merit of encouraging interchange from all class members, too many of whom get lost in the large-group activities. Various types of writing—journals, logs, free responses—similarly encourage active reflection by all students. These are especially valuable at the outset of a discussion to provide a preliminary outlet prior to the influence of assertive students, or at other times to allow for self-clarification or personal consideration of issues under discussion. Other oral and writing activities—role playing, situation expanding, dramatizations—can inspire personal involvement with characters and events to bring about thoughtful consciousness among the readers. (These strategies are elaborated elsewhere in this book.)

By inhibiting their impulses to direct or establish the "correct" interpretation of a text, teachers promote personal growth and allow readers to maintain ownership of their reading. Interpretive skills that are reader-dependent are developed. In the weighing and balancing of class exchanges, the students gain insight into the angles of vision of others as well as themselves. Beyond applying these to the immediate literary work, they adopt these strategies for subsequent readings. They gain confidence to approach a text on their own. In contrast, the teacher-directed interpretation has the effect of curtailing these learnings. The interpretive distance between the readers' initial reactions and the teacher's "solution" is not bridged; understanding is minimized; becoming dependent on teacher and critic, students learn to mistrust or reject their own readings.

The process of exploring the evoked response is itself a learning experience. It cultivates a habit of mind that is provocatively thoughtful and democratic. The dynamics stimulate the expression and recognition of multiple viewpoints; they must be considered and reconsidered against each other, measured and tested against the text. And in considering reactions to the text, readers necessarily reconsider their own belief structures and ideas. Concomitantly, the individual is affirmed in the sense of establishing the significance and value of each person as well as building the level of self-confidence. Altogether, the humanistic focus of literature emerges more strongly within this process. The potential of human activity, the dreams and fears of humanity, the impact of ideas and issues are more immediately explored and evaluated in the context of reader-text discussions.

REFERENCES

Carson, Rachel. *Silent Spring*. Greenwich, CT: Fawcett Publications, Inc., 1964.

Crane, Stephen. *The Red Badge of Courage*. New York: Norton, 1982.

Dostoyevsky, Fyodor. *Crime and Punishment*. New York: Norton, 2d ed., 1975.

Frost, Robert, "Stopping by Woods on a Snowy Evening." In *A Quarto of Modern Literature*. Ed. Leonard Brown. 5th ed. New York: Charles Scribner's Sons, 1964. 426.

Gilman, Charlotte. "The Yellow Wallpaper." In *The Riverside Anthology of Literature*. Ed. Douglas Hunt. Boston: Houghton Mifflin Company, 1988. 171–183.

Hersey, John. *Hiroshima*. New York: Bantam Books, 1959.

Ibsen, Henrik. *A Doll's House*. In *Types of Drama*. Ed. Sylvan Barnet, Morton Berman and William Burto. Boston: Little, Brown and Company, 1985. 31–65.

Knowles, John. *A Separate Peace*. New York: Dell Publishing Co., Inc., 1961.

Kubler-Ross, Elisabeth. *On Death and Dying*. New York: Macmillan, 1970.

London, Jack. *The Call of the Wild*. New York: Dutton, 1968.

Roethke, Theodore. "My Papa's Waltz." In *How Does a Poem Mean* by John Ciardi. Boston: Houghton Mifflin Company, 1959. 1003.

Rosenblatt, Louise M. *Literature as Exploration*. 4th ed. New York: Modern Language Association, 1983.

———. *The Reader, the Text, the Poem: The Transactional Theory of the Literary Work*. Carbondale, IL: Southern Illinois University Press, 1978.

———. "Writing and Reading: The Transactional Theory" *Reader* 20 (Fall 1988): 7–31.

Shakespeare, William. *Othello*. Ed. Mark Eccles. New York: Appleton-Century-Crofts, 1946.

Steinbeck, John. "The Chrysanthemums." In *The Portable Steinbeck*. Ed. Pascal Covici. Rev. Ed. New York: Viking Press, 1946.

CHAPTER 3

"The Guy Who Wrote This Poem Seems to Have the Same Feelings as You Have":
Reader-Response Methodology

Leila Christenbury

The title of this chapter comes from a chance remark by one of the teachers represented in this discussion. This student-centered, reader response-oriented teacher did not praise her student for understanding the poet and sharing his exalted ideas and feelings—she turned the tables and noted that the poet just might have had the same feelings as her ninth-grader. It may seem a small point, but it is a powerful one, a political reversal that underscores a respect for students, even in relation to mature literature and established writers. Through this connection, the teacher insists that the poet and the reader are allied, equal, and in the same human territory. Finally, it has the effect of giving the student intellectual standing and confidence.

Such interchanges can and do happen in classrooms where the reader's response to a text is respected and where a teacher, through both choice of literature that can inspire response and a methodology that allows students to respond, becomes not the knowledge giver or the sole truth teller, but a fellow reader and questioner.

I had a hunch that the primary characteristics of how reader response becomes good classroom practice would be exemplified by gifted high school English teachers who believe in reader response, discussing with their students three poems on a significant, salient topic. I was not wrong. In addition, the discussions represented by the transcripts of these classes also refute two common objections to the implementation of a reader-response methodology in the classroom: (a) attention to student response to literature will deflect seriously from any literary analysis of the work itself; and (b) a reader-response approach, in and of itself, takes too much instructional time to be efficient—it is quicker to tell students than to ask them to explore their own interpretations or reactions to a text. Also, although individual teachers may perceive that large-group discussion involves the majority of the class and that those who participate make extensive comments, such conclusions may be misleading. Accordingly, based on tapes and transcripts, an effort is made to tally the number of student participants and their responses and to measure the length of both comments and periods of silence.

METHODOLOGY AND THEORY

Many teachers reared in New Criticism in undergraduate/graduate training learned to love the close reading of poetry and prose. In this reading we adhered to a consideration of literature as a relatively isolated object to be discussed and analyzed—almost as one would turn a hard object such as a diamond and consider it from all points of view. The diamond itself would not be altered by the turning and handling; it would retain its entire integrity as an object. Thus New Criticism, as defined in John Crowe Ransom's 1941 book of the same name, was literature without the influence of the reader, the historical context, or the personal history of the author. Yet for all its obvious advantages over other forms of literary criticism, many of us reared in this tradition found, when we became teachers, that the technique did not often translate well. For many of us, in first period on Wednesday morning, our tenth-graders were struck dumb at the prospect of close, analytical reading divorced from personal or historical context, and some, we found, were even repelled. What for us was a celebration of the intricate art of literature for our students became a repugnant dissection of an already difficult text, robbing it of joy, making it a task, not a connection to life. We did not fully realize what Louise Rosenblatt calls the "responsibility to the students as well as the discipline" (ix).

I discovered reader response out of my own failure to entice my students to celebrate what I perceived to be the great craft of literature. I think I had forgotten that appreciation came to me after, sometimes long after, I had experienced how a novel or a short story could make me feel, could tell me about my life, my problems, my capabilities. My reading of Louise Rosenblatt told me, and the transcripts of these classes also show that, first, the literature itself must have some connection to the students' lives. Second, in order to capitalize on the students' lives, the approach must be inductive. Third, students must be involved, must be engaged to the point where the discussion leads them "to raise personally meaningful questions . . . [and] to seek in the text the basis for valid answers" (x).

There is an undergirding principle designating that text is a becoming, or as critic Roland Barthes describes it in *Image-Music-Text* as something that is "held in language, only exists in the movement of discourse . . . *experienced only in an activity of production*" (157). Text is, for Barthes and for many others, "the very plural of meaning . . . [dependent on] the *plurality* of its weave of signifiers" (159). Thus for Barthes and others, *signifiers* are not just readers but those who, in their time and place and with their individual backgrounds, make manifest the meaning of the text. In the two classes discussed in this article, the signifiers are different, their weaves of patterns vary, but their engagement with the literature is real and alive.

The two classes that participated in this discussion are at the secondary level in the Richmond, Virginia area. Elaine Younts's ninth-grade class, considered average to below average academically, is at a suburban middle/lower-middle-class public secondary school. Mary Neary-Rice teaches middle-class tenth-graders, considered average academically, at a private nondenominational school from the metropolitan area. Each class discussed three twentieth-century American poems with a common theme of fathers

(Henry Taylor's "Breakings," Robert Hayden's "Those Winter Sundays," and Neal Bower's "Black Walnuts"). Although each teacher's class had some experience with poetry, the students did not prepare for the class beforehand, did not see the poems prior to the class, and were not aware of the project or the taping. All quotations are reproduced virtually verbatim; all names are pseudonyms.

BREAKINGS

Long before I first left home, my father
tried to teach me horses, land, and sky,
to show me how this kind of work was done.
I studied how to be my father's son,
but all I learned was, when the wicked die,
they ride combines through barley forever.

Every summer I hated my father
as I drove hot horses through dusty grass;
and so I broke with him, and left the farm
for other work, where unfamiliar weather
broke on my head an unexpected storm
and things I had not studied came to pass.

So nothing changes, nothing stays the same,
and I have returned from a broken home
alone, to ask for a job breaking horses.
I watch a colt on a long line making
tracks in dust, and think of the kinds of breakings
there are, and the kinds of restraining forces.

—Henry Taylor

THOSE WINTER SUNDAYS

Sundays too my father got up early
and put his clothes on in the blueblack cold
then with cracked hands that ached
from labor in the weekday weather made
banked fires blaze. No one ever thanked him.

I'd wake and hear the cold splintering, breaking.
When the rooms were warm, he'd call,
and slowly I would rise and dress,
fearing the chronic angers of that house.

Speaking indifferently to him,
who had driven out the cold
and polished my good shoes as well.
What did I know, what did I know
of love's austere and lonely offices?

—Robert Hayden

BLACK WALNUTS

The year my father used the car for hulling
was the best. We cobbled the drive
with walnuts gathered in baskets
and cardboard boxes, then rode with him
down that rough lane, forward and backward,
time and again, until the air was bitter to breathe
and the tires spun in the juice.
For years after, every piece of gravel
was dyed brown, and the old Ford
out on the open road would warm up
to a nutty smell, especially in winter
with the windows closed and the heater blowing.

Crouched over hulls mangled green and yellow,
we picked out corrugated shells
even the car's weight couldn't crack
and spread them on the grass to dry.
My father, on his hands and knees, happy
over windfall, talked of how good
the tender meats would taste; and in that moment
I wished with all my heart that he might live forever,
as leaves ticked down around us
and the fresh stain darkened on our hands.

—Neal Bowers

TEACHERS ENCOURAGE STUDENTS TO TALK EXTENSIVELY

If engaging in a transaction with literature, having students make the literature their own, is an instructional goal, then students must be able to join in a conversation. This is to be distinguished from a series of responses to a teacher's question, responses that are ultimately regulated, guided, and abbreviated within the class context. If they are to thrive in a reader-response classroom, students must converse: speak at length, pause, argue, question. They should not be confined to one-word, one-phrase answers in response to a teacher's question and in a pattern determined by the teacher. In a reader-response classroom, teachers encourage students to talk extensively.

From the transcripts, the classes of Ms. Younts and Ms. Neary-Rice could be characterized, in general, as highly lively. Whereas the students in Ms. Neary-Rice's class might be described as more sophisticated in their intellectual analysis, repeatedly citing lines from the text in an almost New Critical fashion and speaking mcre at length than their younger counterparts, the students in Ms. Younts's class also discuss extensively. Students, from the evidence of the tape, remain on task with the three poems during the entire class period, and neither teacher feels compelled to guide students "back to the subject."

Ms. Younts does make one comment—virtually to herself—that a topic is off the subject, but she does not correct the student whose comment precipitates her remark.

The longest periods of silence/wait time are a twenty-second segment in Ms. Younts's class in response to a question on "Breakings" ("What does he [the poet] say he's learned in the end?") and a twelve-second pause in response to a question on "Those Winter Sundays" ("Why [could this poem not take place in modern times]?"). Both periods of silence/wait time are followed by extended, multiple student answers of fifteen seconds or more.

In Ms. Neary-Rice's class, students become so heated over their summary discussion of the three poems, particularly in the area of whether the poems are about fathers and daughters or fathers and sons, they are called to order approximately four times ("Try not to talk at the same time because you want to hear each other" is a typical teacher comment in this passage), and much of that portion of the tape is unclear due to the nature of multiple, overlapping student comments to other students on the interpretations of the poems. Ms. Neary-Rice asks a variety of questions ("What makes you think that?" or "Does anyone else think that?" are representative queries), encouraging her students to expand on their answers. In fact, in both the classes recorded, student responses are not always one-word or one-phrase answers but extended sentences, largely in clusters of five to seven seconds with a dozen or so twenty-second responses. When students do make brief, phrase answers, they occur in the context of a rapid-fire argument/discussion with other students.

TEACHERS HELP STUDENTS MAKE
A COMMUNITY OF MEANING

Because each student's response will draw on individual, even idiosyncratic, personal background and experience, and because exchange and exploration is the goal, reader-response teachers must be patient with factual misunderstanding. Eventually, individual misconceptions are corrected in a community of meaning. In a reader-response classroom, nevertheless, paramount attention is not focused on "right" answers.

Accordingly, Ms. Younts maintains open discussion and explores multiple interpretations. For example, about five minutes into the discussion of the first poem, "Breakings," she initiates a discussion on a passage referring to the breaking of a colt. The colt's experience is metaphorically linked to the poem's speaker's own "breaking" by life/reality, but Ms. Younts waits as the students struggle with the meaning. Later, as a whole class, they do agree on their perception of the poem's major point, but it is a journey of interpretation. As in discussions outside of school, meaning is found and lost and found again:

MS. YOUNTS: What does it ["Breakings"] mean, James?

JAMES: He learned how to be a farmer on his dad's farm and then he left first to find a new job, and he got—he couldn't find nothing better—he couldn't find nothing good—so he had to go back to working on the farm and hopefully . . . (garbled).

KAY: He left his dad and the dad wanted the son to be just like him—so he got tired of it.

MS. YOUNTS: What do you think he's learned at the end [of the poem]?

BILL: I thought he was at a racetrack.

MS. YOUNTS: What made you think that?

JAMAL: Because it said—the colt—he's kicking up dirt. I thought he was at a racetrack.

MS. YOUNTS: What's he doing with the colt on a long line?

JAMES: He's plowing.

KAY: He's breaking.

JAMES: He's plowing . . . he's training.

KAY: He's training.

ANN: He's trying to get it so that he can break the—

MS. YOUNTS: He's trying to break the colt? . . . Ann, you work with horses, don't you? Have you ever seen them when they put them on a long line—what are they trying to do?

ANN: It's a *lunge* line. They're trying to get them to—have them get used to . . .

MS. YOUNTS: Get used to the thing around their head—what do they call that, *halter?*

ANN: Yeah. They call it a halter.

MS. YOUNTS: So what else could they be breaking here?

BILL: Breaking him into a plow . . . getting him used to a plow.

MS. YOUNTS: Breaking on the plow. What does a plow do?

BILL: It plows the field.

JAMES: It breaks up the ground.

MS. YOUNTS: Does it break up anything?

BILL: It breaks up the dirt.

MS. YOUNTS: Okay. What does this guy say about his feelings about his father?

As the discussion goes on, much is said about what the speaker feels about his father and although it would appear the students do not immediately understand the metaphorical significance of *breaking*, they eventually come to the following conclusion:

MS. YOUNTS: What do you think this title, "Breakings," means?

MARY: Breaking of him.

ANN: Breaking the horses.

CURT: Breaking both [of them].

A community of meaning is made.

TEACHERS ASK, DON'T TELL

Teachers who tell students, who talk most of the class time, do not have reader-response classrooms. It must be the students who struggle with the literature, who give the answers, and who make the meaning—their own meaning—of the text.

The major tool, in these discussions, is the question. Whereas Ms. Neary-Rice does give vocabulary synonyms, and Ms. Younts speaks extensively on the variety of walnuts, both women resist almost all direct instruction. When confronted with a student question, both teachers turn to other students rather than become the answer giver.

Ms. Younts does not provide students with a list of preselected terms but asks twice for words the students do not understand ("Find another word that you don't know what it means"), asks for confirmation regarding terms ("Ann, what do they call that, a *halter?*"), and, when she actually looks up one word for a definition, asks students to give her the spelling of the word. She encourages students to struggle to find meaning themselves and, in a typical exchange, tells a student: "Look at *corrugated* in context . . . have you ever seen corrugated cardboard?" When the student responds, "That word doesn't make sense," Ms. Younts does not correct her or argue but acknowledges the fact and tells the student, "We're going to find out why it doesn't make sense."

When confronted with a twenty-second silence regarding the meaning of "Breakings," Ms. Younts gives two prompts but waits for student answers—which do come, from three students. Even when asked for clarification, Ms. Younts turns to her students:

MS. YOUNTS: What do you think changes in the roles that the dad and the son play? Anything?

ANDRE: What do you mean by the *roles?*

MS. YOUNTS: Does anyone know here what I mean by the roles? [*She receives responses to this question, as she does when she asks for an interpretation in "Those Winter Sundays".*]

MS. YOUNTS: He says in here, let's look down at this bottom line, "speaking *indifferently* to him." What do you think that means?

MIKE: Not any differently than . . .

BOB: Not in a different language.

CURT: Same as everyone, everyone else.

MS. YOUNTS: Why would that be that significant if he's talking to his father the same as everyone else?

ALAN: All fathers are like . . .

CURT: It's probably that same weekend routine.

BILL: Does that mean like *indifferently* to, like, than what he usually does—or just to everybody?

MS. YOUNTS: I don't know . . . what do you think?

BILL: It's everybody—he should be talking to his father differently because his father . . .

Similarly, Ms. Neary-Rice, when asking, "Which of these three [poems] seems to be a *father* poem?," receives two student questions: "What do you mean by that?" and "Which one do you like?—or which poem is a *father* poem?" Ms. Neary-Rice, however, does not answer, letting students argue as to the definition. And the students do subsequently argue in what is the most heated discussion of their particular class (depicted in the "Teachers Affirm Students' Responses" segment).

TEACHERS ASK STUDENTS TO MAKE LINKS TO PERSONAL EXPERIENCE

Requesting that students make links to personal experience is a paramount activity in reader-response classrooms. In capable hands, however, it becomes more than students simply venting their opinions. While personal experience is shared and cited, the students in both Ms. Younts's and Ms. Neary-Rice's classrooms also pay close attention to the text of the three poems, using it to buttress their points.

Ms. Younts asks students on two separate instances to relate to the anger of the speaker against his father in "Breakings" and receives multiple answers—some students link their assigned household tasks (such as mowing the lawn) to the speaker; some discuss their general anger toward their parents. During the latter instance, three students share responses, one for twenty-two seconds. Ms. Younts also directly asks, "How many of you think that in twenty years you'll get along a lot better with your father?" Interestingly enough, most students assume they will have an improved relationship, largely because they will be living the same kinds of lives as their fathers.

Fathers and Their Roles

Discussing "Those Winter Sundays," Ms. Younts asks, "What does this dad do that's different from what your dad does?" which leads to a class poll and discussion of weekend sleeping/rising patterns for the students, their fathers, and Ms. Younts. Again, she cycles back to the students' relationships with their fathers, touching on the "chronic angers" aspect of "Those Winter Sundays." Two students responded extensively, one is cited here:

"My dad was like, he started to get—because I knew it wasn't me that my dad was mad at because it was pretty bad you know ever since I was a little kid. It was pretty bad. But once he got to the point where he was losing his job, he started on everything, every little thing—it was getting worse—and I knew it wasn't me."

Ms. Younts, going back to the "speaking indifferently" line of "Those Winter Sundays," asks about students treating their fathers "in a way they shouldn't have"; the request elicits a three-minute, eight-second response from approximately half a dozen students regarding family disputes with both mothers and fathers. In one instance a student goes back to "Breakings" to buttress his point. At the conclusion of this segment, which Ms. Younts does not interrupt or guide other than to call on students, she makes the point that is used in the title of this chapter, "One good thing about this poem is the guy who wrote this poem seems to have the same feelings as you . . . have."

Ms. Neary-Rice's class, discussing "Sundays," gets into a lively argument about the believability of anybody's father banking a fire or actually polishing their shoes. Although banking fires is agreed on as what Ms. Neary-Rice calls a "father thing to do," in general, there is loud dispute about polishing shoes. Yet two students volunteer, much to the encouragement of some peers, that their fathers perform such tasks. And, in the sharing, John, who had loudly proclaimed that fathers just did not polish shoes, links the comment back to "Those Winter Sundays" ("No one ever thanked him") and, essentially, apologizes to Angela:

ANGELA: Yeah, my dad used to polish my shoes for me when I was little—and I wore those Mary Janes and you'd wear them forever and forever—and they were all scuffed up and my Dad would polish them like every Sunday morning, or right before we went somewhere.

JOHN: Did you thank him?

ANGELA: Did I ever thank him? I don't know. Probably not. I hated those shoes.

JOHN: I stand corrected.

Fathers and Their Children

Almost immediately after this interchange, in response to Ms. Neary-Rice's question about "a father's love being lonely" ("What did I know, what did I know / of love's austere and lonely offices?"), two students make long comments twenty- and thirty-second responses respectively). One student literally bursts out:

"I saw some kid smack his father down. He was like at a basketball game, and the father was walking around with his kid; he felt real cool, watching these kids out there shoot baskets and everything. And as they're walking off, the kid goes, 'I want to ride home with Mommy.' And just totally just left the dad.

"And the dad said, 'Well, why don't you want to go home with me?'

'I just want to go home with Mommy.'

"And the Father just walked off."

Students make a number of astonished and sympathetic noises, which leads to a second student point:

"I always felt closer to my Mom than I did to my Dad because my Dad was the one who used to punish me. And my Mom used to say, 'Aw, don't hit him.' "

Later in Ms. Neary-Rice's class, a student says she "can relate" to the poem:

"He [my father] does a lot of things for me that I don't think about, and I never thank him for . . . and a lot of times I'll be not very nice to him, and I won't even realize I'm doing it. And then I'll like think about it and realize and then it's kind of too late, kind of like this [in 'Those Winter Sundays']."

After this remark, three students add their observations about their fathers and the giving and taking of thanks and praise.

The Walnut Experience

With "Black Walnuts," Ms. Younts asks students about their knowledge of walnuts and walnut trees and, uncharacteristically for this instructor and this class, gives the most extensive background yet on the subject. The disquisition of sorts, lasting about three minutes, is almost puzzling. Yet a later conversation with Ms. Younts confirmed what most veteran teachers would assume: The subject matter of the poem, the breaking up of walnuts on the driveway with the family car, is unique enough to worry about. She feared that her students would be hopelessly confused and not understand even the bare surface of "Walnuts," much less the metaphorical significance of the event with regard to the speaker's feelings about his or her father. The discussion of the poem was, also, the last activity of the class period.

Surprisingly, however, not only in Ms. Younts's class, but in Ms. Neary-Rice's class, students had direct experience with a virtually identical event. One of Ms. Younts's students, who grew up in Pakistan, describes how her family used the car to crush black walnuts in their driveway. She tells where her family bought the walnuts, how much they cost, how they broke them open, and so forth. In Ms. Neary-Rice's class a student says she and her family "did this one year" and very briefly describes the procedure.

Certainly the fact that the subjects of the three poems are central to students' lives— parents, if not on-site fathers—makes such an insistence on linkage of personal experience possible. All of the students have stories and opinions and a history in this area; the discussions, as cited here, might not be as rich if the topic were about building highways or going to war. Yet, as the transcripts also show, the students do more than simply link the poetry to their own lives and experiences. Most of the students return to lines, concepts, and ideas in the literature and, while they relate to the text, also do a capable job examining and even analyzing it.

TEACHERS AFFIRM STUDENTS' RESPONSES

In addition, with a reader-response classroom discussion teachers affirm student response to the literature. They can affirm response by overt praise or agreement, but the transcripts of these two classes show that Ms. Younts and Ms. Neary-Rice reinforce their students' responses through two major instructional methods: (a) by referring to student comments in discussion and (b) by asking other students to respond particularly to those comments. Such actions give powerful confirmation to students that their ideas and responses are legitimate.

Ms. Neary-Rice, specifically prompted by the interchange of two students, directs her class to the "chronic angers" line from "Those Winter Sundays":

> CHARLES: Well, it seems like the kid, he feared his father. He doesn't fear him—he doesn't understand his father it doesn't seems like. It says right there, "When the rooms were warm, he'd call, / and slowly I would rise and dress, / fearing the chronic angers." I mean at first it seems like he loves his father for chasing "out the cold," and then it seems like he fears his father.

> KAREN: But does he fear the "chronic angers" of that house or his father? That's not his father.

> CHARLES: It's his father.

> MS. NEARY-RICE: Everybody look at this line and let's see how you first thought about it and see if you think differently on second thought. What are you thinking the "chronic angers" are?

In answer to this question, approximately seven students respond for a total of three relatively teacher-uninterrupted minutes, taking turns looking at the phrase. Another student then moves the discussion to the 'speaking indifferently' section and talks, without interruption, for almost one and one-half minutes.

Ms. Neary-Rice uses this technique repeatedly, moving students to respond to other student observations some half a dozen times during the class period. In "Breakings," for instance, she notes: "Jim said you break the spirit of the colt. If we make an analogy here between the father and son, does that make the son bitter—as Rick said?"

The technique has the effect of inspiring students to continue to respond to each other, as in the case of one student who, with no prompting or teacher-led suggesting, disputes another student's vision of the locale of "Breakings" as a place of "dying fields and dust and storms." The second student objects to this characterization and says that the poem is more a "Kentucky" poem than "Those Winter Sundays," which strikes him as a "New England" type of piece:

"I think these poems are very geographical. They have two geographical distinctions. When I think of horses and breaking horses, I think of Kentucky, and the bluegrass, and like the Kentucky Derby and all that. And when I think of the 'cold' and 'austere,' I think of New England and the birch trees."

Ms. Neary-Rice's response is both praise and an invitation: "Maybe some of you [students] thought that way, too; that makes sense to me." She encourages students to cite instances supporting the geographical hints/nuances of the next poem.

In Ms. Neary-Rice's class, the most heated argument is brought to the fore by the citation of a student's point:

> MS. NEARY-RICE: Did you hear what Charles said? "This [poem "Breakings"] is not about fathers and daughters, this is about fathers and sons." What do you think of that?

The responses, ranging virtually across the entire class, involve approximately six students, and cover the area of inclusive language ("everybody in here [this class] is saying he anyway") and sex of author ("Neal Bowers wrote this" and, from two other students, "They're [the poems] written by men"; "There's not one woman here—*Henry* Taylor"). There are personal examples from families (a girl notes, "my father makes me go out and dig ditches and move gravel and stuff like that"; a boy sarcastically says "my mother never takes me by the hand and teaches me how to sew or do the dishes") and a comment on sex roles ("How many *daughters* break horses?"). One student cites the archetypal aspect of the poem ("on the surface it could be about fathers and sons, but I think it could be the universal relationship between parents and children"). Another student notes the difference between the relationships between fathers and daughters and mothers and daughters ("You never hear," one student asserts, "about mother/son bonding").

From this very heated, wide-ranging argument there emerges a question of whose poem is it anyway, a discussion that is, essentially, about reader response. Theresa starts the discussion, and her comment is almost lost in the uproar. Neary-Rice does not repeat it for the class, but signals the other students to listen:

> MS. NEARY-RICE: Check out Theresa's remark, and let's hear if you agree.
>
> THERESA: I think it [the interpretation of the poem as about fathers and sons or fathers and daughters] is determined by the reader and not the poet.
>
> JOHN: Yeah, it's neutered.
>
> four student voices; garbled. Ms. Neary-Rice calls to order.
>
> MS. NEARY-RICE: Do you agree that there's a different meaning for the reader, that that's possible?
>
> THERESA: Yeah.
>
> RICK: Yeah. Sometimes the poem—you put these allegorical meanings [in it], then it can. But if you just write a straightforward poem, it can't be disputed then. There's, like, no second meaning.
>
> MS. NEARY-RICE: What kind of poem is a "straightforward" poem?
>
> RICK: What the poet wants to write.
>
> ROB: Like a descriptive poem.
>
> KAREN: Like when he says *he*.
>
> ROB: Like a haiku.

KAREN: Yeah.

JOHN: I think you can interpret it however you want—but you may well be *wrong* in your interpretation. Because I think the poet had a set audience in mind and what he was remembering and what he was trying to get out. So if you want to think of it as a father/daughter thing, you may be wrong, but you're welcome to your own opinion.

JIM: The poet's a man.

KAREN: But you don't know the poet.

RICK: But if the author like released what this . . . pamphlet, this book . . . is about, is meant to mean, that would take all the fun out of discussing it.

ROB: Well, you see the poet is writing for the poet himself, and that's how he is interpreting it. But other people can read it, and that's how they interpret it.

[*And how they interpret it, and the very excitement, the very pleasure of discussing it, is surely at the heart of this reader response classroom.*]

CONCLUSION

Certainly there is a place for the literary lecture. Certainly the New Critical examination of that well-wrought urn can also be an illuminating and rewarding activity. But as Rosenblatt and Barthes and others remind us, when we consider our middle school and high school and college students and their engagement with literature, the formation of their joy of literature, we must allow them not only the discussion floor itself but the authority of their own thoughts and instincts. In my school history, like the history of many others, virtually no teachers allowed me that authority—only my reader/guide, my mother, encouraged me to talk of literature in terms of my own experiences and understanding. Certainly no one in English class advanced the opinion that a poet's ideas might be akin to mine or any other student's. Thus, I knew that reading was one thing at home and another in school. This lack of fit should not be the rule in our classrooms, with our students, as we not only take our joy in the words on the page but try to provide an environment where our students can similarly celebrate the text.

The two teachers represented in this article allow their students joy and time, and they honor their ideas. They know and convey that different readers can have different interpretations, and they suggest that poets and young people have similar feelings. What they do is not mysterious or arcane or even terribly difficult. What they do, however, if we care about literature and about developing our students into life-long readers, is absolutely mandatory.

REFERENCES

Barthes, Roland. *Image-Music-Text.* Translated by Stephen Heath. New York: Hill and Wang, 1977.

Bowers, Neal. "Black Walnuts." In *North American Review* 273. 2 (June 1988): 19.

Hayden, Robert. "Those Winter Sundays." In *I Am the Darker Brother.* Ed. Arnold Adoff. New York: The Macmillan Company, 1968. 10.

Ransom, John Crowe. *The New Criticism.* Norfolk, CT: New Directions, 1941.

Rosenblatt, Louise. *Literature as Exploration.* 3d ed. New York: Noble and Noble, 1976.

Taylor, Henry. "Breakings." In *An Afternoon of Pocket Billiards.* Salt Lake City: University of Utah Press, 1975.

CHAPTER 4

Falling into the White between the Black Lines:

When Teachers Transact with Text

Marilyn Hanf Buckley

Imagine a university summer literature institute for educators: a large group of elementary and secondary classroom teachers—both experienced and prospective—and a smaller group of administrators, school board members, and university instructors, all of whom are enrolled in a four-week residential program to teach themselves how to research literature. Research, that is, in the original meaning of the word: to look again. Under the guidance of a director who facilitates the group's collaborative learning, the teachers look again at different ways they might read and respond to literature. The institute calls each individual by the prestigious title of teacher—whether prospective or experienced, primary or college, or working inside or outside the classroom. This chapter uses the term *teacher* in a similar way.

The institute proposes two objectives, one personal and one professional. The first objective focuses on the teacher and asks the questions: How do you read? How might you read? The second objective, pedagogical in nature, asks: How do your students read? Why do they read that way?

THE FIRST OBJECTIVE

The purpose of the first objective is to develop reflective teachers who seriously think about how they themselves read, discerning as best they can the peculiarities of human comprehension. This objective is unusual, perhaps even audacious, involving as it does the grasping of the obscure and intangible processes of thinking. Only geniuses or fools would undertake the task of trying to become observant of the mind's spontaneous and

---

Acknowledgment is given to Dr. Walter Loban for his advice in preparing this chapter.

unconscious ways of resurrecting dead print into that vibrant mental reality called reading. Teachers are neither. If it were not necessary to understand the process of reading, the institute would do best to leave the human mind to its own mysteries and making of miracles. But society, and particularly schools, do not leave reading alone—they teach it and test it; they praise those who excel in it and condemn those who fail; therefore, someone—and who better than teachers?—needs to accept the challenge of exploring, however awkwardly, how reading happens. Whereas the first objective is somewhat impudent, the second is predictable.

THE SECOND OBJECTIVE

Attending to the easier problem of pedagogy, the second objective calls for a new curriculum for teaching literature to elementary and secondary students. This objective, a challenge of serious proportions, is easier only because it follows and benefits from the understandings gained from the first. Generating ideas on how to teach others naturally follows in the wake of discoveries born from self-teaching. To teach literature with poise and confidence, teachers need to experience and internalize the subject. If the institute aspires for a different teaching of literature, then the new ways of literature must first become part of the teacher, not just part of the curriculum. Change the teacher, the institute hypothesizes, and then students will change accordingly. The challenge of teacher education, therefore, is to bring about the teachers' personal re-knowing of curriculum.

A PERSONAL RE-KNOWING OF LITERATURE

In order to understand how teachers engage in re-knowing literature, let us imagine visiting the institute on an ordinary morning. We might see something like the following: A class of thirty teachers, in discussing the assignment, POEMS I GO BACK TO, finish sharing their personal choices of favorite poems and select Theodore Roethke's "My Papa's Waltz" for general discussion. (The text of this poem is printed in full in Chapter 19 of this book, p. 221.)

The class, breaking into five study groups of six teachers each, will take forty minutes to read and discuss the poem, and another twenty minutes to prepare an informal presentation to be shared with the whole group. The group leader inquires: How might this text be read? After silent study, each teacher reads the poem aloud, the reader's initial interpretation shaping its sound. Discussion follows and teachers comment on why they gave the poem its particular reading. After deciding which reading best captures the sense of the poem, the teachers negotiate how that reading might extend itself into a presentation. By defining "presentation" as "offering a gift of interpretation to be viewed or considered," the teachers free themselves from the pressure of trying to craft *the* correct presentation. Three descriptions of presentations are given.

Three Preliminary Interpretations

Group 1.   A teacher pulls the drapes along the windows on one wall, creating a room half in darkness and light. In the lighted section, the teacher who plays the boy sits on the floor, looks up to the Papa, and reads the poem in a narrative tone, as if he were telling the Papa his rememberance of what happened. ("The whiskey on your breath / Could make a small boy dizzy; / But I held on like death; / Such waltzing was not easy.") At the same time the boy is reciting the poem in the lighted side of the room, the poem is being pantomimed in the darkened side. The Papa holds the small boy (who is represented by a newspaper-stuffed suit jacket) at waist height and awkwardly waltzes around the room, banging into things. The mother, sits at a table, scowling. ("We romped until the pans / Slid from the kitchen shelf / My mother's countenance / Could not unfrown itself.") The dual presentation—the boy reciting and the pantomiming—presents a couplet of words and actions.

Group 2.   In silence, the Papa ungracefully waltzes the small boy to bed where he stumbles, and both child and father fall onto the bed. The Papa sleeps; the boy stares wide-eyed into the night and recites the poem to himself. His voice is small, scared, confused. Then the Papa awakes and asks the child what had happened. The boy recites the poem. This time the boy's voice is cheerful, as if the waltzing were good sport.

Group 3.   Off to the side, as if in another room, the boy is sleeping. At center, the mother and papa who have just retired to bed are quarreling. The mother accuses her husband of frightening the boy; the father vehemently denies the accusation. The Papa and Mother turn away from each other and pretend to sleep. Both recite the poem, with one voice following the other, both saying all lines. The Papa's saying of the poem is matter-of-fact; the mother's recitation is angry and denying. The very same words, but very different words, reverberate, but without resonance. The conflicting interpretations clumsily bang into one another, much like the Papa's waltzing.

Response to the Interpretations

After each presentation, the teachers write about four impressions: What I saw; what I heard; what I felt, and what I wondered about. Then, teachers reread their comments on all the groups, and begin discussion. After sharing general reactions, the teachers identify the commonalities among the diverse presentations and reread the poem to find textual justification for such consensus. To prevent the majority point of view from being *the* meaning, minority interpretations are called for. Sometimes, a minority interpretation is good-naturedly shouted down, the audience exclaiming that the text—no matter how liberally read—could not support such an interpretation. Other times, a silence will follow a teacher's minority report, then someone will insist: "Why, of course. I never saw the text that way, but I do now." Other teachers will nod in agreement.

Part of the discussion usually includes the nagging question: But how would we evaluate the different interpretations? Teachers have been reminded many times by Walter Loban that whoever controls evaluation, controls the curriculum. Designing new methods of evaluations are an integral part of designing new curriculum.

The morning session ends and teachers leave for a two-hour break, an hour for lunch and an hour for journal writing. Part of the teachers' writing will be to respond to "The question for the week." For this particular week the question is: How does change in teaching literature happen? At the end of the institute, different study groups collect all papers pertaining to a particular question and write a summary. The summary to this question follows.

HOW DOES CHANGE IN LITERATURE HAPPEN?

Two conditions are needed for curriculum change: one, an inspired theory that disturbs the staying power of the status quo; and two, an inspired teacher who challenges the complacency of her own teaching. The equilibrium of both the theoretical base and the teacher who instructs from the base must be upset—discreetly if possible—if change is to happen. In education neither one nor the other of these conditions makes for substantial conversion; only the two together disquiet the steady poise and intractable position of conventional schooling. By combining forces, the two conditions generate the strength required to uproot the established ways of doing things, in particular, the ways of doing literature; that is, the ways of its teaching and learning and whether such ways can be changed. Change in theory and teacher behavior, a demanding fusion of intellect and emotions, constitutes the criterion for measuring the validity of any educational experiment, including the present reform in literature.

PRESENT REFORM IN LITERATURE

In the United States, England, Australia, New Zealand, and Canada, the beginning of one curriculum change is happening; namely, the integration of English Language Arts through literature. It is, to be sure, premature to predict whether or not this reform will be just another fashion or a substantial shift in how literature is taught. For five years I have been involved with the new curriculum, studying, more or less informally, the strength of the theory and the resolve of teachers, and working with the California Literature Project, and the Alaska Literature Consortium:[1] Both projects and my own work are persuaded by the transactional theory of Louise M. Rosenblatt, a theory of considerable influence at the present time in this country and abroad.

Rosenblatt's respect for readers and the process they use to comprehend the text makes her theory particularly amenable to today's educators who are primarily concerned with developing reading comprehension. As the school population becomes more culturally and linguistically diverse, teachers look for a theory that both explains why thirty-three students read a single story in thirty-three different ways, as well as a theory that encourages teachers to take advantage of the diverse ranges of comprehension.

Teachers realize that the word *comprehend* derives from Latin, *comprehendere* meaning to seize, to grasp, to capture. To comprehend is to act. And it is an act that is done by individuals, not something done to them. If readers are to comprehend—that is, if they are to seize, grasp, or conquer—a text, then the readers must initiate and accept responsibility for the making of meaning, asserting themselves intellectually and emotionally. Rosenblatt's profile of a reader describes the type of reader many teachers are eagerly trying to develop. Rosenblatt's theory provides teachers with the security of a theory they can use once they have engaged in their own change.

TEACHER CHANGE

The problem of teacher change, so easy to talk about and so hard to effect, is not unique to the literature institute. The question as to the best way to effect teacher change is being asked in schools across the country. My approach to teacher change in literature, one among many proposed approaches, involves four steps:

1. Teachers concentrate on the general conditions required for change.
2. Teachers focus on the process of reading, particularly how they themselves read, and construct different hypotheses on how reading happens. Comparing their processes with other participants, teachers write a draft of the reading process.
3. Teachers study Rosenblatt and several other theorists on reading, to determine the commonalities between their personal hypotheses and those by the theorists.
4. After teachers describe a reading process that holds somewhat true for them, their colleagues, and theorists, they design a plan of action to investigate whether their students use a similar reading process or one idiosyncratic to the students. Let us examine the first step.

1. THE PROCESS OF CHANGE

Rosenblatt's contention that no one can make meaning for readers other than the individual readers themselves, can be extended to suggest that no one can make a "new" teacher other than the teachers themselves. This means, of course, that the teacher accepts the responsibility, consciously and deliberately, of participating in decision making. To make change in how one teaches is no simple matter and does not get enacted with the facility of—let us say—a change of mind. Teaching is a behavior, deeply rooted and in action more spontaneous than reflective, so change is primarily psychological. It involves not so much a change of mind as a change of heart.

And without the change of heart, it is my observation that teachers will continue repeating their established patterns of instruction whether or not they *intellectually* adopt a new curriculum idea or verbally boast of academic acquaintance with this modern theorist or that.

Understanding and accepting the complexities of change must be the first step in curriculum revision. Schools are political institutions; thus, not to consider the politics of change is either ignorant or naive. I am not yet confident about the best way to engage teachers in some hard thinking about the process of change, but I suspect it begins with asking ordinary questions about change and not giving up until you get honest, and thus extraordinary, responses.

The questions should be calculated to bring about a political awareness, requiring the teacher to decide if she is willing to assume the role of change agent. I have used statements such as the following: Who are the important change agents? Do materials create change? Can teachers create changes in others that are not already in themselves? What are the consequences of change? And so forth.

In summary, the first step concentrates on teachers becoming aware of both the political and personal aspects of change, particularly the power of persuasion that is afforded to those who accept responsibility for change. A new curriculum, such as one based on Rosenblatt's transactional theory of literature, is *new*—it cannot be successfully put into practice by a teacher who does not explicitly agree to change. If the first step is successful, individual teachers accept the responsibility that they—as individuals—can effect a significant difference. Teachers grow in awareness of their own behavior—what they think, how they read.

2. HOW DOES A TEACHER READ?

When we talk about the purpose of Rosenblatt's transactional theory of literature we are, in one analysis, talking about teaching students to read. The teaching of reading, thought by many to be the raison d'être of schooling, is usually part of the professional preparation for elementary or secondary teachers. However, most teachers with whom I have worked report that they do not feel confident or independent in teaching reading. As one teacher put it, "I follow the manual and hope for the best."

To be honest, I am not surprised that teachers admit to such ignorance. In my opinion few people know about reading, because few people understand the nature of the mind: what thinking is, how it happens, and how it fails to happen. Reading, an act of verbal thinking, is heir to all the mysteries of how the mind composes and comprehends symbols.

I believe it is best for a teacher to admit the formidable complexities of verbal thinking and, with humility and wonder, proceed to observations of how oneself and others engage in the miracle of reading. I use "miracle" in the sense that A. N. Whitehead used it when he said that even though the miracle of a child's learning language is explicable, to the wise it remains a miracle.

Describing the Reading Process

The question: how do you read? If when asking teachers this question they infer it to be evaluative, it is best to remind them that the answers, if they are to be helpful, must be descriptive. Teachers are not being asked how they think they should read or how they would like to read? Those are easy questions with hypothetical ideal answers. But, how does one read? This is a difficult question that lacks definite answers.

Caution needs to be taken in trying to observe and objectively report the mercurial associations of the mind. Over millions of years of evolution, the brain has developed ways of doing the business of making meaning. These ways are not directly observable or explicable. If poets' brains were opened by scientists while they were creating, the poem could not be found. Much chemical electrical activity, to be sure, but no poem. The same of course can be said for the analysis of the brain of the reader of the poem.

If respectful of the profound mysteries of the imagination, a teacher can begin, ever so modestly, to reveal them. Through their attempts at introspecting how their mind makes experiences from a few oral or written symbols, teachers—finding their "answers" untidy, disorderly, unreliable, and full of contradictions—should become properly overwhelmed, frustrated, and full of awe. Teachers, more than anyone else, should expect and tolerate ambiguities. Once they realize they can only describe a few, simple, superficial behaviors from the vast, extraordinary complexities of the reading process, they will be educated.

To facilitate teachers observing their own reading, the following procedure is recommended.

A. A teacher reads assigned and self-selected texts in five genres: poetry, short story, drama, novel, and essay. Assignments provide common texts so that readers can engage in group discussions. They also have the secondary purpose of provoking teachers to analyze how they react to assigned readings, which is the common school practice imposed on students, as opposed to self-selected readings, which is the preferred way most people outside school read literature. The readings, selected from adult literature, challenge the teachers how they, as adults, read. If time permits, teachers should read the genres in adolescent and children's literature. But reading "as a teacher" follows, and should not precede or substitute for, reading "as an adult."

The purpose of a variety of readings is for teachers to determine whether they read different texts differently. For example, do strategies for making meaning apply to all readings or only to some? Are some texts more difficult than others? Are there better ways of reading poetry or essays, ways that are somewhat exclusive to the genre? And so forth. The essay, an example of exposition, represents a type of school reading. Its inclusion provides teachers with experiences in efferent reading which they will compare with aesthetic reading.

B. Titles of assigned readings varied according to group leaders and teachers, but readings previously used include titles from Grace Paley's "Enormous Changes at the Last Minute," to Robert Graves's "Warning to Children" and Ralph Waldo Emerson's "The American Scholar."

C. The assignment of readings includes the teacher keeping a journal. In this journal teachers write their responses to the text and descriptions of their behavior before, during, and after reading. Behaviors include all intellectual, physical, and emotional activities. Each page of the journal is divided in half. One half is for notes about the text and a running commentary of reader reactions: opinions, predictions, evaluations, and quotes. On the other half, teachers reflect—talk aloud to themselves, if you will, about *how* they read.

The readers' primary concern is to make meaning; how they individually make meaning—that is, their observation of their process of thinking, is secondary. Literature demands and deserves full attention. It was not written to provide analysis of the reading act and in no way should it be violated for purposes of research. After some initial self-consciousness, readers can both simultaneously read and crudely observe their process of reading.

D. Getting at the process of reading may be helped by the following questions. Teachers should not try to answer all of them or even most of them. I suggest that teachers read over the questions for a general sense of what is meant by process, and then forget about the specifics. The objective is for teachers to gently observe themselves read without distracting from the text. That is all that is expected.

A few sample questions for guiding reflection follow. Questions concern three stages: before, during, and after reading.

Questions Guiding "Before Reading" Commentaries
• What are my feelings about the assignment? Am I enthusiastic, casual, angry? Why do I feel this way? Do I predict my feelings will influence my reading? If so, in what ways?

- Does the fact that I will discuss the text in class influence my mood? Am I worried that I will not "get" the text? Do I fear that I will miss important aspects of the text?
- What do I already know about the text and/or author? If I do have information how do I think it will affect my reading?

Questions Guiding "During Reading" Commentaries
- What does my reading sound like? (Reading voice)
  When I read silently, do I hear the words, as if someone is reading the text? If so, whose voice is it?
  Does the voice change for different characters and descriptions?
  How does my "silent" reading differ from my reading aloud?
- What is my reading rate? (Reading speed)
  Do I vary my rate of speed, that is, slowing down, reading rapidly, skimming, rereading certain parts, and so forth?
  In silent reading, what happens to my reading voice(s) when my rate changes?
  Do I establish reading rates for particular types of reading? For example, do I usually read pleasure reading fast or slow? Assigned reading? Readings I expected to be tested on? Readings, assigned or self selected, which I enjoy?
- What does my reading look like? (Mental visualization)
  Do I see pictures of the text? All of text? Only some parts?
  How and when does the clarity of visualization change, if it does?
  Am I unaware of pictures or images but seem to have a felt sense that I am "seeing," perhaps in another way?
- Does my reading make sense?
  Do I vicariously experience any or some or all that I read?
  Do I put myself in the role(s) of characters, feeling their feelings as my own?
  Do I stand outside the characters and actions, watching as a sympathetic spectator? An uninvolved spectator?
- How does meaning happen?
  Am I conscious of the text's language? For example, do I particularly note unusual words, images, sentence style, effective phrases, figures of speech, and so forth? Or do I move through the language to the meaning, not paying particular, conscious attention to the words?
  If I do note the language, how do I note it? Do I check or underline selected words, phrases, or sentences? Do I stop and appreciatively reread?

Questions Guiding "After Reading" Commentaries
- When the text is finished, how do I feel? What are my immediate reactions after finishing a text?
  What might help me to reflect? What would probably distract from my reflecting?
- How would I react to a True/False or multiple choice test?

From this sample of questions, the reader may gain a sense of the investigative disposition that the teachers assume. The questions and journal help teachers to summarize how they read.

Preliminary Summarizing of the Reading Process

The individual questions, as I mentioned before, are not important. Teachers want two things from their readings: (a) emotional and intellectual involvement with the text, and (b) assumptions about how they process the text. The more important objective, we should not forget, is the first. Discussions about the text and how one "gets at" a text are kept separate until the discussions naturally integrate with one another. In this chapter my focus is on the process, and I do not include—because of space—the teachers' core discussions on the literary works.

By studying the descriptions in their journal, teachers identify patterns. From these patterns they make tentative generalizations about their reading and write a first draft of the reading process. Parts of two teachers' drafts follow, written before the teachers compared their reading processes with others.

A Teacher Thinks about Reading

"I like to read and think of myself as a good reader. But my high standards for reading probably hurt me as much or even more than they help me. I've discovered that I don't read with my heart, I read with my ego. I read to talk about the reading, impressing friends with clever interpretations of motive, character analysis or boasting of intimate knowledge about what the author is REALLY saying, etc. I'm careful to note details, characters' and places' names, so I can speak with exactness. I'll even memorize a particular, well expressed description, so I can quote it in my discussion. Or do I discuss? Perhaps I only lecture.

"I tried to read for reading; not to talk cleverly about my reading. It was a Wallace Stevens' poem, "Two Things of Opposite Natures Seem to Depend," which I hadn't read before. I monitored my reading. Even the very first reading degenerated into my "teaching" the poem (in my mind) to some invisible friend or student at the same time that I was reading it. There were two voices: one a reading voice and the other a what-this-poem-really-means voice.

"I tried to shut off the pedantic mutterings of asinine instant revelations and just let the reading voice sing the words. I tried only to listen. I imagined Stevens reading aloud the poem to me as I reread it. (My reading voice changed to masculine.) As soon as the imagined poet finished reading, I cleverly quoted—in reference to his reading—the lines from the poem "Music falls on the silence like a sense / A passion that we feel, not understand . . ." My imagined Wallace Stevens beams a radiant smile.

"The ego won again. I was disgusted with my need for approval, my compulsion to rush to judgment or comment about the poem before I even finished reading it. I realized my enjoyment was not in the words or rhythm or ideas, but in how quickly and cleverly I could talk about it. When did I make this Faustian bargain, giving up that which once pleased me for some cheap excuse of knowledge? I wasn't always this type of reader; the 'pedant' inside of me wasn't always there. I told the members of my group that I really didn't know how to read. They said, 'Of course you know how to read. You're a good reader.' Obviously they don't understand. Two questions nag me: One, can I relearn how to read? And two, how many students, particularly in my top groups, am I making into 'nonreaders' like myself?"

And Another Teacher Comments

"Reading, whether of literary or expository language, is a process of trying to make sense. The greater the sense or meaning, the better the reading. If I read a short story or a biography and don't get much meaning from it, I am not reading these texts well.

"How do I make sense of a page of print? I realize I translate the print into oral language. To put it another way, I hear what I am reading. Comprehension, then, could be explained if I knew how I comprehended spoken language. Listening to a string of words and knowing what they mean, what they imply, and what they are not meaning is amazing. My three year old can do it and do it well. Does that mean he'll be a good reader? I don't know.

"Emotions are also part of listening comprehension. What I hear can make me laugh, weep, overthrow the government, or sign a contract for life insurance that I don't need. In reading literature, my emotions are in charge. They drive my intellect. Emotionally, I have to want to read a text. If I can't get into a text, I can't lose myself. If I can't lose myself, I can't become the book. If I can't become the book, there is no reason to read literature. Surely, I don't read literature for information, even though I get a lot of information whenever I read. I guess I read for pleasure. The same pleasure I get from listening to a story, watching a good film or play. I change consciousness, forgetting time and place, and enter into an imaginative world. It's the story that does it. My brain particularly likes stories and can learn quickly and easily if information is given through the narrative.

"I learn quickly and easily if I connect with the text. I don't try to read well, I just offer myself to the text or is it that the text offers itself to me? I'm not sure. It's like meeting a person, and very quickly liking or disliking the person. If I like a person, it's easy for me to relax and talk fluently, understanding what he or she has to say, even if the person is from a background unlike mine. On the other hand, if I dislike the person, I get tense, acting and talking like a fool, and not paying attention to what is being said.

"It's the same with reading literature. If I like the text and make a connection, I understand almost everything, even the so-called hard stuff. My comprehension is good because I experience the text rather than read it. In discussions, I'm brilliant. No, not brilliant, but I'm full of good ideas and opinions. When I can't get into a text—and I don't know the reasons for this detachment—I try to read but I'm unsuccessful. If I have a choice, I put the book away and seek another. But if I'm compelled to read it, I suffer. My eyes go over the lines but all I get are words. If I try to discuss or write about the text, I fail. A professor would think that I was a retarded reader.

"No one should be made to read literature. It's like making someone listen to Mozart or look at Manet's paintings. If they want to, they'll be enriched; but if they don't, to force them is act tantamount to blasphemy of the artist and diminution of the reader's humanity. Literature is not a requirement, a chore, a duty. When it is reduced to a requirement, it loses all its secrets. A professor can become exasperated that his insensitive students don't appreciate Pound or MacLeish, but a student cannot read literature. He can only experience it. And the prerequisite for experiencing is genuine affection. Without emotional involvement, there is no comprehension."

3. COMPARING PROCESS WITH OTHERS

After teachers generalize about their probable processes of reading, they meet with a study group, consisting of seven or nine members. The purpose of sharing observations of processes with each other is to determine the similarities and differences among the group. What behaviors do all members do that make for comprehension? Are there behaviors shared by all members that interfere with comprehension? What are the typical behaviors of the majority? What are the minority behaviors? Are there many right ways of reading literature or only one way? What are the patterns among the group in influence of the following: reading voice, mental visualization, reading aloud, reading speed, identification with characters, predicting, judging or suspending judgment, concentration or distractability, language appreciation, reflecting while reading, handling unknown vocabulary, relations between pleasure or boredom and comprehension, relations between comprehension during reading and after reading (that is, recall), and any of the behaviors that the group commented on in their journals.

In comparing their suspicions, guesses, or assumptions of how they read with their colleagues' estimates of their processes, they may appreciate, perhaps for the first time, the incredible individuality of reading. If these insights occur to teachers, I contend, they will never again be satisfied with the simplistic, fatuous, delusive explanations of reading proposed by educational technicians. Nor will such teachers be apt to arrogantly prescribe rigid methodology to their students. Instead teachers may realize that what they need to know about teaching reading to elementary or secondary students is to be found in the students themselves.

Teachers Write Second Draft

From their own analyses and the group's, teachers rewrite their paper on process to include their revised thinking. The paper contains not only their speculations on how they and others read, but includes the conditions necessary to read literature with maximum comprehension and enjoyment. A small section of a teacher's paper follows:

> "The assignment to reflect on my reading has left me more confused than I ever was, particularly as it affects my teaching. Before the Institute I was confident that I knew what I was doing. I've been a teacher expert for three years and only came to the Institute to update my thinking. Now I'm not sure about teaching, and frankly I'm angry at the Institute for causing this insecurity. After I sort it all out and have my kids go through the process of reflecting on their reading, I'll probably evaluate this experience as seminal to my professional growth. But right now, I'm disconcerted. In reflecting upon my reading I've found some surprises.
>
> "The first is that my thinking and feelings are interconnected. I don't enjoy what I don't understand, and I don't understand—at least not at the deeper levels—that which I don't enjoy. For example, I didn't like Robert Graves' poem "Warning to Children" and frankly couldn't care less what it meant. Others in my group did like it, particularly the cleverness of how Graves kept reversing descriptions, and they struggled for a long time to figure out the warning and what might be in the package. I didn't participate because I had no intellectual energy. I'm reminded of a quote, I think it's by D. H. Lawrence. "Blood leads and the mind follows in the wake." I frankly dislike thinking of myself as a person who has to be emotionally pleased with something before she can study it. Such a dependency puts me in kinship with all the adolescents I teach. Troubling thought. After all I'm 36 years old and have a master's degree. Doesn't age and education ever triumph over the "blood"? No wonder it's like pulling teeth which aren't ready to come for me to get my kids involved. Most of them neither understand nor enjoy what we read.
>
> "When I read I either read for meaning or style. Awareness of both are always present, but one seems to predominate. In Doris Lessing's "To Room Nineteen" I was so caught up with

the story that I couldn't remember anything about Lessing's style. I honestly couldn't re-member how the story was made. All I know is that I was in room nineteen and it was painful. In Katherine Anne Porter's "Flowering Judas" I was more the spectator, watching how the character of Laura was made, appreciating how skillfully Porter created the somber moods and denials.

"Yet I was not the character Laura, I was a reader, an observant. In "To Room Nineteen" I was . . . what was her name? I forget. Imagine I forgot the name of the character with whom I became one and I remember clearly the character I did not identify with. What does this mean? I guess when the emotions don't get in the way, the brain can do its business more tidily.

"In reflecting upon my reading, I suspect that I am only 'moved' by literature when I'm in the mood to be moved. That sounds cute, but I am serious. If I can't or won't give permission to the text to be all it can be—because I am distracted or tired—then the text has minimal affect on me. At certain times I can read quality literature with the same insouciance that I read third rate novels, and be totally insensitive to the differences. The text is not independent of the reader, *Hamlet* is boring or extraordinary depending on how and when the reader meets it. Could we parody Hamlet's words (act II?) 'There is nothing either good or bad, but thinking makes it so,' to 'A text is neither good nor bad, but reading makes it so'? No, I don't believe that. There must be something about truth and art which makes them inviolate to the capricious whims of readers.

"I am confused. How can I return to school and reprimand, however subtly, students for paying no attention to the particulars of a text, when I read Saul Bellow's "The Thief" with little comprehension and no appreciation. If an exam were given on it, I would have flunked. Yet I am a good reader. Are the students whom I flunk also good readers who simply got the right book at the wrong time? I don't know."

This teacher and her colleagues now have an opportunity to study theory and research to learn how experts describe the reading process.

Reading Rosenblatt and Others

The teachers read and discuss their drafts with each other. They realize they are all teachers who are desperately trying to make intelligible how reading—the fundamental subject of all schooling—happens. They help one another to identify the important state-ments in the position paper and changed them into questions. Questions are then arranged in order of importance to the teacher. With questions in mind, the teachers are ready to read theory and research.

Study groups are organized according to interests and the readings are distributed accordingly. In addition to Rosenblatt, teachers read other theorists including Bruno Bettelheim, David Bleich, Kenneth Burke, Umberto Eco, Wolfgang Iser, Walter Ong, and Robert Scholes. Particular attention is also given to practioners, including Walter Loban, Dwight Burton, Charles Cooper, Robert Probst, Alan Purvis, James Squire, and others.[2] Each group is responsible for reading and discussing several texts; they prepare a presenta-tion on their readings for the large group. Discussions, many times quite animate, follow these presentations.

As teachers study, they find substantiations for some of their position paper opinions, none for others. Original assumptions in the position papers are expanded, qualified, and deleted. New hypothese are added. Again the teachers collaborate with each other, listen-ing and learning from one another. The second draft is revised so that each teacher has a final draft, consisting of reflected opinions, substantiated by theory and research, on the reading process. Teachers will use this final paper to guide investigation of a new group of readers—their students. Even though teachers must first begin by teaching themselves, their career objective is to teach students. The question teachers must take back to their classroom in first grade or twelfth is: How do students read? This brings the teachers to classroom-based research.

4. HOW DO STUDENTS READ?

The teacher's final draft describes the reading processes used by adults and supported, at least in part, by theoreticians. Students, however, are not adults and that which is true for adults is not necessarily true for children and adolescents. I suggest that teachers assume they do not know how students read literature, regardless of their years of teaching experience. What we think we know about students' reading may be incomplete if not misleading. It has not been the educators' style to learn from their subject, that is, the student, the way other scientists do. Astronomers study stars, botanists plants, but teachers do not study children. Our arrogance has kept us ignorant. Without such study, what we say about learning is suspect.

Students are the teachers of teachers in the same way as the organization and the structure of the earth is the teacher of geographers. Teachers, armed with their cautious descriptions of how they read and the latest theoretical thinking, are prepared to observe their students with minimum bias or prejudice. As the teachers learn to describe objectively, avoiding prescriptions and evaluations, profiles of how students read literature will emerge.

Children, at different ages, have peculiar ways of seeing and explaining the world. Do their "peculiarities" also pertain to how they read and experience literature? Would not the way they know the world also include the way they know the word? For example, does an eight-year-old forage for meaning in a story in the same way as a twelve-year-old? Are children, with their developing cognitions, precluded from knowing a text as an adult might know it? Or is there a constant quality of the human mind that intuitively understands the story, regardless of age or cognitive level? Do the readers of literature progress through definite stages as they mature, or is there basically one stage that simply varies in quality? If stages, do readers have to realize each stage before they proceed? On the other hand, if readers do not grow, do the readers forever stay at their particular stage of development? In a heterogeneous class of tenth-graders, how many different types of readers would there be? Can students introspect on how they read? What would a personal theory of reading composed by a nine-year-old or fifteen-year-old tell us?

SUMMARY

There is no end to the questions that teachers may ask. But teachers will probably not begin to ask the right type of questions until they (a) decide they are responsible for change; (b) observe how they and others read; (c) study transactional theory and teach themselves what they need to know; and (d) research, in the true sense of scientific inquiry, how students read and how they might read. Guidance on how best to teach literature in elementary and secondary schools will come from the student. Students must tell teachers what happens when they fall in the white space between the black lines and transact with text. Students are after all the readers, and what they make of the text is the teachers' first concern. Rosenblatt writes: "What the reader makes of the text is, indeed, *for him [or her]* the poem, in the sense that this is his [or her] only direct perception of it. No one else can read it for him [or her] (105). And no one else should read it for the reader. In literature institutes all over the country, teachers are learning why this is so.

NOTES

1. California Literature Project, directed by Dr. Mary Barr, California State Department of Education, Sacramento, California. Alaska Literature Consortium, directed by Annie Calkins, Alaska State Department of Education, Juneau, Alaska.
2. Recommended readings are cited in the culminating bibliography of this volume.

REFERENCES

Roethke, Theodore. "My Papa's Waltz." In *The Pocket Book of Modern Verse*. Ed. Oscar Williams. New York: Pocket Books, 1972. 433.

Rosenblatt, Louise M. *The Reader, the Text, the Poem: The Transactional Theory of the Literary Work*. Carbondale, IL: Southern Illinois University Press, 1978.

Whitehead, Alfred North. *The Aims of Education and Other Essays*. New York: Free Press, 1957.

PART II

Initiating Readers' Responses: Classroom Processes

The chapters in this section focus on beginnings—ways teacher can draw out in the classroom readers' responses to a text. The authors of these chapters propose strategies through which teachers initially engage students and cause them to explore their responses. They demonstrate how, although the teacher may provide the catalyst to open the discussion, it is the students' responses that are at the heart of the activity. In these chapters we see teachers resist using techniques that have the effect of predicting or directing response—thus limiting responses, such as reference to the writer's turn of mind or critics' understandings of the text.

The chapters offer a variety of approaches for initiating reader response and illustrate a range of audiences and situations. The strategies described were selected in each case because they fit specific teaching occasions, but they may well be adapted to other audiences and situations. Readers are invited to adapt these strategies to their own teaching situations and to think about how they can use them in their future classrooms.

In Chapter 5, Ron Luce reacts to a basic challenge in teaching literature— students who have been turned off, who have lost confidence in themselves as readers. His technical college students groan in dismay at the assignment of a poetry reading. Aiming to reverse their negative attitudes, their concern for "never get[ting] the right meaning," he effects a line-by-line response experience with Robert Frost's "Mending Wall." The students' initial tentative reactions and their developing interpretations are illustrated through their journal entries, which move from initial transaction with the text through a summary response to a connected personal experience. A transcript of a follow-up class discussion demonstrates the dynamics of such group interactions as the students, testing and refining their insights, wrestle with their sense of the poem. Luce offers additional suggested activities to augment his iceberg-breaking strategy.

The initiating approach described by Anne Sherrill in Chapter 6 is to use a pre-reading strategy prior to asking students to write a journal entry about their emotional response to Anton Chekhov's "The Lament." She shows her students several paintings and asks them to speculate about the communication taking place among the people depicted in them. The succeeding discussion exhibits meaningfully how the students' attitudes and social experiences affect their transaction with the text and how their perceptions are engaged and expanded. Sherrill incorporated into the response discussion aspects of the text's artistry; these flow from the students' reactions and promote their reconsideration and expansion. Sherrill also offers insight about the application of the transactional theory of literature by contrasting alternative options for teaching "The Lament" within the framework of several other literary approaches.

In Chapter 7, Patricia Kelly considers the consequences of two reader-response approaches. Particularly, she explores how the students' perceptions develop in response to Sylvia Plath's "Words," given the stimulus of a pre-reading experience and that of readers theater. The role of each in focusing or opening the students' responses is examined, in relation to the issue of directing or limiting students' transactions with the text. The potential effects of these strategies on the students' interactions are illustrated and discussed. Kelly's representation of these two approaches illustrates reader-response methodology and suggests guidelines for classroom application.

Deborah Appleman, in Chapter 8, first makes a case for the suitability of reader-response methodology to "the developmental and intellectual charac-teristics of adolescents." She then points out features of texts to which these readers respond, using the novel *Ordinary People* as her example. Within this framework, in tune with reader-response theory, she identifies criteria for select-ing texts. Furthermore, she argues for the enhancement of student's interpretive abilities by introducing them to "basic tenets of transactional theory" and then asking them to complete a "response diagram" in which they identify features of the reader and the text that affected their personal transaction. Appleman discusses the outcomes of these procedures and offers several additional follow-up activities to foster readers' developing responses.

James E. Davis identifies several strategies for preparing readers for texts in Chapter 9. He promotes the writing of a daily journal by students prior to and during the reading of Arthur Miller's *Death of a Salesman*. Initially, journal topics cause them "to examine their own knowledge and feelings about one of the themes"; subsequently, the topics encourage them to explore their reactions. Davis provides follow-up activities and questions for the teaching of this drama. Several additional examples of initiating strategies, written by students from Davis's methods of teaching literature class, are included.

CHAPTER 5

Mending Walls:

Using a Reader-Response Approach to Teach Poetry

Ron Luce

In his poem "Mending Wall," Robert Frost places two seemingly different men on opposite sides of a stone wall that is in a state of deterioration. Then he sets them about the task of making repairs. One of the men, the speaker of the poem, is ambivalent about whether he truly wishes to repair the wall year after year (though he initiates the activity in this instance) or whether he simply uses mending as a way of sharing time and verbal exchange with his neighbor while sharing a philosophical discussion with those of us who listen in on the poem. He would appear to be motivated by a strong desire to destroy the barriers that inhibit the total enjoining of minds and space. At first, the neighbor appears to serve only as a foil to the insight of the speaker; he is motivated by simpler thought regarding the purpose of mending the wall, stubbornly insisting on maintaining a barrier of stone and minimalist human interaction as the only effective means of getting along in the world.

However, as the poem unfolds, the distinctions between the men, their motives, and their deceptively simplistic dichotomies about the human condition begin to disintegrate; in fact, it is possible, with careful reading, to imagine and support the notion that the neighbor may well be motivated by the same powerful urges to enjoin the human spirit as is the speaker of the poem. He speaks only twice, saying, "Good fences make good neighbors." Admittedly, this is not much to work with. On the surface, it appears that the neighbor is making an attempt to maintain distinct space, to be left alone. However, ironically implicit in the neighbor's statements and *actions* is the suggestion that the eternal *sharing* of the "mending" is as much a part of making good neighbors as is the idea of maintaining separate identities, a perception that is too easily attributed only to the narrator. This ambivalence has come full circle, feeding a paradoxical reading of the title suggesting that the wall gets mended and it does mending; it is both obstacle and source of unification bound by the complexity of human interaction.

MENDING WALL

Something there is that doesn't love a wall,
That sends the frozen-ground-swell under it,
And spills the upper boulders in the sun;
And makes gaps even two can pass abreast.
The work of hunters is another thing:
I have come after them and made repair
Where they have left not one stone on a stone,
But they would have the rabbit out of hiding,
To please the yelping dogs. The gaps I mean,
No one has seen them made or heard them made,
But at spring mending-time we find them there.
I let my neighbour know beyond the hill;
And on a day we meet to walk the line
And set the wall between us once again.
We keep the wall between us as we go.
To each the boulders that have fallen to each.
And some are loaves and some so nearly balls
We have to use a spell to make them balance:
'Stay where you are until our backs are turned!'
We wear our fingers rough with handling them.
Oh, just another kind of out-door game,
One on a side. It comes to little more:
There where it is we do not need the wall:
He is all pine and I am apple orchard.
My apple trees will never get across
And eat the cones under his pines, I tell him.
He only says, 'Good fences make good neighbours.'
Spring is the mischief in me, and I wonder
If I could put a notion in his head:
'Why do they make good neighbours? Isn't it
Where there are cows? But here there are no cows.
Before I built a wall I'd ask to know
What I was walling in or walling out,
And to whom I was like to give offence.
Something there is that doesn't love a wall,
That wants it down.' I could say 'Elves' to him,
But it's not elves exactly, and I'd rather
He said it for himself. I see him there
Bringing a stone grasped firmly by the top
In each hand, like an old-stone savage armed.
He moves in darkness as it seems to me,
Not of woods only and the shade of trees.
He will not go behind his father's saying,
And he likes having thought of it so well
He says again, 'Good fences make good neighbours.'

In the preceding synopsis of my reading and derived meaning of the central conflict
and force in Frost's poem is the essence of the dilemma teachers face in the classroom

when we try to teach students literature. In a sense our students are that neighbor of whom Frost's narrator speaks. They, like the neighbor, are called to the task of picking up (analyzing) "loaves and balls" of stone (literature), often handling them savagely; they are called to lift them, grasp them, fix the walls of their assimilated versions of American culture—a culture that has been shaped for them by powerful competing, often unarticulated forces and philosophies. They seem to feel it all differently from teachers; many refuse, like the neighbor, to answer the central question that is asked: Why do good fences make good neighbors?

The teaching of literature has suffered in the past not for a lack of material (loaves and balls) with potential to excite and encourage students. There is more than enough material with which they can become engaged. The teaching of literature has suffered because of teacher-perceptions that the written *text* (the wall) is the source of meaning and joy and students must somehow be forced to come to the text to which they are called, not for participating in laying up stones, but for participating in admiring the fence (text), as though this will eventually make them "good neighbors." As the narrator might be doing to the neighbor, some teachers might be misreading the situation created within their classrooms. Insistence on clinging to what a text *says* rather than *does* keeps both their students and them from venturing into the realm of one another's symbolic structures and dealing with the wall between them.

LEARNING HOW TO TEACH POETRY

When I first began teaching, I had no formal training in *how* to teach. I thought I knew a great deal about writing and reading and that was enough. All I had to do was share all that knowledge with those who had not yet arrived at the place where I was standing (somewhat like the narrator of the poem). I taught subjects. I taught Frost poems, for example. I wasn't teaching students. Fortunately, through the support of a few friends and colleagues and because I was studying the components of effective writing, I came to terms with the idea of "audience" and how I must think about them and their needs—a major revelation to someone who already believed himself to be a most conscientious humanist. I thought I had arrived. I had uncovered the secret. Now I could teach Frost poems *to people.* I just needed to figure out how to get them involved as active participants in the classroom and then they would learn from me. That all seems so arrogant now.

I am not sure of just how it happened; perhaps it was the culmination of many things (not least of which was reading reader-response theory), but somewhere along the way my whole concept of teaching changed. I found myself losing the need to focus on presenting material to students and began to focus more on helping them discover their own thinking processes. As I grew, I had to question what my real objectives for my students were. For example, did I want them to *know Robert Frost?* Or did I want them to know *about* Robert Frost? Or did I want them to know Robert Frost's *poems?* Or did I want them to discover how to think about a *poem in general?* Or did I want them to learn to read carefully, to feel a powerful emotional response rise up within themselves as a result of reading, to think about what they had read (regardless of what it was), to ask questions, to analyze, to read more, to question more, to explore from numerous perspectives what turned out to be a Robert Frost poem and then share their thinking with others for the purpose of refining their own thinking and feelings? This was an important line of thought, one I was ashamed to say I had not fully contemplated before; up to this point, I had always accepted, without ever effectively articulating it, that the real goal was to help students to come to terms with what *I* knew to be "true" about literature as I had been taught and as I had learned it through my own reading and interpretations.

Through the presentation of her transactional model—a model that promotes helping students experience literature and create meaning as they transact with a text—Louise Rosenblatt helped me to find my way. Reader-response theory, as Rosenblatt presents it, embraces a level of concern for students that other theories either have not addressed or have widely abused the student reader. In this model, meaning emerges from the transaction of reader and text, each affecting the other; it does not reside in the text from which the student gleans meaning as perceived by an author placing words inviolably in a text. Readers bring their experiences and culture to bear on the text; the text serves to isolate and focus the students' realms of meaning.

Rosenblatt's view of literature as part of the fabric of individual lives—all lives (not just an elite few)—provides a great challenge to the way literature is taught. It forces an awareness that many who teach literature or are preparing to teach literature are already good learners and are well-adapted to the limitations imposed by New Critical theory—close, objective analysis to establish the meaning within the text, to discover the "correct" meaning—and most likely have been exceptions to the "norms" in English classes throughout their educational experiences. Reflection on Rosenblatt's theory challenges us to ask what happens to those who do not find literature exciting and interesting and what can be done to keep the English class malaise of previous generations from infecting classrooms. It does not allow teachers to participate in the deliberate perpetuation of the dichotomy between the common reader and the literary elite.

ADAPTING THEORY TO THE CLASSROOM:
AN EXAMPLE

What follows is a very brief example of the use of the transactional model to introduce "Mending Wall" to technical college students in a writing course as a way of trying to engender some critical thinking and to promote confidence in themselves as readers. The class, made up of sixteen second-year students majoring in diverse areas, including nursing, forestry, medical records, and accounting, had revealed in conversations that they did not feel "smart enough" to work with literature. No one in the group had ever stated (or even joked about) any interest in leaving the technical college to become an English major, and no one expressed a love of writing or reading, though a couple of students admitted to liking to read as long as it was "interesting." Several students expressed downright hatred of any kind of reading except reading purely for escapism (the *National Enquirer* was mentioned as good escapist literature in at least two cases).

Prior to the class where I was to introduce the poem, I had met with the group several times to discuss writing and to work with them on essays they were creating for the class. On one occasion, I had presented them with a well-written student essay from a previous quarter, uncovering it little by little on an overhead screen while they reacted to the language. In that experience, they learned that their own reading and the text are shaped by the interaction of the words and their own interpretation; they perceived and formulated responses that shifted and reorganized themselves as they worked their way down the pages. We took time to share what happened when they visually struck a period or question mark or when their eyes came to the white space at the end of a paragraph. We discussed how they had been trained and had trained themselves over the years to have a visual, emotional, and logical response to the stimuli before them. They were surprised by the experience and impressed by how much they were able to agree on the essence of the essay even though different readers had slightly different interpretations of individual lines and words. Before beginning the Frost poem, I reminded them of the essay project and of the fact that they bring many skills to the reading experience and the goal was to simply react to the new "document" they were about to encounter. (I determined not to refer to the term *poem* until they did.)

HELPING STUDENTS "EXPERIENCE" THE POEM

I walked around the room, put a sheet of paper face down on each student's desk, and asked them not to look at it until I told them to do so. I had carefully scribbled across all the letters on a copy of the poem, leaving spaces and punctuation intact, so that I ended up with what looked like words that took up the correct amount of line space but which had no meaning other than as visual representations:

When the copies were distributed, I asked the students to turn the papers over and react. At first, many seemed somewhat startled, not knowing what the "gibberish" was. I told them I had taken away one of their tools for analyzing: words. Then I asked them to think about what this document might be. "How might we analyze it?" "Does it *do* anything?" "How might we react without the words to help us?" After a pause, a few comments started coming forth. The students began to grasp for meaning. They identified the title because it was bolder and bigger than the rest of the words and because it was centered at the top of the page. They talked about the short line length and capital letters at the beginning of each line. Finally, someone said it looked like a poem. And then I heard the grunts and groans.

I asked them why they reacted as they did. "What does the word *poem* do to you?" I got vague responses, such as "boring stuff" and "I can never get the *right* meaning." They had framed a negative attitude and set themselves up for being inadequate to the task of reading the poem (they wouldn't be able to get the "right meaning") based on previous experiences. We shared the baggage that they were bringing to the task of reading without having read a word as yet, factors that were triggered by visual impressions that ordinarily would be unarticulated but would color every word they were going to read if they did not try to come to terms with their responses. They were surprised at how much they shared a lack of confidence and how much they created stumbling blocks to the potential for meaningful interaction with an, as yet, undisclosed text. I simply stated that this document need not be a revisitation of past experiences and they should try to keep an open mind.

The next step in the process of helping the students to experience the poem involved something with which they were already familiar. I had the poem on a transparency and uncovered the title, "Mending Wall." I asked them to take out a sheet of paper and respond to the words they saw on the screen. I read the title, and stated, "This is not a test. There is no 'correct' meaning; there is only you and the words. What do the words *do* to you?" Then, after a moment, I began to uncover the poem line by line and to read it, giving them a brief period of time to write. At first I uncovered only a line at a time and let them write whatever they wished; then I began uncovering groupings of lines that completed a single image or idea. (The poem contains no stanza breaks.) When they were finished with their notes, I handed them a typed copy of the poem (I had removed Frost's name so that they would not be influenced by recollections of past experiences with his work), reread the entire poem from beginning to end, and asked them to write a very quick summary of their reactions to the poem. After a few moments, I asked them to write down their own mending wall experience. The following notes demonstrate the kinds of responses I received:

STUDENT A: TERRY

Notes

Title: I want to know what it means and what the poem is about.
Does it have to do with a type of barrier or is something being fixed?
I'm confused. What doesn't love a wall?
The top of the wall faces upward to the sun.
Two can pass over or around it.
Hunters have gone over the wall and caused stones to fall off.
Come spring you find gaps on the wall.
Two people fix the wall so that it separates two different places.
They had a hard time making the top of the wall level.
The wall separates woods and an orchard.

If they didn't meet to fix the wall they wouldn't be as good neighbors.
It keeps them from crossing each other's paths.
But why do they need the wall?
They can each have their own privacy.

Summary

One neighbor feels that if he doesn't have the wall between them, they wouldn't be such good neighbors. It keeps them from trespassing on each other's territories. One neighbor feels it is just in the way and wants to know why the other one needs and wants it so badly. He feels that it is a waste of time to mend because it will be torn down again. He wants to know what kind of Elf is causing it to fall down. The other one feels his father was right and still abides by that same saying "Good fences make good neighbors."

Personal Mending Wall

I'm the type of person that needs a small wall. Some things I keep to myself and I try to deal with by myself. Although other things I'm willing to share. Usually I'm an open person. For example, if I worked somewhere and was having problems with a certain job or task, I would want to figure it out by myself. But if I was having problems in school with a class or essay, I would want someone to explain to me and tell me what's wrong. It just depends on the problem and how big it is.

STUDENT B: MARK

Notes
Vietnam Vets Memorial.
Resents confinement.
Cold feelings.
Knocking down the wall.
Love.
Doesn't like hunters.
He found holes in his fence.
Fixing the fence between their property—maybe.
How people separate from each other.
Stone fence.
Respect other's things.
Fences only make good neighbors to keep something in, not out.

Summary

Fences or walls are for keeping something in, not out—at least between good neighbors. If there is not a need for the wall, why have it or repair it? The neighbors respect each other's property. By respecting each other's property, you will be good neighbors. Kind of like the saying, "if you never lend it out, you don't have to worry about not getting it back." Friends don't believe that and they don't need walls either. Maybe tearing the wall down will make them better neighbors and better friends. But neither will suggest it or say anything; they'll just leave it be like it has always been and fix it every year.

Personal Mending Wall

When my wife and I were dating, there were parts of me I didn't want to share with her. Even when we were engaged, there were thoughts and ideas that were mine only. As time went on, she showed me that it's ok to be afraid and vulnerable and that brought us much closer together. My fears didn't go away, but someone else knew them. And she cared and was concerned. It helped make our love what it is today. We make it a point to not let a wall get started before it's too big to knock down.

STUDENT C: MIKE

Notes

Mending Wall—where you go to reconcile differences.
There are things that don't like barriers.
These things can't get through, so they go around it and break it down.
Slowly tears down the wall?
Breaks through and allows communication to be easily done.
So we have broken this wall/barrier down for petty reasons. The author attempts to reconstruct.
No one is aware of this problem until they decide to reconcile.
The holes represent communication, and rocks are blocks in that communication.
Some blocks are large, some small.
We get perturbed at this.
People should keep to themselves and not intervene, or get to know people—according to the neighbor.
Are walls good? Should we not get to know one another?
A fence is a means of protecting one's self from others.

Summary

This poem is about how we build walls between ourselves and others, and how they are torn down by some who want to hurt us, and also by love. The wall is the barrier between us that doesn't allow us to know each other, for if we do get to know each other, there is room for love or hurt. The apples won't eat the cones. This means "I won't hurt you." Why should there be a wall if I'm not going to do anything to you? The neighbor wants the wall because he/she does not want to risk being loved or hurt by the other person. They can co-exist, but there need not be any communication.

Personal Mending Wall

The walls that I have built to keep people out are few. I like to have the freedom to talk personally with people. I hate it when people build them to keep me out, especially if there is no real reason for the wall. Sometimes people will instantly put a wall up if they feel that we are getting too close. I try to tear walls down, to get inside to see what is happening.

It seems to me that some important experiences were articulated here. For example, notice that the students go through some reactions to the poem that involve questioning and struggling to answer their own questions. They go through the processes of checking initial responses as the poem unfolds. Mark, for example, begins with an image of the

Vietnam Veterans Memorial, and then has to discard it in light of the evidence he finds. Terry starts with several questions and then admits confusion about what doesn't love a wall, and finally comes to terms with her own central question, "Why do they need the wall?" Many of the notes are simplistic restatements of the events in the poem. But several go beyond that point. For example, Mark says, "Fences only make good neighbors to keep something in, not out." And Mike speaks of reconciliation, and asks, "Are walls good? Should we not get to know one another?" In each case, it seems to me that these students are struggling with the ambivalence that Frost presents in his poems.

Notice also the desire to find answers to their own questions in their summary statements. Mark deals with his question, "If there is not a need for the wall, why have it or repair it?" He responds with "By respecting each other's property you will be good neighbors. Kind of like the saying, 'if you never lend it out, you don't have to worry about not getting it back.' Friends don't believe that and they don't need walls either." And his final "summary" sentence is a great response restatement of the closing mood of the poem, "But neither will suggest it or say anything; they'll just leave it be like it has always been and fix it every year." He seems to be indicating the same kind of communication gap between the narrator and the neighbor that is articulated by Mike, who focuses on reconciliation; "They can co-exist, but there need not be any communication."

Notice also in their own "mending wall" statements how the poem begins to help them articulate and draw on the components of their everyday lives. Each speaks of needing other people, vulnerability, care and concern, love, sharing, communication—all universal concerns of human beings. These are their initial responses to the poem. Not mine. And they have reached this point without concern for what the poem "means."

HELPING STUDENTS SHARE THEIR RESPONSES

After they dealt with their initial responses, they were then ready to move on to a closer examination and sharing. I broke them into three groups and asked each group to discuss different sections of the poem (fifteen lines each) and prepare to share their perceptions with the whole class. I set up the session by asking them to look at the lines and ask themselves what makes the poem work. I asked them to consider what the writer does that they responded to, that carried them through the poem gracefully, that allowed them to feel whatever it was they felt about the poem. I determined to intervene in the small groups only if the discussion were clearly outside the poem or related topics or if the groups were clearly unable to proceed on their own. I spent most of my time walking around the room, listening and working at not jumping in to explain the poem—an extremely difficult task. As it turned out, I did not need to intervene, but I had prepared myself for the possibility: I had predetermined that I could ask the group to summarize their discussion for me and that I could question why they had come to the conclusions they had, and I could question how they could defend their responses by pointing to support from the poem or to specific details from their shared responses.

After the discussion period, I asked students to designate a speaker for each group, then I brought the class back together and asked speakers to share their group's perceptions. I planned to allow students to comment freely after each presentation and to openly discuss their reactions to the responses of their classmates. I planned to intervene only when the discussion got off track or when their "meaning" needed to be clarified by the text. As it turned out, until close to the end of their presentations and discussions I found myself being involved very little, except to control the potential chaos of several people speaking at once. I expected students would get side-tracked and begin to drift in directions not consistent with the poem or the heart of the discussion. I feared losing momentum. Again, I had a plan: If that happened, I would simply respond with appreciation for the subject matter and ask how the text had inspired the direction of that particular line of thinking or sharing. Sometimes I asked questions like, "Are you saying . . . ?" and then attempted a summary statement to elicit a reaction when it appeared that other students were confused about what a speaker had stated. Other than that, I waited. Essentially, the class agreed on the basic flow of the responses and discussion and seemed to have little difficulty with the poem—up to the point of the last five lines:

> He moves in darkness as it seems to me,
> Not of woods only and the shade of trees.
> He will not go behind his father's saying,
> And he likes having thought of it so well
> He says again, "Good fences make good neighbors."

The following is a transcript of the class discussion to demonstrate the basic flow of the ideas raised. In it I have attempted to use my students' own language—taken from audiotape (revising only to the extent of changing pronoun referents, eliminating redundancies, and making transitions between different speakers; my additions to their words and phrases are printed in italics). Several students' comments are grouped together about a particular idea as they occurred:

Whether it is lack of communication or love, something there is that doesn't love a wall. Hunters tear down the wall not out of love or lack of communication. They tear it down to please the yelping dogs. There are these gaps that stay until we take a look in spring. This person [the narrator] says his wall is down and it needs repair. *It is similar to a situation (for example) where* two people get to know each other very well. They break up. They set up a wall between themselves. Then a couple of months later they get together again, but the wall is still there. They don't share. They don't have much in common any more. We all feel this way *sometimes.*

   Even though they [the narrator and the neighbor] are two different people, why would they need this wall? That's the way it is in real life. *For example,* cultures may be very different. We need protection. *We are like them . . .* they [the narrator and his neighbor] are never going to be able to get close as long as they have this wall between them. *They remind us of incidents from our own lives.* We made a comparison to these two people. *We* envision these two people trying to put this fence up and then trying to figure out why . . . *mostly saying to themselves,* "You take care of yours and I'll take care of mine." There are parts of *our lives* where *we* don't want anybody in. *What we really* want *are* gates! *We* can expose too much of *ourselves* to just anybody, *and we need to be able to control it. The neighbor—the "guy on the other side of the fence"—knew this.*

   The *neighbor* is not necessarily bad. There's nothing to say that he's not a friendly person or willing to have a friendship with the *narrator.* It's just that he wants his privacy and property respected. *This reminds us of a great* example: *a woman* had these neighbors *with whom she and her husband* were super friends, and they did things together. *But* the neighbors just kept coming over and making themselves at home until they became really annoying. *They didn't know when enough was enough! But it doesn't have to be that way among people who care about one another. For example, a man and his* wife have differences. *His* wife likes to go shopping. *He likes* to go hunting and fishing. *They've* always from the start given each other that *essential* space. Yet *they've* always shared everything about each other. *They* just *know enough to* give each other space. *They* have walls, but they are little . . . *yet* very important *walls. People* should not give *themselves* totally out or *they* won't have anything left.

The poem speaks about darkness. "He moves in darkness, it seems to me." Darkness speaks of loneliness. *The neighbor* can't break the wall down *because he is locked in by tradition.* He won't change or see the light. He feels like he has to do this thing—the wall. What he really wants is to build a gate.

It all gets strange . . . we are looking at the elves thing again. Sometimes we *all* wish someone would take the magic wand and hit someone over the head and get the message across to *him.* The [narrator] is saying, "I could say Elves to him . . . " Little bells go off in the head . . . *The narrator would* rather this neighbor would see it for himself, *see* that he needs to come out of the darkness *on his own. This is like a true life story in which* for four years *a woman* has been struggling in a marriage where *she* wanted *her* husband to be hit over the head by a magic wand. *She* found after a great deal of time—*after threats of divorce, marital problems, and all-round difficult living*—in some things he *would finally say* it for himself. He [the husband] saw that he needed to change; bells went off in his head.

Darkness probably does represent some kind of *similar* sadness. We tend to associate darkness with sadness. *The neighbor* will not go behind his father's saying. He would like to, but can't do it. Maybe that's the way it is—tradition. Despite what he wants *personally,* the walls will stay. Perhaps it is unsurity. Maybe he could *or should* let this person in. But having the wall makes it safer. *It all comes down to a safety factor, kind of an* "I-can't-get-anything-out-of-it, but-you-won't-hurt-me" attitude.

. . . *But then* . . . on the end of that line about darkness he is not necessarily in darkness . . . this guy [the speaker] is seeing him [the neighbor] in darkness. *We* had been thinking about the guy not being able to change . . . but now *we* see it [the poem] *coming from* this guy who's been talking about this as his feeling . . . he wants to tell this guy [the neighbor] how wrong he is and that he shouldn't be building this fence or wall. In reality this is just his opinion. All this time, he [the narrator] is helping to build the *same* wall he is complaining about.

The last half of the previous transcript is a result of one young woman's follow-up comments to her group's presentation and the subsequent discussion in which the class and I became involved. The last fifteen lines of the poem generated the largest percentage of class discussion and interest, so it is worth explaining a bit more about the dynamics of class interaction and how students arrived at what I perceived to be a significant level of sophistication. The young woman began by saying no one in her group really knew what "darkness" meant in the line, "He moves in darkness as it seems to me." The urge to explain almost overwhelmed me. But I was determined to help the class find its own way. I told her to forget what it means and to think about what it does. She then went on to say that she thought it had to do with the fact that the neighbor really wanted to make gates in the wall, but he didn't know how—it equated with sadness. I asked her how she came to that in the poem. She was unable to point to anything that would support her view beyond the statement that she felt it to be so. To help her and her group out, I asked what the class made of the "darkness thing." Responses seemed to evolve into the idea that darkness means the neighbor did not want to get hurt or it shows the neighbor's lack of knowledge. One student got off into a sidetrack about her husband of four years who had only begun to communicate recently about his feelings. The discussion screeched to a halt, and I found myself wanting to cut her off and get back to business, but I gave her the time to explain. She became involved in talk about magic wands, and the like, as articulated in the transcription. It was interesting, but seemingly a rehashing of material already discussed. (The class was visually expressing disapproval with the sidetrack.) I let her have her say, thanked her for sharing the experience, and said I wanted to get back to the "darkness" issue because so many people seemed interested in coming to terms with it. The young woman who began the discussion of the meaning of "darkness" asserted once again that the darkness has to do with how the neighbor wanted to make gates. I asked again where she saw this in the poem. Again, she could only say she felt it to be true.

Several more students took a stab at coming to terms with the "darkness" issue, some suggesting that there was something not quite right about the image of darkness hovering over the neighbor. In several instances, students read out loud the line containing "darkness" prior to making their comments. With each statement that was an "I think it means . . . '' or an "I feel it means . . ." I kept asking, "Why?" "Where do you find it in the text?" "How do you get that from what the text does?" Suddenly, the young woman who initiated the discussion was struck by the repetition of the line and by my insistence on getting at the how and why, and leaped back into the conversation: "He moves in darkness *as it seems to me*. He is not necessarily in darkness. This guy (the narrator) *sees* him in darkness. So he [the neighbor] may not actually be in darkness. He's just *seen* in darkness." I asked, "So what does that do for you?" "Changes it all around." "How?" "Well, I'd been thinking of the guy as wanting to change something and being in sadness. Now I see it where this guy [the narrator] is writing [narrator and author are obviously perceived as one] and talking about this as *his* feeling as if that guy [the neighbor] is in darkness. He [the narrator] wants to tell that guy how wrong he is and he [the neighbor] shouldn't be building this wall. In reality, this is just *his* [the narrator's] opinion."

LEARNING WITHIN THE READER-RESPONSE CLASSROOM

Clearly, these students had come a very long way in the course of an hour. They began with the restatement of lines from the poem. Then they shifted away from the poem toward concrete examples from their own lives that helped them to focus on their initial grasping for meaning and back again to the poem. And then there was the revision process of testing their ideas against what the poem actually says from the perspective of the narrator—a perspective they came to see as being potentially biased, perhaps unintentionally misleading. Here the poet was cast aside as students explored the role of the narrator and his shaping of the initial reading (or misreading). This is, I believe, a sophisticated examination of how to read a poem, one they came to with little more from me than coordinating the division of labor and the means for sharing their responses and creating a forum where revision was possible and where "correct" meaning was set aside for the purpose of finding *legitimate* meanings on which they could grow, meanings that were refined and expanded, readings that were personally varied.

Critical to this methodology is tolerance of students' legitimate readings of texts that are given them amidst the texts of their own existence. Analysis of poems requires a vast network of resource experiences on which the reader can draw for comparison. This takes time to develop. The more well-read the readers, the more they can draw on memory banks of literary resources, language, and personal successes and sort through the abstractions presented by the shaping of words in new forms and modes. If we do not allow students their honest initial responses, we perpetuate forcing them into an impossible situation of groping through limited resources for the *one and only answer* the teacher wants and feeling frustrated with the text that will not immediately give up its meaning:

> Such an effort to consider texts always in relation to specific readers and in specific cultural situations, and to honor the role of literary experience in the context of individual lives, has powerful educational implications. . . . At least this can be indicated: a primary concern throughout would be the development of the individual's capacity to adopt and to maintain the aesthetic stance, to live fully and personally in the literary transaction. From this could flow growth in all the kinds of resources needed for transactions with increasingly demanding and increasingly rewarding texts. And from this would flow, also a humanistic concern for the relation of the individual literary event to the continuing life of the reader in all its facets—aesthetic, moral, economic, or social. (Rosenblatt 161)

We must help students learn that meaning lies not in us (the teachers) or in the symbols placed on a page, nor solely in themselves; it is something that happens in the *transaction* of a reader's mind and a writer's recorded symbols. A "web of feelings, sensations, images, ideas," woven as the reader experiences emotional and logical responses to the text is the all-important beginning place (136–37). That does not mean the first reading should be the only reading or that *any* meaning is acceptable. The notion that any reading is legitimate as a first response is simply a starting point. After that first reading, the readers reflect on what has been read and on what has been experienced as they have read and then revise thinking accordingly, perhaps with enough success to get involved in further study of language and literature. Before students can acquire such zeal, we need to change what we do to them:

> The capacity to participate in verbally complex texts is not widely fostered in our educational system, and desirable habits of reflection, interpretation, and evaluation are not widespread. These are goals that should engender powerful reforms in language training and literary education. But none of these are attainable if good literary works of art are envisioned as the province of only a small, highly trained elite. Once the literary work is seen as part of the fabric of individual lives, the gap may be at least narrowed, without relinquishing recognition of standards of excellence. (Rosenblatt 143).

Instead of passively participating in the learning of literature, students at all grade levels can learn to take responsibility for living in the literature. There are countless ways beyond what has been shown in the previous pages to make opportunities for them to actively engage and reflect. For example, students could read a poem silently to themselves and then frame one or more key questions; then they could be put in groups of three or four and each person could ask a question(s) of the group and attempt to collaboratively sort through their various readings to arrive at some possible meanings. The groups could then choose the best of their three or four questions to pose to the class for collaborative learning. Students could rewrite a poem in light of their own experiences and share the poem with small groups or the class for discussion of similarities and differences between the rewritten poem and the original, looking for whether or not the copy accurately reflects the class's derived meaning of the original. Small groups could put on plays (or create video portrayals) that characterize their collaborative interpretations of a poem; and then the whole class could discuss the interpretations in light of their responses to the original poem. Students could be taken to settings similar to the setting of the poem for the purpose of reenacting it as a living art form and then discuss this *experience* of language— what the poem *does* as a living thing rather than as a motionless object, ink and paper. Any of these projects could be adapted to individual or group activities. Any of these ideas could be used by small groups for focusing on different poems of one author, group (confessional, imagistic, etc.), or period; then the whole class could discuss the interpretations and make a project of charting similarities and differences among poetic styles and poets, examining texts within larger texts or fields of study. The point of the projects would be to provide opportunities for students to first engage poems without fear of disapproval or being wrong, then to reflect on their assertions; then to test their responses against a collaborative experience and verbal sharing of their derived meanings for further revision and growth.

Helping students develop into readers who can explore the world of literature and its myriad possibilities requires a long-term commitment. Louise Rosenblatt seems to know that it is not something forthcoming in a single poem or a single quarter or semester and she realizes that it requires a concern for each student, regardless of whether the student will be forever an "ordinary" reader or literary scholar. Opportunity for "literary events" to take place, are needed, opportunities that will be perceived as representing a meaningful way of being and that can be verbally articulated.

Our approaches have too long been limited to taking students to the carefully piled rocks of literature that we place before them each year. We want them to raze the walls. Always we have in mind the making of a way over and through, but what we often get is a pulling—our pulling—of the students, leaving not a stone on a stone of the literary event. For the victims of that approach there is often no tradition, no articulation, no wall, only the so-called "pleasing." They have heard us say, "Spring is the mischief in us, and we wonder if we could put a notion in their heads," as though they could not possibly have the experience of literature for themselves, as though they are simply empty and waiting to be stuffed by our "greater" perceptions. There are a few—like Louise Rosenblatt—who remind us that "notions" are already there waiting to be made manifest: "We'd rather they said it for themselves." Reader response gives students a way to say it and an ability to move toward the critical perception that perpetuates their desire for more joyful events in the creation of their own texts—their existence within a time and culture—that literature helps them to build. Yes, *good* fences do make good neighbors.

REFERENCES

Frost, Robert. "Mending Wall." In *The Poems of Robert Frost.* New York: Random House, 1946. 35–36.

Rosenblatt, Louise M. *The Reader, the Text, the Poem: The Transactional Theory of the Literary Work.* Carbondale, IL: Southern Illinois University Press, 1978.

CHAPTER **6**

Through a Glass Darkly:
Seeing Ourselves in Chekhov's "The Lament"

Anne Sherrill

Imagine a host of literary critics gathered to discuss Anton Chekhov's "The Lament." In the story, set in nineteenth-century Russia, a cab driver, Iona Potapov, attempts unsuccessfully to tell people of his sorrow over his son Barin's recent death. In the course of one evening his attempts at communication are rejected four times: twice by people who engage the cab, then by a porter and finally another cabby. The selection ends with his telling the story to his horse.

VARIOUS APPROACHES TO READING "THE LAMENT"

To the student of genre studies "The Lament" offers the classical plot structure connecting it to many other early short stories. There is a complicating incident as an officer engages the cab and Iona first tries to communicate his sorrow. Other similar incidents afford rising action to the climax, which occurs at the end when Iona, overcome by grief that he can no longer hold inside, tells the story to the horse.

For the New Critic examining the complex interrelationships and interactions of words and symbols as they intertwine with and support meaning, the descriptions of the snow parallel Iona's sense of isolation and the coldness of human beings. In the first paragraph of the story the snow is described as all encompassing, having settled on roofs, horses' backs, people's shoulders. From this panoramic view Chekhov moves to the figure of Iona bent double and seated in his box on his cab. He and his horse are motionless as the snow settles on them. Iona is described as a white phantom and the horse as a gingerbread horse. In this first paragraph Chekhov sets the stage for the grief Iona feels.

At other points he returns to the description of the snow and always it underscores Iona's all encompassing grief and isolation from the warmth of human companionship.

A structuralist examining the structure underlying the work may note the story divides itself into scenes: the initial scene of Iona and the horse in the snow, the officer who engages the cab, the three young men who subsequently do, and the return to the stable.

A student of biographical studies most certainly would examine Chekhov's life as it might shed more information on how he came to write the story. Similarly a student of literary tradition would consider the influence of other works, both earlier and contemporary.

Iona's laughter and joviality even though the three young men who hire the cab abuse him would be of interest to the critic examining the story from a psychological viewpoint. The surface friendliness is a mask to hide the despair that makes him reach out to others in an effort to make them listen. The need for people to communicate with other humans is a theme running through the story that is firmly rooted in psychology.

Iona is a poor cab driver who must endure the cold in hope of earning a few kopecs. He is not of the class of the officer and the three young men who engage the cab. Their evening is not relegated to work as is Iona's. They are of a higher social class and are insensitive to one of Iona's station. Their treatment of him shows he is not worthy of their respect. He should not even bother them by attempting to tell about the son's death. The story thus offers opportunities for students of historical and sociological (particularly Marxist) criticism to interpret conditions in Russia during the time of the story.

After Iona returns to the stable and a fellow cab driver falls asleep as he attempts to tell him his story, Iona thinks that perhaps the best audience would be women because they are stupid and cry easily. Feminist critics who study stereotyping would certainly find it in that observation.

APPLYING THE TRANSACTIONAL THEORY OF LITERATURE

Reader-response theory similarly lends itself well to a story such as "The Lament." In response theory, finding meaning involves both author's text and what the reader brings to that text. Each conditions the other and out of that transaction comes in Rosenblatt's term the "poem" (12). In this sense the text is not static. Meaning is recreated each time a work is read. In response theory, making meaning begins with acknowledging the importance of the personal response of the reader and is necessarily exploratory. In a classroom, the teacher's role is to set the stage for the performing art as it were, a setting for the sharing and meshing of many ideas based on a given piece of literature. Thus making meaning becomes a shared endeavor moving on a continuum from an individual's initial tentative construct to that of the group. The teacher becomes a cicerone of sorts as the group under guidance of the text shapes the "poem."

As a preface to the reading of "The Lament," I presented my class of upper-division college students with some paintings that show people communicating in some way. I asked them to comment about the communication that might be going on in each. "The Long Story" by William Sydney Mount shows two men at a table and another in the background. Speculation ranged from the men's reminiscing to their contemplating a sinister act. They saw Judith Leyster's "The Jester" as mischievous, friendly, someone that would be fun to be with and who would probably never be at a loss for friends. In Georges de LaTour's "St. Joseph and the Carpenter" they saw an older person lovingly teaching a younger one a trade or a grandfather spending time with a grandchild. Picasso's "The Lovers" suggested a couple who had reached some new understanding of one another or were making up after a quarrel. Such examples of communication are absent in the Chekhov story.

After all had finished the story (about ten minutes), I asked them to write for three minutes on the following questions: (a) What emotions did you feel as you read the story and on its completion? Why? (b) Were you prepared for Iona's telling the horse the story?

At the end of the three minutes I asked for a sharing of their answers to the first question.

STUDENTS: I felt very depressed. It was really sad at the end. It seemed like he had tremendous guilt about his son's death and he couldn't communicate it to anyone.

He couldn't find anybody with the compassion.

Nobody seemed to have enough time.

And it's typical. Even now we get preoccupied with what we're doing and we sometimes don't let people talk.

Even though they didn't know him they could have helped him. He just needed somebody there.

TEACHER: So you felt a definite emotion when you finished the story. How about as you read it?

I wanted to punch these guys who wouldn't listen.

I felt sorry for him. I thought he needed human comfort. He just needed to get it out to hear himself say it.

At least he told it to the horse so maybe he felt better.

[Representative Segments of Discussion]

TEACHER: Let's talk for a moment about a writer achieving an emotion in the reader. If I were to say to you "I'm very happy today" and leave it at that, you're not going to feel happiness. I need to give you some details perhaps to make my happiness contagious. Even my posture might convey my state of mind to you. If you were to create a picture of Iona, what would he look like?

STUDENTS: His whole body is withdrawn into him. He's making the world go away and he's into his own sadness.

It just looks like it's been hurt.

His arms are dragging on the ground.

He's not doing anything. It's like he's just overwhelmed.

Well, it says in here that when he was alone he was humped over, stuff like that.

He held his head down.

TEACHER: Those are some of the ways you would depict him then if you were a painter or perhaps a sculptor. They suggest a sense of isolation, of sorrow perhaps. Now let's look at what the writer does to create an emotional effect in the reader and to build the character of Iona. One way is to detail the incidents when Iona comes in contact with these different people and, as you said, they ignore him. Let's look at the story carefully for a moment. Were you able to identify some scenes when he tries to communicate and he's rebuffed, ignored, or made fun of?

STUDENTS: The people one right after the other reject him.

TEACHER: Who was first?

The policeman. He tried to talk to him and he said "Well, that's what happens."

TEACHER: Is he a fare? Does he get into the cab? What happens in that scene?

STUDENTS: I think the rejection really starts before, in the first paragraph. The picture that the author gives starts before he meets the fares by things being so wet and thick and snowy. He's been alone in the same position. It's almost dark and he's lonely.

TEACHER: Could you read us the parts that best show that?

STUDENTS: " . . . he is bent double as far as a human body can bend double; he never makes a move. The evening mist is descending over the town."

I'd like to mention that scene with the officer. At first you think he's going to be interested because he says "What did he die of?" but then he just cuts it off.

The officer is just making that remark so he can get it out of the way and get on with it.

TEACHER: We've all done that, haven't we. You're polite, but you don't want to take the time.

STUDENT: It seems like there was kind of, you know, a come on by the officer. I'm open. Then he cuts him off.

TEACHER: So he's not interested at all. Do we have another encounter?

STUDENTS: Three young men come up and they want a ride.

They offer him a real cheap price, and it's not as much as he would like but he appreciates anything. They abuse him the whole time

He even tried to forget his grief, and he tried to get caught up in the merriment of them but nothing seemed to help.

TEACHER: Did you get the feeling that Iona really has any joy at that point?

STUDENTS: I felt that he was kind of numb. Especially when they hit him and it said he heard rather than felt the blows.

I think they remind him of his son. He's trying to picture that young man as his son.

TEACHER: How did you take the laughing? Is it reasonable that someone with that much grief would joke?

STUDENTS: "He wanted to be happy. He wanted to be part of their merriment."

I thought he was laughing because he thought maybe he could get in with them and they'd listen to him.

TEACHER: It's a desperate attempt, isn't it, to join in in any way.

STUDENT: I can relate to this personally because, you know, it's like after the funeral is over everybody goes back to how it's supposed to be. You need people more then after it's all over than you do when you're going through it. I was sitting here thinking that the author really captures that gut feeling because this is it. A lot of people don't have time for you. Some of them are scared.

TEACHER: And this just happened last week to him.

STUDENTS: It's a good picture of the stages of grief. Who did that book?

Ross. Keebler Ross?

Kubler Ross.

TEACHER: Does anyone want to comment on that?

STUDENTS: You're right. He's still in the first stage of shock and needing to hear himself say "This has happened."

He may be in the denial process. You know this has happened but mentally it hasn't set in yet.

TEACHER: So are you saying Chekhov has given us a universal stage of grief?

STUDENTS: Yeah.

He has another comment about the way he jokes around about the moist ground and that death took his son and not him. I don't think he was glad to be alive.

TEACHER: And what do you make of that? Does he feel some guilt? Someone mentioned that at the very first of the discussion.

STUDENTS: No, but he's trying to act like it really doesn't affect him as much as it is.

I think he really does wish it was him instead of his son.

I thought this pointed up the irony of the situation. He really should be the one to have gone. It's not normal to bury your own child.

He tries to rationalize it.

The way he said it, too. They're in a jovial mood. If he talks dark and depressing, they won't listen. Maybe if he acts kind of "Guess what happened?" then maybe they'll listen for a minute.

TEACHER: Most of you said Chekhov evoked a feeling of sadness or depression in you after reading the story, and he did that by having you live through Iona's frustrations in trying to communicate his grief. It's the same principle as if he had said "Iona is a lonely old cab driver." You don't experience that unless he gives you the details that show he is lonely. We might want to go back to that first paragraph of the story that you mentioned earlier as establishing that sense of isolation. Can you give us the best phrases that show that?

STUDENTS: "bent double." That gave me the impression he was drawn into himself like the sculpture we saw. He was motionless. The horse was motionless. The only activity was a little bit of snow that was building up. It was real white and real serene, and you could tell it was all leading up to something pretty dreary.

Some of that was a little different for me. Like "phantom" suggested something had happened but that he was like one of these lonely old men you just don't like being around because they're so unhappy. But then the story goes on and explains why he's unhappy. I pictured him differently in the beginning—lonely but more like a grumpy old man and you don't want to bother with him.

TEACHER: Does that say anything about the way we sometimes relate to people like Iona? Can someone put him in a contemporary setting in which he would appear to be to us just a grumpy old guy we didn't want to fool with?

STUDENTS: You always seem to have someone in the neighborhood like that, but if you got to know them it's probably because they're really lonely. They don't know how to interact with other people. Really they're kind of pitiful, but you don't know because you don't know their story.

TEACHER: And so they remain isolated, don't they. Is there any other place where Iona goes back into himself again and the snow figures in?

STUDENTS: I think we missed the part in that first paragraph about if the snow drifts fell on him he wouldn't find it necessary to shake it off. That really reminds me of somebody who's so sad and so lonely he doesn't even care if he froze to death.

TEACHER: That's a good point. Are there some other places?

STUDENTS: After he's tried and failed to communicate with that officer he sits alone again and the snow falls on him. It's like he came out of his shell and now he goes back in.

What she just said and the feeling you get that he might really want to die when he says he was lucky it wasn't him, that death mistook his door and took his son.

You know he has a wife but I guess he's too macho to cry to her.

He says women are good listeners because they cry at anything.

Boo!

TEACHER: So far we've talked about the character of Iona and the events that show us his loneliness and frustration. We've also talked about the emotional response you had during and after reading the story, the overall feeling it generated.

In a story that you remember, there is something about the total picture that you take away with you, a central idea that grows from the story but is larger than the story itself. It's not just the characters or a series of events but what they all add up to. A writer like Chekhov presents his characters in situations and lets their reaction to events illustrate some point.

What is the central idea that you take away? That you'll probably remember long after you've forgotten the details of the plot?

STUDENTS: We're social and we have to interact with others.

We were talking about the people he was trying to say something to. I think the author was making a point about human nature. If we're walking down the street today and we see an old bum, you know, asking us for money we'll act like we don't hear him. We'll pick up our pace and be on our way, and I think the author is suggesting every one of us is like that and we need maybe to listen to other people.

TEACHER: Do you think we are like that?

STUDENTS: I think so.

Not necessarily.

TEACHER: You're not that way?

STUDENTS: Well, no, I've done it too, we all have. You can go to a hospital and ask somebody 'How are you?' but you don't want them to tell you how they are. So you just get on to something else. I think we're all guilty.

Well, I think the story is just plain human nature. There is loneliness and there's going to be. That's real life. Nothing's going to change.

TEACHER: So that's the way it is and people like Iona ought to just accept it.

STUDENTS: [Laughter]

No. Ideally, we'd go out and try to be different but realistically we'll do that for a day or two.

Like realistically you're only going to have a few people in your life that you talk to and you've got to realize not everyone is going to care about you and want to listen to you.

Yeah. You're lucky if you can find a couple people who will.

So realistically that's how it is. Everybody should concentrate on finding their one or two people.

When people get old most people aren't there anymore, and at least in our society young people avoid them. They are lonely and it's a vicious cycle. The young people have so much that they're doing they just don't want to sit forever. There's an old lady that lives down the street, and if I go over I know I can't get away for about an hour and I have all this stuff to do, you know, and I like to talk to her a little bit but you keep thinking in the back of your head "I have this book to read." So I kind of avoid going over there.

Maybe it's just my nature but none of this has been true of me. My husband says I'm the biggest sucker born because every bum that comes up, I give to him. That's just the way I was taught. I believe I'm my brother's keeper.

This reminded me of *The Pigman*. That old man talks to the animals at the zoo.

TEACHER: A writer can present a problem or a comment on human nature without having any desire to make you go off and do good. But at least you're aware of it. You think about it, perhaps in a new way. I wonder if we could expand on these ideas a little more, perhaps in our society as a whole. [At this point I presented a slide of George Tooker's "Government Bureau."] Is there anything in this picture that relates to a key idea in Chekhov's story?

STUDENTS: It looks like the walls have eyes and ears. Watch out what you're saying. It makes us seem really sneaky and suspicious.

It's very impersonal.

You can listen but the person doing the speaking can tell whether you're truly interested. These sure aren't.

TEACHER: What about the picture led you to that thought?

STUDENTS: A lack of humanity there. The faces in the wall aren't looking toward each other. There's no interaction.

TEACHER: Do you think that Tooker in 1956 is relating the same idea as Chekhov did a century earlier?

STUDENTS: Things have gotten worse. It's like we were talking about the family in the forties and now. They're just not as close now.

It's almost like society is forcing us to be withdrawn into ourselves and cold because who really wants to listen. If you were to make a mistake the walls or Big Brother or whoever is listening would know. Is it the right movement? Is it the right thought? And society today is making us the cold people that we are."

TEACHER: How is that?

STUDENTS: We all have numbers for everything.

Well, even here on campus you have to be careful.

It's not just common sense being careful. It's just that we go so fast just normally. It's like she said we just don't have time to sit and listen.

TEACHER: So it's not society? It's us?

STUDENT: No, it's both I'd say.

TEACHER: [I then offered them a slide of Edvard Munch's "The Scream."] Take a look now at the painting by Edvard Munch. What do you notice about the lines in the painting as they relate to the title?

STUDENTS: This artist has done the same thing Van Gogh capitalized on. You have your background all woven in. It's a frenzy. There's nothing to do but get upset when you look at this.

The waves are like a scream. They echo and go back.

It looks like an echo going across everywhere. The world.

It seems loud like everyone in two miles of this woman could hear.

The more you look at this the more it affects you. It's disturbing.

TEACHER: In the painting you have the artist making a great deal of use of line. The subject and the technique blend especially well. In the story you have words, scenes, and so on that set up the effect Chekhov offered us. In effective artistry all the parts work together to create the success of the work. Do you, by the way, see any parallels in the painting and Iona?

STUDENTS: Yeah. This person's screaming and the people in the back don't seem to be noticing.

She's so lonely and frightened.

TEACHER: One aspect of successful craft is to make a story believable. Look at the second question I gave you just after you finished reading the story. Were you prepared for Iona's telling the horse his story?

STUDENTS: Yes. He's said he has to tell someone.

It's beyond sad. You can't comprehend that someone has to go to a horse.

TEACHER: Did the author present us with enough build up so that the ending was inevitable?

STUDENTS: Yes. The horse has been with him throughout the story.

I was shocked but then again I wasn't.

You knew he was going to get it out somehow.

He had to say it out loud.

People talk to their pets all the time. They won't talk back, they'll listen, and at least we think they understand.

TEACHER: I usually ask you at the beginning what you think of the story but I waited on this one. How did you like it?

[Chorus approval, nodding of heads]

I liked the descriptions.

You hate those people being so rude.

It was just like watching TV. You could really picture it.

CONCLUSION

Though the discussion seemed to contain digressions, each feature was useful in helping the students to examine their reactions and what within their own experience produced that reaction. In the interest of the organic nature of discussion, it is probably best for the teacher to interrupt the flow as little as possible. My own interjections are attempts to synthesize or summarize the points students have voiced and to guide the discussion gently without forcing my own ideas on them. The two questions they answered immediately following the initial reading were designed to encourage personal response as well as set the stage for later consideration of the artistry involved in Chekhov's preparing the reader for the ending.

After the discussion I asked students during the last five minutes to answer two questions:

1. After you finished the story, was there a single incident from any point in your life that the story made you think of? Briefly tell what it was.
2. After you completed the reading you had your own ideas about the story's meaning. As a group, did the contributions of the class members build any new dimensions that hadn't occurred to you? What were they?

Responses to question 1 ranged from deaths to a dislocated shoulder. In connection with transactional theory, I was particularly interested in individual perceptions about meaning evolving from the discussion (question 2). Several remarked they had not noted the artistry in the initial paragraph of the story nor realized the story lends itself to scenes. Others commented that they felt more sympathy for Iona and became more aware of the need to take time to listen to people in need. Some had not considered the several reasons for Iona's laughter with the three young men who abuse him. One comment summarizes well an example of the individual construct growing with the creation of that of the group.

> Yes, most of us agreed that the world is full of people who want to care for others but just do not have the time that is necessary. I hadn't really thought about the importance of listening to people in need; I had basically thought of the tale as a man who felt sorry for himself because he lived and his son died.

Student comments about such topics as Iona's laughter are rooted in their having themselves experienced or seen others laugh when it was not a sign of merriment. Their ability to see the thoughtlessness of all of these people toward Iona probably stems from their recollection of a time when they needed to talk and no one was there. The people who rebuke Iona are varying reflections of themselves because they too have been guilty of not taking time with others.

These insights reflect a certain amount of life experience that these college undergraduates bring to a literary work. Moreover, high school students also bring significant experience to their reading of "The Lament." I presented the story in the same manner to high school sophomores; they felt the same degree of sympathy for Iona as did the older students. They readily recalled times when they needed someone to talk with and no one was there. Instances included parents yelling at them for not being home on time, a grandfather's death, a lack of interest by another in something very important to the teller, a fight with a friend. They readily saw how the story relates to how they sometimes do not take the time to listen to another or the difficulty in finding someone who will listen. Overall, however, most felt they did have a good friend they talked to a lot. (I was reminded of the lengthy telephone conversations most of us had in high school in which we analyzed one another's current problems.)

They did not have much insight beyond the school, family life, or popular entertainment. For example, they responded to George Tooker's "Government Bureau" with comments that it looked like something out of a science fiction movie. They had no comments in connection with our society as a whole being impersonal.

G. Robert Carlsen has presented a flow chart indicating what persons in various age groups primarily respond to in their reading (26). Persons in late high school and college years are more likely to be concerned with philosophical questions and problems of humankind. As one gets older there is a natural process of decentering, moving from an intensive concern with self and adolescent life toward broader issues. His chart suggests why certain works are particularly appealing at certain ages. It is important to keep this concept in mind as we think about transactional theory. There are aspects of "The Lament" that strike a chord in high school sophomores but the meaning they build will be somewhat different from that of an older group. Each meaning is valid, just different based on the set of life experiences of each member in a particular group.

For students in a classroom in which the teacher attempts to develop an atmosphere conducive to "literature as exploration," the poems created have several ramifications: those initially created through the individual's transaction with the work and those created by the group as a composite greatly dependent on the different life experiences of those in that group. Finally, there is the poem that individuals take away as their own, usually a modification of the original insight enriched now by the collective responses of the group. Ideally, in the best Rosenblatt tradition, students are encouraged to approach literature personally and to feel their own responses are not just encouraged—they are cherished.

REFERENCES

Chekhov, Anton. *The Best Known Works of Anton Chekhov*. Freeport, New York: Books for Libraries Press, 1972.

Carlsen, G. Robert. "Literature Is." *English Journal* Feb. 1974, 23–27.

Rosenblatt, Louise M. 1978. *The Reader, The Text, The Poem: The Transactional Theory of the Literary Work*. Carbondale, IL: Southern Illinois University Press, 1978.

CHAPTER 7

Two Reader-Response Classrooms:

Using Pre-reading Activity and Readers Theatre Approaches

Patricia P. Kelly

I vividly remember several years ago a student, trembling with frustration, standing before me at the end of a class near the beginning of the year, clutching her notebook with pencil poised, and asking intensely: "What *was* the reason Sammy quit?" after we had discussed multiple possibilities for Sammy, in John Updike's *A & P,* quitting his job. Breaking such student expectations for definitive answers to problematic situations in literary texts is not easy even with a reader-response approach to teaching literature.

To help students learn to reconcile the dissonance caused from multiple views, to see those views as useful, to make sense of a literary selection, and to assume more control for the discussion of literature, I use Readers Theatre. This reader-response approach not only provides oral performance possibilities for students but also encourages them to discuss in depth a literary selection in order to know what "interpretation" they want to get across to an audience. When students prepare for a Readers Theatre presentation, their discussion of a text evolves differently from a discussion generated by a pre-reading activity. So what follows is a look into two of Kathryn Atkins's tenth-grade classes when they read and discussed "Words," written by Sylvia Plath in the last weeks before her death. One class discussed the poem using a typical reader-response approach initiated by a pre-reading activity and one class talked about the poem in small groups while preparing a Readers Theatre performance.

WORDS

Axes
After whose stroke the wood rings,
And the echoes!
Echoes travelling
Off from the centre like horses.

The sap
Wells like tears, like the
Water striving
To re-establish its mirror
Over the rock

That drops and turns,
A white skull,
Eaten by weedy greens.
Years later I
Encounter them on the road——

Words dry and riderless,
The indefatigable hoof-taps.
While
From the bottom of the pool, fixed stars
Govern a life.

—Sylvia Plath

PRE-READING FOR READER-RESPONSE DISCUSSION

The first tenth-grade class in her rural high school, where classes are generally small, had eleven students, which allowed us to use a whole-class discussion model and still provide plenty of opportunity for all students to participate. I began the class by asking students to write in their journals about a time when words hurt: When was it? What was the situation? Why do you remember it now? What did you learn? Kathy and I wrote with them, and because these were sensitive remembrances, I began the discussion by telling them of the incident I had written about. Although students did not choose to share their journal entries at that time, in the discussion of the poem that ensued, students referred not only to my experience but also their own.

After this pre-reading activity, I read the poem aloud to them and initiated the discussion by asking: "Do you see any similarity between your own experience and what Sylvia Plath describes in the poem?" David began by saying, "Well, like us, someone said something she didn't like and it hurt her feelings and made her feel bad."

Immediately students began sharing their personal connections to Sylvia Plath's experience, situations they had written about in their journals. They talked of being called a liar, of being disowned by family members, of comments about having big feet, and being betrayed by friends. The only reason I can offer for students' sharing personally at this point but not earlier is they had connected so strongly with the poem and the depth of hurt feelings that there was safety in a shared experience. Nothing had occurred after their personal journal writing except the reading of the poem.

Throughout the ensuing discussion Kathy and I commented only in ways to keep the interaction going, for example "Do you want to say more about that? Does anyone else have a different view? Is that idea like anything anyone else has said?" We wanted the students to control the direction and nature of the talk as much as possible.

After the recounted instances of hurtful situations, the discussion shifted to the text of the poem when Michelle said, "Axes sort of cut out your feelings"; followed by Susan's tag comment, "Yea, scars your mind"; and Kim's observation, "Brings tears."

To which John added, "The tears are like sap out of a tree after you've cut it; someone hurts your feelings so much it makes you cry."

Robert teased, "Would it make you cry?" and John ducked his head and said firmly, "Naw."

After some good-natured laughter, Kim pointed to the poem and read, "Like the water"; she looked up puzzled, "Where did they get that from?"

Julie answered, "She's describing a lake like a mirror . . . when you're trying to make yourself feel better."

And Jeanne added, "She's trying to cover up the hurt and hide her feelings."

The discussion of water brought the students naturally to asking about the "white skull, eaten by weedy greens." One student said the skull was a rock; another said it was "old memories; the hurt's still there." At the end of the short silence that then occurred, Mark said, "Like death. . . ." Several students in unison rejected that idea, and it was never brought up again. The reaction was not to Mark himself but to the idea. He continued to contribute to the class discussion. It is my contention that the students felt good about the direction they had taken; their "analysis" was fitting together, and they did not want to entertain as a possibility an idea that would lead them in a different direction.

After that slight diversion, the students went straight to the text again, agreeing that "Years later I encounter them on the road—" referred to meeting the same person or situation again. But they also concurred that she, the persona, might be just remembering the situation and that would have the same effect on her.

Students decided that "dry and riderless" showed that the words didn't affect her any more. And they expressed surprise at "hoof-taps"; Karen said, "Look, she comes back to horses." However, they did not attempt to connect with or to understand that part specifically. Instead they talked about the last stanza in general terms.

For example, Mark said, "She's showing that she can go on with her life . . . but that rock will always be there."

But Robert qualified, "That may depend on how big the pool is."

"Yea, if it's a little pool," Susan began explaining, ". . . like if she's a shallow person and it's a big rock, she'll not get over it. If she's pretty deep or it's a little rock, it won't continue to affect her as much."

Looking at the last line of the poem, "Govern a life," Michelle connected the hurtful experience I had shared with them in her comment: "The hurtful words can make changes in your life; for instance that could have been a beautiful dress," referring to my story about another teacher who had made fun of a dress I was wearing, which I subsequently threw away.

At this point the students had worked their way straight through the poem, making personal connections in some places, and all had participated in some way. To encourage them to take another look at problematic sections of the poem, however, I told them that, though I had read the poem many times, it still puzzled and confused me in places. I then asked them to circle three places in the poem that still confused them a little and then to choose one of the circled places and write about it: why the section was confusing, how the section made them feel, or some possible meanings of the section. The three sections selected most often were "Echoes travelling / Off from the centre," "Eaten by weedy greens," and "fixed stars." No one, however, wrote about or talked about "fixed stars." The discussion of "weedy greens" was similar to their previous conjectures about the line.

Students puzzled over "Echoes travelling." Interestingly, they had skipped that section entirely in their class discussion.

Traci finally said, "It's the echo of the wood ringing from the axe; it sounds like it's crying." The boys grinned and shook their heads, good-naturedly disassociating themselves from the consideration of crying.

Michelle selected no part that still puzzled her, saying: "She [Plath] puts it in the right words; she knows what she's talking about. It happens to me every day." Kathy said Michelle later chose this poem as her favorite for the year's study.

We then asked each student to select an object, similar to axes, that could also be used as a metaphor for hurtful words. Students compiled quite a list, for example: knives, cactus, razors, thorns, darts, hammer, and stick pins. Kathy suggested they take a favorite metaphor from the list and use it to describe the situation they had written about when someone hurt their feelings, in the way Sylvia Plath had or in any way they chose. After the students wrote—most tried poems—they chose to pass them around the circle to read and compliment each other. One girl's poem began:

> Like darts,
> Propelled by insignificant means,
> Struck me the same as the voice. . . .

INTERPRETATION OF PRE-READING ACTIVITY DISCUSSION

This class discussion was fairly typical of a lesson where a pre-reading activity helps students connect their personal experiences with literature. The students understood the text, not from a literary stance but from personal associations, and they were pleased with their understanding of the poem. Despite the students' perceived satisfaction, I have two concerns about the class discussion. First, although pre-reading activities are necessary to provide the bridge between a student's experience and the literature, such activities sometimes can push the discussion in a direction suggested by the pre-reading to such an extent that students reject contrary views or do not deal with a section of the literature that has them consider a different view. In other words pre-reading activities are both a blessing and bane.

Students do need some type of pre-reading experience, of course, especially with difficult material; however, those pre-reading activities must be directly, not obliquely, connected to the literature. In a study using simulation games as pre-reading, a group that played games conceptually unrelated to the stories they read had fewer student responses and slower responses than in either the group using no pre-reading games or the group using conceptually related pre-reading games (Kelly 102). Unconnected pre-reading activities seemed to confuse students, making it more difficult for them to respond to the text. But we must be cognizant that a pre-reading activity has the potential to inhibit divergent thinking. For example, the students in Kathy's class probably cut short Mark's tentative idea about death because the focus on personal hurt of the pre-reading activity did not include the concept of death.

I am also concerned with this particular discussion because students conducted their discussion of the literary selection as a teacher-led class, even though Kathy and I were managing the student discussion rather than asking text-related questions. Students proceeded through the literary work with the goal of somehow explaining most of it. Though they were actively participating, their preconceived notions of what constituted a discussion of literature were evident, thus limiting their personal exploration of the text.

READERS THEATRE AS READER RESPONSE

What I describe next is another tenth-grade class of Kathy's, in which we used Readers Theatre as the process for discussing Plath's poem. Kathy had engaged these students in creative dramatics activities on many occasions, and they enjoyed performing although they were not particularly adept at Readers Theatre. We divided the fourteen students into a group of five boys, a group of four girls, and a group of five boys and girls. I wanted them to cohere as groups, so I gave them the task of performing selected sentences so that they projected specified moods and emotions, such as anger, happiness, sadness, mystery, fear. They had five minutes to prepare their readings so that the class could guess the mood/emotion being conveyed. These mini-performances began the process of their working as a group, reminding them that the purpose of Readers Theatre is to convey with the voice an interpreted meaning to an audience, and got them performing in front of the class to abate any initial self-consciousness. I then gave them large print copies of the poem, glued to colored paper so that each group had its own color-coded identity when performing. We did not provide any pre-reading writing or discussion because we wanted the students to wrestle with the meaning of the poem and how they might present that meaning to an audience.

The group of five boys was initially governed by the task. (I have found this to be true for most groups at any grade level.) Kevin said, "We've got to figure out how to present this poem."

Bobby filled the anxious silence, "Somebody read the poem. . . ." Actually two boys read the poem twice.

After listening to the second reading, Kevin asked, "Can we present this in any way we want?" They decided they could do as they wanted with the presentation and immediately got down to the task of understanding the poem when Will, who had been silent thus far, said, "What are the axes? I got it; look at the title!"

At first they thought they might have one person read the title and author and the other four boys read a stanza each. That soon changed as they talked about the emotions in each stanza, for example, Patrick proposed, "Tears should be said softly."

Then Greg said excitedly, "I know; words . . . like sticks and stones will break your bones, but whatever they say, words hurt like anything." They laughed and punched at each other good naturedly, punctuating their knowledge of the truth of the words just spoken.

With that understanding they discussed how they would read each line, conveying the emotion they wanted: anger, sadness, deep pain, and resignation—or as they put it, "There's nothing she can do about it." They read the poem several times, discussing the effectiveness of their arrangement for communicating their meaning. Their Readers Theatre presentation was a sophisticated blend of choral and individual reading.

The mixed group of boys and girls settled quickly into discussing the poem for developing a presentation with Debbie's first task assessment remark, "We've got to read this to the class. We've got to figure out what it means; what's the emotion?" This group concentrated on the notion of echoes: The sound of the axe echoing and the fact that years later the feelings come back is also an echo. They decided to repeat the last word in each line in order to provide that "echo effect." Other words, such as "the rock and axes," they saw as important and decided all group members would read them for emphasis.

Their discussion led them to conclude that one line in each stanza carried a lot of meaning, for example "To re-establish its mirror" in the second stanza, and those lines would be read by all the group members "to echo and make the ideas echo in your mind," Mark said. Like the other group they practiced their reading several times. Their presentation was almost musical and certainly projected the echo effect they wanted.

The group of four girls also settled into the task quickly. Melanie read the poem twice before Kari said, "We have to figure out what axes are."

Susan answered, "Words that hurt you."

And Becky, pointing to the poem, said, "Tears."

Melanie explained further, "Something you always remember for years." With that, they ceased dealing with the poem's meaning except indirectly as they worried about presenting it. They experimented with several arrangements, reading the poem multiple times but generally not discussing the meaning they were giving the lines. Only the line "Eaten by weedy greens" generated any further meaning-making attempts. Instead, they treated the task as *who* would read *what;* the how and why of the interpretation was not discussed. Ultimately they chose the least imaginative and safest reading arrangement— each of the four girls read a stanza.

After the students had enjoyed each other's Readers Theatre presentations, we asked the groups to spend the last ten minutes talking about their "readings" and why they had decided to present the poem as they had. Two of the groups shared reasons for their very different emphases, the "echoes" and the "emotions," but they also concluded that the major idea each was presenting was similar: the lasting hurt caused by unkind words. The group of girls reported that they had considered some different ways of presenting the poem but had liked the way each of them could be responsible for a stanza. But, through their body language and facial expressions, I sensed they wished they had risked a more creative approach. The class also talked about a poem they had read earlier by Plath called "Mirrors," remarking on the occurrence of the mirror image in both poems. Throughout this culminating discussion students seemed not only comfortable with differing ideas but also appreciative of the diversity of interpretation. Unlike the whole-class discussion, these students liked having viewed the poem differently.

INTERPRETATION OF READERS THEATRE APPROACH

These whole-class discussions following Readers Theatre presentations broaden students' understanding of the literary work because they hear the thinking that underlies different interpretations. The discussions are not a "reporting" of the group activity; neither are they like a class discussion of the poem. And therein lies their benefit. They are similar to an "expert" group approach because each group is an expert on its presentation, but the motivation is somewhat different. Each group wants the others, who have appreciated its rendering of the literary piece, to understand the uniqueness of its interpretation. Although they are teaching each other as "expert" groups do, students do not perceive the discussion in that way; they see it as an informal sharing.

Kathy was surprised by the presentations. The four girls were her best students, but for some reason they did not take the risks necessary to carry out the task creatively. Even their short discussion revealed they had the skills to discuss the poem, but for the presentation they played it safe by assigning stanzas and reading with no evident interpretation. On the other hand, the boys, who never shone academically, were willing to risk playing with the ideas in the poem because the Readers Theatre process did not resemble any other type of class discussion that might hold them accountable for "knowing" the poem. Furthermore, I have found with other classes that both the small-group discussions and Readers Theatre presentations evolving from them improve dramatically in subsequent experiences. I assume, therefore, that with additional exposure to this approach the group of four girls would learn to discuss and perform literature more independently, more freely, and more meaningfully than with this first endeavor.

With Readers Theatre students read a selection, in this case a poem, many more times than occurs with other discussion arrangements—large or small group. First they use many readings as a way into meaning; then they practice readings to project their intended meaning to others; and last they listen to readings with the meanings others have derived. I am always amazed that students seem unaware they have read the literary selection half a dozen times or more, for they would most surely resist that many readings in a regular class situation.

In some ways, however, the students in the Readers Theatre class did not "cover" the poem as well as the other class; perhaps the whole-class setting and more familiar structure of the pre-reading activity influenced them to consider most lines of the poem in a traditional way. The Readers Theatre students did not discuss possible meanings for the more difficult images in the poem, but instead related to the sensory impressions and emphasized those in their interpretations. Like all readers these students made meaning at their own level of literary and personal experiences. Consequently, it is not surprising that they seemed unable to connect with three specific images in the poem, images using sensory language drawn from Plath's own literary and personal experiences. However, the students' choice of relating to the poem from a sensing, emotional approach rather than an explicative one was a useful strategy for them. Their discussions and presentations showed they understood the poem in a holistic way and had personal experiences that connected with the poem. These students were approaching the reading of and talking about difficult text as autonomous learners who accepted and even delighted in varying interpretations. (For this to occur the Readers Theatre activity must come first, becoming the vehicle of response to and interpretation of the text; if interpretation comes first, then Readers Theatre becomes performance rather than reader response.)

CONCLUSIONS

Whatever the differing surface features of these two classes using reader-response approaches, there is a common factor in both because students were moving from their "personal responses and interpretations back to the text" (Rosenblatt 282). In the first class their personal responses were triggered by an external stimulus, the pre-reading activity, whereas in the Readers Theatre class something in the text stimulated their personal responses. When Greg said the "sticks and stones" children's rhyme, he was bringing personal experience to explain the poem for him. His addition of "words hurt like anything," was offering personal knowledge to contradict a widely disseminated myth. The reaction of his group members showed they not only understood his connection but also shared feelings about it.

Rosenblatt cautions that in adopting various teaching strategies for literature we must

> be very careful to scrutinize all our procedures to be sure that we are not in actuality substituting other aims—things to do *about* literature—for the experience *of* literature. We can ask of every assignment or method or text, no matter what its short-term effectiveness: Does it get in the way of the live sense of literature? Does it make literature something to be regurgitated, analyzed, categorized, or is it a means toward making literature a more personally meaningful and self-disciplined activity? (279)

Having students read and discuss literature for Readers Theatre performances is not an activity *about* literature but provides the experience *of* literature by giving life to literature through performance. This reader-response teaching approach purposefully engages students with literature in a way that encourages the sharing of personal meanings, requires self-discipline to carry out the task, and fosters the diversity of ideas.

REFERENCES

Kelly, Patricia P. "Can I Know How You Feel If I Haven't Walked in Your Shoes?" *Focus: Teaching English Language Arts* 2 (1983): 98–102.

Plath, Sylvia. "Words." In *Ariel*. New York: Harper & Row, Publishers, 1961. 85.

Rosenblatt, Louise M. *Literature as Exploration*. 3d ed. New York: Noble and Noble, 1976.

CHAPTER 8

"I Understood the Grief":

Theory-Based Introduction to *Ordinary People*

Deborah Appleman

> *In the education given the adolescent in America, there is still little to enlighten him. . . . He will sense needs and curiosities, and here again, it will often be only from the reflection of life offered by literature, that he will acquire such insights.*
>
> (Rosenblatt, 88)
>
> Ordinary People *was about finding your self-identity. It was like a guide to dealing with people. It showed how people dealt with death and an attempted suicide. It showed to the reader that ordinary people deal with these things every day. This means that Joe Average isn't alone in this world.*
>
> (Chris G., grade 11)

READER-RESPONSE THEORY AND THE ADOLESCENT READER

For decades, theorists in the field of English education have been heralding reader-response theory as an approach to literature well-suited to the developmental and intellectual characteristics of adolescents. Teachers, too, have begun to adjust their teaching styles to acknowledge readers' responses and have selected texts with which adolescents could identify.

Adolescent readers, preoccupied as they are with their own developing identity and the acute need to make some sense of the complex and bewildering world around them, bring their personal experiences to the reading of a literary text and project those experiences onto the textual world, whether or not the teacher encourages or facilitates that process. The very characteristics of adolescence that might prove intrusive to a purely critical reading of the text, leading to what I. A. Richards called a "mnemonic irrelevance" are the very qualities that can enable young readers to respond richly and personally to literature within the theoretical context of reader response. As Probst explains:

> The adolescent, characteristically preoccupied with self, should be an ideal reader. That is not to say that he will read well, or even read at all. He may despise literature, the

The author wishes to thank Martha Cosgrove for her skilled teaching and the Modern Literature students of Henry Sibley Senior High School, Mendota Heights, Minnesota for their responses to *Ordinary People*.

literature classroom and the literature teacher, and express great pride in his inability to make sense of the written word. But unless he is very unusual, he has the one characteristic essential for a reader—an interest in himself. He is concerned about his relationships with peers and parents and his gradual assumption of responsibility for himself. . . . Preoccupation with self should make adolescents uniquely receptive to literature, for literature invites their participation and judgment. (4–5)

Rosenblatt further reminds us of the importance of consonance between a reader's preoccupations and those that arise in reading a literary text:

Any insight or clarification the youth derives from the literary work will grow out of its relevance to certain facets of his emotional or intellectual nature. The whole personality tends to become involved in the literary experience. That a literary work may bring into play and be related to profoundly personal needs and preoccupations make it a powerful potential educational force. For it is out of these basic needs and attitudes that behavior springs. Hence, literature can foster the linkage between intellectual perception and emotional drive that is essential to any vital learning process. (182)

By refusing to overlook or ignore the nature of their adolescent readers, teachers can encourage students to bring their personal experiences, values, questions, and concerns to the reading of a literary text, making the "transaction," as Rosenblatt calls it, the very point of the reading experience itself.

ADOLESCENTS AND TEXT SELECTION

Ordinary People is a touching story of male initiation, of a young man who is growing into adulthood against incredible psychological odds. The locale is in the Midwest and the time is the early 1970's, but the novel could be happening anywhere and at any time, which is one of the reasons students respond to it so easily. Conrad Jarrett could be any of us in adolescence; full of awful secrets, trying to gain control of his own world, worried about how others view him, wishing just to become "ordinary." (Peck 43)

The passage from adolescence to adulthood, never an easy trail to blaze, has today become a perilous and stressful journey.

Contemporary American society has struck teenagers a double blow. It has rendered them more vulnerable to stress while at the same time exposing them to new and more powerful stresses than were ever faced by previous generations of adolescents. It is not surprising, then, to find that the number of stress-related problems among teen-agers has more than trebled in the last decade and a half. (Elkind 6)

The contemporary challenges that have created this increase in stress among today's adolescents, in Elkind's terms—the "perils of puberty," "peer shock," and "family permutations"—are precisely those issues that face Judith Guest's adolescent protagonist, Conrad Jarrett, in *Ordinary People*.

Developing an integrated sense of identity is a daunting task, one made even more difficult by our confused and confusing times. That search for self-definition is the focus of Conrad's psychological odyssey as he attempts to derive an "integrated" self-definition after the layers of sibling rivalry, parental expectations, and peer-imposed roles have been pulled away.

Conrad's struggle to define himself within the context of his family, his peers, and his personal history, mirror with remarkable accuracy the process of self-finding faced by many adolescents. The fact that both Conrad and the adolescent reader are immersed in the same difficult and troubled search for self will facilitate the students' ability to identify with and respond to the text.

But it is not merely the adolescent quest for identity that makes *Ordinary People* a novel with which adolescent readers can easily identify. As Conrad sifts through the details of his life in order to make some sense of them as well as of himself, he peels back the layers of artifice that have surrounded his life and the life of his family. His mother's preoccupation with appearances and "good taste," the troubled emotional truths that bubble under the smooth facade of his parents' marriage, the falseness of many of his brother's friends and their expectations are all a crucial part of this contemporary coming-of-age story set in the plastic veneer of suburban adolescence. Becoming aware that all is not as it appears is a necessary if painful part of adolescence.

Conrad's suicide attempt, his family's (especially Beth's) reaction to it, and his struggle to recapture a commitment to living are clearly central to the novel and thus will figure significantly in any reader's engagement with the text. Although suicide is a troublesome and potentially dangerous topic for any reader, for adolescents it is an especially difficult topic.

Adolescent suicide has reached nearly epidemic proportions and is currently the leading cause of death among young people, after car accidents. For life's counterparts to Conrad, white males between the ages of sixteen and nineteen, the rate of suicide has nearly tripled since 1960 (*Newsweek* 15).

Recently when I asked a group of forty high school students if they had personally known anyone who had committed or attempted suicide, thirty-two responded that they had. Nearly half admitted to having considered suicide at least once, and more than a third said they considered it sometimes or frequently. As one student put it, when asked what experiences she brought to the text that might affect her response, "The fact that I've thought about committing suicide. I know someone who's tried to kill herself and I realize how much she needs to feel liked and normal."

However, some teachers may resist the prospect of discussing suicide with their students. One college student, rereading the novel before he student-taught in a suburban high school English classroom wrote:

> I found myself shocked by the admission in the book about how exactly to slit your wrists. Frankly, I'd be worried about this in the classroom. But you can't not teach this. Just because we have atomic bombs doesn't mean we'll use them. And if we do, the problem runs much deeper than reading to see how they work. If you can't head it off long before it happens, it may already be too late.

But Rosenblatt tells us that "the emotional character of a student's response to literature offers an opportunity to develop the ability *to think rationally within an emotionally colored context*" (228, her italics). By making the discussion of suicide an integral aspect of the response process, then, more than a literary response is enriched; students may, indeed, be able to make sense of a seemingly non-sensical phenomenon.

In addition to the relevance of the issues presented in *Ordinary People,* the style of the book also facilitates a literary response in adolescent readers. Beach and Appleman summarized research that underscores the importance of accessible and realistic, "reader-friendly" language in literary texts. When familiar language is used to convey strong emotions, as it is in *Ordinary People,* engagement with the text is far more likely.

The following passage is representative of the language in the novel as well as Guest's sense of internal dialogue:

> All connections with him result in failure. Loss. Evil. At school it is the same. Every-where he looks, there is competence and good health. Only he, Conrad Jarrett, outcast, quitter, fuck-up, stands outside the circle of safety, separated by everyone from this aching void of loneliness; but no matter, he deserves it. He does not speak to anyone. He does not dare to look at his classmates in the eye. He does not want to contaminate, does not wish to find further evidence of his lack of worth. (107)

This type of painful self-scrutiny is all too achingly familiar to adolescent readers. Students easily recognize the similarity of Conrad's struggle with self-acceptance with their own struggles. The relevance of the novel's issues to adolescent readers in language that is both real and familiar makes *Ordinary People* a text that will foster an engagement with reading on which the following strategies for teaching can be built.

PULLING BACK THE CURTAIN ON LITERARY THEORY: THE READER-RESPONSE DIAGRAMS

> What, then happens in the reading of a literary work? Through the medium of words, the text brings into the reader's consciousness certain concepts, certain sensuous experi-ences, certain images of things, people, actions, scenes. The special meanings, and more particularly, the submerged associations that these words and images have for the indi-vidual reader will largely determine what it communicates to *him.* The reader brings to the work personality traits, memories of past events, present needs and preoccupations, a particular mood of the moment and a particular physical condition. These and many other elements in a never-to-be-duplicated combination determine his response to the peculiar contribution of the text. (Rosenblatt 30–31)

Students' interpretive abilities can be enhanced if they are more aware of the theoretical context in which their responses occur. Thus, as teachers discuss specific literary texts with their students using a response-based approach, they should introduce students to the basic tenets of reader-response theory so that the oral and written responses to literature that follow are framed in a theoretical context not only for the teacher, but for the student as well.

What follows is a description of one approach we used with a group of "college-bound" eleventh- and twelfth-graders. The strategies described, however, are equally appropriate for undergraduate college students.

Before reading *Ordinary People,* the students responded to several poems and short

stories that were selected for their ambiguity and openness to a wide variety of interpretations. As a prelude to each whole-class discussion, students wrote brief response papers
on each literary work before any teacher or whole-class explication occurred. Students
then shared their response papers and were encouraged to listen, not for the most plausible
or seemingly "correct" interpretation, but for the diversity represented in their peers'
responses. We then discussed some of the general factors that can influence an individual
reader's response to a literary text as well as the specific factors that were at play in their
own responses. Students were then introduced to the basic tenets of Rosenblatt's transactional theory of reading and were asked to list both the textual and reader characteristics
that had influenced their response to the literary texts they had been discussing.

After several pre-reading activities, including an anonymous suicide survey to elicit
and discuss their attitudes about suicide, the students read *Ordinary People*. We then
asked them to complete a reader-response diagram identifying *Ordinary People* as the
"text" and themselves as the "reader."

Reader Response

context

reader (   )————→ meaning ←———— text

Under "reader" and "text," students were then asked to identify specific characteristics of
each that might affect the particular nature of their "transaction" with the novel. This
information helps to bring to the reader's consciousness the values, assumptions, and
beliefs brought to the text; it also helps to inform the teacher of the factors that affect these
students' responses to the text.

The resulting diagrams demonstrate the students' remarkable ability to assess their
characteristics as readers that were relevant to their reading of *Ordinary People*. Under the
"reader" heading, many students mentioned the following factors as influencing their
response:

1. parents' divorce: "Suddenly the family was ripped apart—by choice"
2. depression: "Get depressed sometimes. Sometimes I close up and won't talk
   about my feelings"
3. relationship with parents, specifically, inability to get along with their mothers: "I
   get along with my Dad better than my Mom," "I know what it's like to have
   someone act like Beth did," "Don't get along with my mom"
4. feelings of insecurity: "doubting yourself," "not thinking people will forgive
   you"
5. thoughts of suicide: "The fact that I've thought about killing myself," "I thought
   about suicide, what it would do to my family"
6. experience with close friends or relatives who committed or attempted to commit
   suicide: "my best friend tried to commit suicide," "my cousin tried to kill
   himself this year," "my best friend's brother killed himself in April"
7. sibling rivalry: "older sister/brother who's perfect," "the way I feel I have to be
   perfect like my brother," "Having to follow a sister's perfection"
8. "feeling like an outcast"

9. experience with death: "I understand the grief: I know what it feels like to have someone die in my family"

In terms of text characteristics, the following were the most commonly offered:

1. realism: "This book was the most realistic book I ever read," "People seemed like real life"
2. language: "The language was strong. It was written in simple language and not with all these scholarly words." "I liked the swearing"
3. characteristics of protagonist: "Con's age was close to ours." "Thoughts were some that I've thought"
4. narrative structure: "Switching from one person to another"
5. settings: "you could relate it to our time," "It was written in the late 70s rather than hundreds of years ago"

After the students listed both personal and textual characteristics, they were asked . several statements of meaning that arose from their transaction with *Ordinary Peopi* statements ranged from personal insights to general comments about families and so The following are representative:

1. "Most answers to problems lie within yourself."
2. "Families that look perfect on the outside are not always perfect on the inside.
3. "I have to learn to deal with my feelings and face them better."
4. "Communication is important to keep a family together."
5. "Everybody needs to feel normal, to be accepted."
6. "You can't hide from life and its problems."
7. "How complicated family life is."
8. "Life isn't fair, right or nice, it just is."
9. "Everyone has problems, even "ordinary people." The only difference is in the way people deal with their problems.

In addition to making reader-response theory explicit to the students, the reader-response diagrams, especially the reader characteristics listed by the students, helped the teacher gain some additional insight into her students. In the teaching of literature, teachers' knowledge about students is as important as their knowledge of materials. Both are critical to creating the "vital sense of literature" that Rosenblatt celebrates (51).

Through this approach the students saw more clearly that as individuals, they brought salient personal qualities that were not irrelevant or unimportant but were actually critical to the act of reading. They also learned that the self-knowledge they might be gaining from the text was not incidental but central to the literary experience. This notion of self-discovery through literature is clearly explained by Probst:

Thus, exchange with the text can become for the reader a process of self-creation. The entire process—responding, correcting errors, searching for the sources of the response, speculating about the author's intent and weighing the author's values and ideas against one's own—culminates in a sharpened, heightened sense of self. Some part of the reader's conception of the world is either confirmed, modified, or refuted, and that changes the reader. (21)

The reader-response diagrams help foster the kind of "self-creation" Probst describes. It also encourages personal exchanges with the text that can be built on in whole-class discussions as students develop their responses to a text in both an individual context and the community-of-readers context that a literature classroom can provide. The context of a classroom discussion does not merely provide an outlet for reporting previously constructed responses such as those generated by the reader-response diagrams; it can serve to help the student develop additional responses.

DEVELOPING READERS' RESPONSES:
ORAL AND WRITTEN STRATEGIES

Steig describes the importance of communicating responses:

> It is also my experience, and that of my students, that attention to one's own or reports of another's reading experiences and associations *does* frequently lead to "dramatic encounters," "surprises," and a sense of "discovery" of something that seems to be in the text. (12)

Ideally, classroom discussions should provide opportunities for readers to express their reactions and their perceptions about the text. The classroom atmosphere should be open and accepting so that these perceptions can unfold and develop. This contrasts from those (often teacher-dominated) discussions that are designed to arrive at a predestined point. These deny response development.

One approach a teacher may use to encourage oral responses to texts that are compatible with the reader-response perspective is described by DeZure. She argues that the structure of a classroom discussion should match the narrative structure of the novel being discussed. Focusing on the multiple-perspective technique of *Ordinary People* as well as on the theme of family mythology, she advises using the "jigsaw" technique in the teaching of *Ordinary People*. Briefly described, the jigsaw technique involves having students participate in "small groups to discuss a focused problem. Second, they rotate to other small groups composed of different students to share their new insights" (17–18). DeZure used the jigsaw technique to explore the complex family structure of the Jarretts by having preliminary groups focus on individual characters (a Beth group, a Cal group, a Conrad group), then rotating to secondary groups that were comprised of students who had analyzed different characters. In the secondary groups students focused on general questions about the family. Although this procedure is a bit more complicated than traditional group discussions, as DeZure points out, "Complex problems often require and deserve complex analytical procedures to solve them. Simple is not always best" (19).

Response journals can help both secondary and college students further develop and refine their responses to literary texts. For neophyte interpreters who often lack confidence in the validity of their own individual responses, the private, personal quality of a journal encourages them to explore literary response through writing and to reflect on the nature of their responses by reviewing what they have written.

These written responses can help students clarify interpretations that arose in class discussions. They can also be a place to reflect on class discussions, to weigh the results of public discussion about literature against their own personal responses and to discover the degree to which their own responses have been influenced or even altered as a result of classroom discourse. Thus, the kinds of journal assignments offered here should be viewed as both extension and support of the responses that will emerge from the approaches already discussed.

Students can be asked to keep a running response to the novel as they read it, jotting down almost epigrammatic responses as they occur during the act of reading. Sometimes called a learning log, students can write on one side of their notebook, leaving room for the teacher or another student to comment on their responses. The following are some excerpts from a college student's reading journal (page numbers refer to Guest's *Ordinary People*):

> p. 3 How important is it to find something that you're good at? Pressure of trying to show everybody else that it's all right. Everything will be fine.
>
> p. 8 What is fatherhood? Not applying pressure, yet talking about what to wear? Isn't that pressure?
>
> p. 20 Uncertainty, the bane of adolescent existence. But Con has experienced, lived with uncertainty, now back in the real world, he's forced to face uncertainty again. His father shows that the adult world is uncertain as well.
>
> p. 32 The question of obedience has come up a couple of times. Is that what makes you a good boy? "Protecting yourself from further grief." That's the motto, the bumper sticker. Live to avoid problems. This takes us back to the epigram. You can't just live on. Make plans.
>
> p. 87 Being *"Ordinary People,"* that's what's important. Is it? They try and try to be ordinary. The illusion is to make some appear ordinary, happy, unfazed. The reality is individuality, subversion, pain.
>
> p. 207. Here it is. Guest gives the answer. Con lost his direction. Himself when he lost Buck. . . . Keep reading. Berger the wizard sets it down. Social pressures and all. But Con isn't unique. Everyone wants perfect kids. Con just has a legacy.

What is provided here is almost a transcription of the reader's interaction with the text, as it occurs. Some comments react directly to the language or the events presented in the text. Others are more metacognitive in nature, noting the readers' self-reflection on their own response process. The sum effect of this type of journal is to create what Steig calls, after Culler, "stories of reading":

> Associative response papers are not just relevant as evidence of the nature of the process of reading, or of the reader's personality, but can actually become new interpretations— or readings not obtainable through other approaches. (41)

Another type of journal assignment is the dialogue journal. Students write entries about a text in their own journals and then exchange them with another student. Students are then able to read other student's literary responses as well as receive commentary on their own responses. The following is a dialogue exchange based on *Ordinary People:*

This book has made me understand more of what my friend is somewhat going through. It has given me hope that things will work out for her just like they have for Conrad. I really didn't like Beth, I thought she was extremely cold and didn't really seem to care about her child. I think she needed help in dealing with her problems. She actually made me more appreciative of my mother because at least I know she cares. I could also relate to Conrad in the way that he had to follow his "perfect brother." That is something I have had to deal with because my brother was extremely smart. It has helped me see that I compare myself to my brother a lot more than other people do. Just like Conrad felt like he had to be so great but no one really expected it from him. He was not really compared like he thought he was. While I was reading this book, I could really get involved with what was happening to Conrad. I would get happy for him when good things would happen or upset if bad things happened. I thought that all the feelings Conrad had were explained well. It gave me the feeling the author knew what Conrad was going through. (Jennifer, grade 11)

I think it has made me appreciate my mom more, also. When you see such a "bitch" for a mom, you see how much better you have it. I don't know about your friend but maybe this showed you some of the things you should say or not say, for that matter, to her. I can see how you think that you have to compete and be up to the standards of your brother, but obviously no one is exactly alike and no one expects you to be like him. I thought I could really get involved in the book, like I was really there, also. Now I feel I understand what people who commit suicide are somewhat going through and be able to cope with it better. (Teressa, grade 11)

CONCLUSION

When Louise Rosenblatt first published *Literature as Exploration* in 1938 and described the importance of a transactional approach to literature with adolescents, she could never have imagined the kind of teenagers that inhabit today's high school and college class-rooms. Yet, as we have seen, her insight into the nature of adolescents and the qualities that they bring to literature is especially relevant to students of the nineties. When such an approach is used with a novel such as *Ordinary People*, students and teachers are likely to be engaged in vital and poignant literary exploration. The responses of many of the students presented in this chapter reveal how deeply they were affected by their reading. By Rosenblatt's standards, the criterion for a successful literary experience has been fulfilled:

> The criterion for judging the success of any educational process must be its effect upon the actual life of the student; its ultimate value depends on its assimilation into the marrow of personality. (p. 182)

Ordinary People found its way into the very marrow of the personalities of many of the adolescent readers who were quoted throughout this chapter. Perhaps Mark (grade 12) said it best:

> I read this book in just a few days because it was important to me. I had to find out if Conrad made it. To make sure he didn't kill himself. I really got into it. My life helped me understand the book. The book helped me understand my life.

REFERENCES

Beach, Richard, and Deborah Appleman. "Reading Strategies for Expository and Literary Text Types." In *Becoming Readers in a Complex Society: Eighty-Third Yearbook of the NSSE Part I,* Ed. A. C. Purves and O. Niles. Chicago, IL: National Society for the Study of Education, 1984. 115–143.

DeZure, Deborah. "Matching Classroom Structure to Narrative Technique: Using "Jigsawing" to Teach *Ordinary People,* a Multi-perspective Novel." *CEA Forum* 19: (1989): 17–20.

Elkind, David. *All Grown Up and No Place to Go: Teenagers in Crisis.* Reading, MA: Addison-Wesley, 1984.

Guest, Judith. *Ordinary People.* New York: Random House, 1976.

Newsweek. spec. ed. Summer/Fall 1990.

Peck, David. *Novels of Initiation: A Guidebook for Teaching Literature to Adolescents.* New York: Teachers College Press, 1989.

Probst, Robert E. *Response and Analysis: Teaching Literature in Junior and Senior High School.* Portsmouth, NH: Boynton/Cook, 1988.

Richards, I. A. *Practical Criticism.* New York: Harcourt, Brace, & World, 1929.

Rosenblatt, Louise M. *Literature as Exploration.* 3d ed. New York: Noble and Noble, 1976.

Steig, Michael. *Stories of Reading: Subjectivity and Literary Understanding.* Baltimore: Johns Hopkins University Press, 1989.

CHAPTER **9**

Evoking Reader Response among Students Preparing to Teach:
Ideas for Creating Openings

James E. Davis

There are few printed reader-response examples available for my students taking the course in the teaching of high school literature, so I have them create their own. Over time we are building up quite a bank of approaches to commonly taught works. After reading and discussing some of the theories behind reader response (such people as Rosenblatt and Probst), and illustrating the approach through the teaching of a literary work, I give my students three major ideas to keep in mind: (a) Much of the response to a work depends on what the student brings to the literary work (experiences, values, beliefs, etc.); (b) the work(s) chosen must be worthy of reflection—this means that the selection should appeal to students' interests and should contain some ideas of substance, appropriate style, and interesting language; and (c) an atmosphere must be created in the classroom that allows students to express themselves without being ridiculed.

ILLUSTRATIVE TEACHING MODEL:
DEATH OF A SALESMAN

One of the works I find most amenable to this approach is Arthur Miller's *Death of a Salesman,* the drama that explores Willy Loman's dreams of success and his false values that lead to his and his sons' downfall. Over the years I have developed several means to accomplish my end of getting honest responses from students and capitalizing on them. I use small- and large-group discussions, oral reading of segments of the play, viewing one or more film versions, a journal/notebook, daily topics for the journal/notebook, and culminating topics that underline the general and specific changes of attitude and feeling to which the whole process has contributed. The daily journal topics help readers to think through the play, and also contribute to more interesting and informed group discussions in class.

For the journal/notebook and class oral discussion I have used such topics as family relationships, mental illness, American values and/or beliefs, death, suicide, the "salesman" mentality, loyalty, popularity, and urban decay. I use such topics because they are important to young adults and have impact on them. They also correlate well with the themes and actions of the drama itself on a day-to-day basis as our exploration progresses. I also encourage students to read ahead of our daily assignments to gain more insight for their discussions.

I want to prepare students for their reading of *Death of a Salesman* by first getting them to examine their own knowledge of and feelings about one of the themes of that play—the American dream. I believe we have to discover a common denominator between the work and the experience of the reader. When readers are given enough rein they may express some point of identification with the work. This may not be a point that is obvious to the teacher. One way to get students to think about the play is to have them write in their journal/notebooks their own definition of the American dream. I also ask students to write about where they acquired their information on the American dream. From friends? Parents? Teachers? Movies? TV?

Next I conduct a class discussion of the students' concept of the American dream and where they got it. I often have the class sit in a circle with a student leading the discussion. There are not "right" or "wrong" answers. Typical answers are:

Being rich and powerful	Youth
Good looks	Strong body
Super stardom	Happy family
Likeable personality	Comfortable income
Enough to eat	A warm place to sleep
Clothes to wear	Friends
Approval	Power
Doing your own thing	Independence

The group soon concludes that there are many variants on the American dream. An obvious follow-up question is how they would go about fulfilling their version of the American dream. They respond with things like:

Marrying rich	Getting a good education
Knowing the right people	Developing your talent
Having good relations with others	Developing self-reliance

Someone writes the responses on the board, and I ask students to write in their journal/notebooks characteristics with which they agree. For the next phase I ask students to write in their journals whether they possess these American dream characteristics. How much importance do they attach to the degree to which they possess the "success" characteristics? To the extent they do not possess them, how will they deal with their "failure"?

Now students are more ready to approach the reading of *Death of a Salesman,* and it is time to provide activities to assist them *during* their reading. Both small-group and large-group discussion are helpful. After a close reading of Scene One in the play, for example, students can come up with their own lists of family problems and how they are handled in the Loman household. Here are some items students have identified:

1. Willy criticizes everyone around him (he berates his wife, calls Biff a lazy bum, and ignores Hap).
2. Biff runs away from his problems by drifting from job to job.
3. Hap fills the void in his life by whoring around.
4. The whole family tries to voice their problems through the creation of their own fantasy lands where they see things from a narrow, short-term perspective.

Students can then come up with their own examples of family problems and how they were dealt with, for comparison with how problems are handled in the Loman household.

The daily journal/notebook topics are statements that try to get students to think and ultimately to write about the topic for discussion on the following day. This is important for two reasons. First, it encourages students to analyze their own opinions. Second, it gives them something to talk about and share the next class period, thus promoting active rather than passive learning. Some examples of journal topics for *Death of a Salesman* include the following:

1. Describe what the term *family* means to you.
2. What are some of the daily frictions within your family?
3. What are your attitudes about mental illness?
4. How are the mentally ill portrayed in some books or movies you have read or seen?
5. What are some of the reasons that people commit suicide?
6. How are older people usually portrayed or looked upon in our society?
7. What are some examples of the ways that adults or certain organizations force or at least foster competition with adolescents' lives?

Following are some sample student responses to such questions:

"In reading *Death of a Salesman* by Arthur Miller, we find several instances or circumstances parallel to those in today's society. The play deals with a rather pitiful family that seems to be preoccupied with the excitement of athletics. The position of education within the family structure is secondary."

"Willy Loman places sports as a top priority in his sons' lives. He tells Biff that he will be great and that he should continue to improve his athletic talents. Willy places far more emphasis on his son's athletic prowess than he does on his study habits."

"Willy Loman's family structure seems to be shaky; there is little family unity. Willy does not communicate with either his sons or with his wife. He lives in a dream world and cannot face reality. Willy is not honest with family members or with himself. He makes barely enough money to support his family, and when he borrows money to make ends meet, he lies to his wife to cover it up."

"I see three areas in the play that are very parallel to the problems faced by families today. First, education is given little emphasis. In my own family, my father is exactly like Willy

Loman; he lives his old football days again through my brother and me. Also, like the Loman family, I believe that my family places too much emphasis on material things. I have no friends without a VCR, stereo, and at least one television in the house. Also, I feel that one of the biggest concerns to modern families is the lack of communication. Sometimes, a whole week passes, and the members of my family barely see each other long enough to sit down to dinner together."

Following the reading of the drama, I show a film version (such as Dustin Hoffman's portrayal of Willy, though there at least two others available) in order to show a director's conception of such things as the set, the dream sequences, and the characters themselves. The film version is compared with how the students envisioned the play.

Finally, after the students have written in their journals, discussed concepts, read the play, and watched the movie, I further challenge my students with culminating journal topics—questions or statements posed to determine what effect or impact the play ultimately had on them. Generally, I find most of my students have a changed attitude or deeper awareness of the conflicting principles depicted in this play, such as family and society and how the individual relates to them. Some possible topics:

1. Everyone has delusions of grandeur. What are some of the things that you have fantasized about and have they ever come true?
2. How has your view of the American way of life (capitalism, profits, competition, striving to be number one) changed after your reading of the play?
3. In ancient times, a tragedy usually involved an historic, or at least influential member of society (such as a king—Oedipus Rex, Macbeth, or Hamlet). Why do you think Arthur Miller wrote a play about the death of a virtual nobody?

It is easy to see that these questions require more than a memorization of a few terms or token understanding of the plot. They call on students to put their own thoughts into words while still keeping them related to what they have read. These culminating journal topics sometimes are the basis for a more involved, fully developed paper that tests not only a student's ability to comprehend an issue in the play, but also asks them to form their own opinion concerning it. Some possible paper topics students could try:

1. Write your own version of Willy's interpretation of the American dream.
2. Describe an instance when someone ignored your needs and how you reacted (consider how Willy reacted in his boss's office).
3. How do you think Willy would be treated nowadays as compared with when this play was written? Do you think he would be given more respect?

Activities such as these make the reading of *Death of a Salesman* an enjoyable and rewarding experience for most of my students. They question some of their preconceived notions about the way they live and develop an awareness of the needs of the people around them. Some students are more deeply moved and changed than others by this drama, but all seem to be moved and changed in some way by being allowed to have their own individual, personal responses.

TEACHING STRATEGIES CREATED BY STUDENTS

My *Death of a Salesman* example gets my students to think about their own approaches to teaching literature and to critique my approach. They say such things as, "Is that really reader response?" or, "I could do that." And, of course, I let them. In fact, I require them to create examples for teaching literature based on the reader-response theory. They come up with interesting possibilities. Some students have difficulty writing out the approach. One of the techniques I have found most helpful is to suggest that they think of where they want to start and then write the script for what might happen.

SCRIPT FOR CLASS DISCUSSION
OF "THE SWIMMER"

Here is one of those scripts based on John Cheever's short story in which Neddy Merrill decides to swim home through the broad circuit of the neighborhood swimming pools. At the start this seems like creative daring, but the story evolves into a revelation of loss. The script is the most open, nondirective approach possible. It is an edited version written by one of my students, Dan Timko, after several suggestions from me.

Characters

MR. TIMKO: *First-year teacher attempting a reader-response approach for the first time.*

KARA: *An average student from a blue-collar background who aspires to go to college. She works very hard but has some difficulty in her interpretation skills.*

JOHN: *A very intelligent student who expends his energy being a class clown. He is an excellent athlete and feels that football will get him a scholarship.*

MIKE: *A straight "A" student who is always well-prepared for class. He aspires to go to any Ivy League college. He seems to lack popularity because he takes no part in extracurriculars.*

KIM: *A student from a very well-to-do family who is somewhat spoiled, very popular and trendy; she tends to be a good student.*

JACK: *A classic unmotivated learner. He comes from a divorced family and is generally more worried about his afterschool job than his studies. It is a real challenge to get him involved.*

LYNN: *A co-captain of the cheerleading squad, but not in Kim's social circle because of her economic status. She is very intelligent, but allows herself to act like an airhead in order to be less threatening to guys.*

Script

MR. TIMKO: Good morning, class. Today we're going to discuss the short story "The Swimmer." Who wants to start us off? (silence)

MR. TIMKO: Come on, we need someone to start us going! Surely you had some reaction to this story.

JOHN: I thought it was stupid. (laughs)

MR. TIMKO: Okay, at least that's a start, John, what was stupid about it?

JOHN: Why, don't you think it's stupid that this guy went around swimming through people's pools?

MR. TIMKO: Why do you think he did this?

MIKE: Because he lost everything: his wife, his daughters, and money.

JOHN: He didn't lose his wife. She was there in the beginning, idiot.

MR. TIMKO: All right, let's settle down and show respect for other opinions. Anyone else have any suggestions about the beginning with his wife?

LYNN: If the guy is crazy then it could be a dream.

KARA: The beginning is the most normal part of the whole story. It's a realistic look at rich people.

KIM: It is not! I live in a good neighborhood and it's not like that.

MR. TIMKO: Do you think that the author thought that the rich were like that?

MIKE: Maybe it's a satire of life.

LYNN: I agree it's a satire.

MR. TIMKO: Are we pretty much in agreement on that point?

ALL: Yeah.

MR. TIMKO: What do you think about his swimming through the pools?

JOHN: I still think he's crazy.

MR. TIMKO: Maybe he is crazy, but then what is the author's purpose in Ned Merrill, and why do you see through his eyes?

JOHN: It's a crazy man's mind.

LYNN: Well, how can you believe anything then?

MIKE: Maybe you can't.

JACK: So what's the point then? If you can't believe anybody?

KIM: What about the people that he meets?

KARA: They were right about his family.

LYNN: Yeah, they were right.

MIKE: Maybe that's how we're supposed to know what happens, through the people he meets.

MR. TIMKO: Who were some of these people?

MIKE: The Hallorans are the first people that bring up his problems.

LYNN: When they said that, I thought they were crazy because Ned ignored them.

KARA: I didn't get real suspicious until he was at the Biswanger's.

MR. TIMKO: That's an interesting passage. How about reading it? How about you, Jack?

JACK: What page?

MR. TIMKO: Page 529, the last three lines.

JACK: "Then he heard Grace at his back say: They went for broke overnight—nothing but income—and he showed up drunk one Sunday and asked us to loan him five thousand dollars."

MR. TIMKO: What did you think about this while you were reading?

KARA: At first, I thought it was just the gossip of the rich, but at the end of the story I felt that it made sense.

MIKE: I think that when I read this, I realized that something was not quite right.

JOHN: This guy is swimming through all the pools in his neighborhood, and it wasn't until then that you noticed something was weird?

MIKE: You know what I meant?

JACK: I felt sorry for him at the end of the story.

KARA: I sure didn't think he was rich and got greedy and lost it all.

LYNN: I agree that it was all his own fault.

MIKE: They portrayed Ned to be really pathetic at the end. I thought it was tragic when he came face-to-face with the fact that he had lost everything.

JOHN: You would feel sorry for him, you're a loser just like him.

MR. TIMKO: Okay John, let's confine our comments to the story itself.

KIM: I guess I felt sorry for him too. It must be really hard to have money and have everyone know you lost it.

MIKE: And the people at the party showed no sympathy for him.

MR. TIMKO: It seems like half of you felt sorry for him and the other half didn't.

KIM: So who's right?

MR. TIMKO: Maybe there isn't any definite answer. It seems as if both sides have valid arguments. Look there's only a few minutes left. So, I'll give you the homework assignment for the weekend. Please read the first five chapters of *A Day No Pigs Would Die*. All right everyone, good discussion today. Have a nice weekend.

Dan said at first he thought it would be easy to write a paper on a reader-response approach, but the project turned out to be quite a challenge. It really caused him to think very seriously about his role in the classroom. Yes, reader-response approaches will surely do that. As he created the scenario he kept wanting the teacher to say more because of the conditioning he had been exposed to through most of his education. But he managed to restrict the teacher's comments to only those that were absolutely necessary. Obviously, he had learned much about both the advantages and the difficulties of reader-response approaches.

A RESPONSE GIMMICK FOR INTRODUCING "THE MOST DANGEROUS GAME"

Another strategy I use to get students started on their reader-response projects is to suggest they think up an attention-getting device. Students are not necessarily self-starting. To get discussion started (sometimes) I tell them, "Ya gotta have a gimmick." They do come up with some rather bizarre ones, such as the following example, devised by Tammy Morgon. In this story by Richard Connell, an expert big game hunter is swept overboard in a storm but manages to reach an island safely; there, his host sets up a "game" in which the hunter becomes the hunted.

Tammy began with a pre-reading role-playing situation. (I do not necessarily recommend it, but the way she worked it out tells a lot about reader response.) Two competitive males are chosen to arm wrestle in front of the class. They are told that "something" is at stake and are given the option of refusing to perform. What is at stake? If they perform, she will not require them to take the final, but the winner will automatically receive an A and the loser will fail. The students begin to question her sincerity. She assures them that she is serious because the activity is part of an experiment to determine how motivation factors influence strength. The students choose to participate; she records the grade and extends the invitation to the rest of the class. A student raises his hand. He seems surprised when she tells him to pick a partner. He starts to pick a girl, then laughs and picks another boy of similar build. After all willing participants have been allowed to arm wrestle, the class discusses the activity guided by these questions:

1. How fair was it that one student got everything while the other lost everything?
2. How do you feel about competition?
3. If you are competing for high stakes, would you prefer to compete with someone who is no challenge for you or with someone who is highly challenging?

After discussion Tammy introduces the short story and asks them to read it for the next class period. She hopes that she has started bringing out feelings in the students that will probably be brought out again as they read the story. Next period she begins by asking the class what they thought. Some possible responses:

> It was cruel and awful—no humans would do that.
> It's a vindication because of all of the animals that hunters kill without a thought.
> It was unrealistic.
> It was very realistic. Men like a challenge.

As students give their responses, she writes them on the board and encourages discussion. She then asks, "Have humans historically done anything so cruel and awful?" The second issue might raise the idea of the superiority of man. The third and fourth comments, direct opposites, might lead to a discussion of the differing perspectives among peers.

When the students have exhausted their ideas on these topics, she gives them the option of applying the story to the previous day's activity or introducing a new activity. If they choose to use the arm-wrestling example, such questions as these might be used:

1. Why do you think Zarof chose someone who would be a challenge to him? Did we do that?
2. Did Rainsford enjoy the challenge, or was he forced to participate? From here discussion will probably move on to characters. Did the characters remind the students of anyone in society today? After suggesting several sample ideas, students can have a few minutes to recreate the story in their minds, using modern characters from our society, before they share those ideas and give a rationale for their choices.

TRANSITION FROM THE TRADITIONAL MODE

Not infrequently I have students who either are sure they do not believe in the reader-response approach or have serious doubts about their abilities to carry it out. For these doubters I suggest they simply think of what they would do to introduce a work, what would happen while it is being read, and what would happen after. Students often produce what I would call a blend of traditional and reader-response approaches that can serve as good transitions from one to the other.

PRE-READING, READING, AND POST-READING ACTIVITIES FOR *ANTIGONE*

One such doubter, Mary Raines, began by making a series of journal assignments that she hoped would lead her students into thinking about issues they will encounter when they read *Antigone*, the tragic drama of Oedipus's daughter. Antigone is condemned to death by her uncle Creon after, in defiance of his order, she buries her brother to properly honor him.

1. Write about your relationship with your siblings or a close friend.
2. Discuss your understanding of or feelings about the concept of family loyalty.
3. Write about what you think it would be like to be held in isolation.
4. Discuss your feelings about suicide and those who commit suicide.
5. Pretend that you are in a situation where your peers are trying to talk you into something you don't want to do. How would you handle it? Demonstrate the scene with the use of dialogue.

Writing about these five items in the journal provides background that should help students in reading the play. Mary asks the students to read the play aloud in class and provides questions to be discussed as appropriate. Some of her questions follow:

After the prologue: How do you feel about the way Antigone and Ismene are talking to each other? What do you think the long-term effect of their words will be?

After Scene II: Why did Antigone refuse to allow Ismene to share in her punishment? Explain in what way she could still be mad? In what ways she wanted to protect her?

After Scene III: Describe occasions when you feel like Haemon does in this scene. Talk about times when people do not listen to you because of your age. How is this fair (or not fair)?

After Scene IV: Toward the end of the scene Antigone says that if Creon is the guilty one, she hopes his punishment is equal to hers. Explain whether or not you think this will happen? What would be equal punishment?

After Scene V to the end of the play: What do you think was said between Haemon and Antigone in the tomb? Do you think Antigone was dead when Haemon reached her? Why or why not?

After the oral reading, Mary divides the students into groups to discuss their reactions and reminds them of the guidelines for small-group discussions. For example, everyone is given ample time to say what they want. No one is to criticize what is said. Students should take notes on things they find interesting or original, and ask questions about things they do not understand.

After the small-group discussions are completed, Mary has each group share with the class a few things they discussed in their group. As the presentations take place, the teacher (or some other designated person) takes notes, being careful to identify the differences between the groups' reactions. Next, Mary has the class discuss the differences in interpretations and determines whether or not a mutual consensus can be reached.

The final step in Mary's plan is to ask the group what they would like to do with the play as a follow-up activity. Some suggestions to get them started (if students do not come up with enough of their own): (a) Do a newscast on some of the events in the play with a commentary as you go along; or (b) do a dramatization of the play and make the masks, costumes, and stage to provide a real atmosphere for the play.

FINAL COMMENTS

Through discovering and writing their own reader-response approaches to literary works my students are learning much, and so am I. I have presented here only a few of the approaches they have suggested, and I have barely scratched the surface of the infinite possibilities individual teachers can invent. I present these as alternatives to what has all too frequently happened in the past (and still does) when teachers present predigested texts to their classes and ask students to regurgitate "right" answers to test questions. Students have been taught *not* to speculate about what they would or would not do in a given literary character's context. They have been taught *not* to try to draw parallels and contrasts between their own lives and the characters in the stories. They are *not* encouraged to synthesize what they have experienced personally with what they have read. Implicitly if not explicitly, they are taught *not* to have a transaction with a text in any meaningful way.

It is clear that both the teacher's and the student's role in reader-response approaches is different. Patience and tolerance are required of both teacher and students. Success with reader response takes varying amounts of time depending on the teacher's and student's abilities. Therefore, I have set no rigid timetable for any of these activities and approaches and would recommend only the most general guidelines. Approaches like these could spark expanding on topics impossible to predict in advance (if the approach is moderately successful).

With a reader-response approach, what is written down on paper in the lesson plan should probably be written in pencil keeping an eraser handy to make changes to suit the readers and to guide them in whatever direction they may go. What should be most important to us in every case is what our students will do after they leave our classroom. What will the student be able to get out of reading when the teacher is not there to give the "answer" and then test to make sure it has been learned? Isn't it more beneficial for the teacher to find ways to lead students to their own conclusions about what they have read, to find ways to show readers they can learn from reading the experiences of others, to find ways to help them relate what they are reading to their own lives?

REFERENCES

Cheever, John. "The Swimmer." In *Story: Fictions Past and Present*. Ed. Boyd Litzinger and Joyce Carol Oates. Lexington, MA: D. C. Heath and Company, 1985. 623–630.

Connell, Richard. "The Most Dangerous Game." In *The Most Dangerous Game and Other Stories of Adventure*. New York: Berkley Publishing Corporation, 1957.

Miller, Arthur. "Death of a Salesman." In *Types of Drama*. Ed. Sylvan Barnet, Morton Berman, and William Burto. Boston: Little, Brown and Company, 1985. 225–271.

Sophocles. *Antigone*. In *Sophocles I*. Ed. David Grene and Richmond Lattimore. New York: Washington Square Press, 1954. 101–209.

PART III

Developing Readers' Responses: Classroom Processes

Going beyond the initial responses to literature is the focus of the chapters in this section. The authors recognize that causing readers to understand a relationship with a character or topic in a text or to express their preliminary feelings or ideas is comparable to only unlocking a door, perhaps to open it slightly. In their chapters they describe and illustrate approaches that cause students to develop and expand their preliminary notions, to consider and reconsider, to measure and test their evolving understandings against the text. The strategies practiced include writing of several types, oral discussions, activities, and simulations.

There are two pertinent features of the strategies to attend to: the general methodology, that is, the processes by which expansion and refinement of thought and feelings are provoked; and the teaching techniques exemplified that express the nondirective posture of the teacher. Of course, the activities, the processes and questions may readily be reoriented, recombined, and adapted for other literary texts and teaching situations. (Chapters in other sections also present teaching strategies to evoke and develop readers' responses or suggest activities for this purpose.)

In Chapter 10 Robert E. Probst relates two concepts that inform current English teaching: the unique relationship of reader to text, reflecting the individuality of response to literature; and the broadened range of written discourse to accommodate the variety of perceptions and needs of students. He proposes alternatives to the standard analysis paper, illustrating three types:

the personal response growing from the text, focusing on feelings, memories, and conceptions; the creation of imaginative texts, building, perhaps, on a powerfully evoked image; and assertions about the text. His central thesis states that there is more than one perspective to bring to those responses. He argues that "we should invite students to engage in those other ways of experiencing literature and in those other modes of writing."

In Chapter 11, Marshall Toman first acknowledges the evolution of his own perceptions of Eudora Welty's "Petrified Man," using these, particularly his earliest reading, to anticipate his students' responses. In class he reads aloud from his students' preliminary reactions to what they liked or disliked about the story, these comments being a springboard for discussion. He asks open questions that lead students to support and build their understandings with textual evidence. Variant student perceptions and comments by critics are used to expand the framework of responses. Toman considers in detail the nature of transactional discussion: the teacher's avoidance of becoming the dominant reader, which he exemplifies in his classroom processes; and the handling of the types of comments—plausible/implausible and positive/negative—while valuing open expression and using all comments to clarify perceptions.

Two aspects of teaching literature are particularly developed in Chapter 12: connecting the students with the text and assuring carryover. Mary Jo Schaars, teaching Thoreau's *Walden,* builds student experiences that connect their lives with Thoreau's concepts to provoke thoughts and feelings. The discussions that emerge are not predictable; as excerpts of two classes' interactions indicate, each class follows its own lead to establish its understandings. The culminating activities turn the students inward to measure Thoreau's values and to compare themselves with him. Samples of students' writing illustrate the personal and intellectual connections that have developed, bearing out the potential for carryover into subsequent readings and students' lives.

Elizabeth A. Poe addresses the concern for individual differences among students by using multiple texts. In Chapter 13 she represents her approach with a group of World War II novels. She explains the use of journals as a method of establishing knowledge and feelings about the topic and the use of small-group interaction as a way of exploring and expanding understandings of the texts. Subsequent class discussions develop comparative and contrastive insights that reflect variations among both readers and texts. Poe asserts that class exchanges and culminating activities enrich and intensify each student's experiences. She also portrays her active facilitating role and the processing of insights.

"Lots of questions, lots of discussion" will promote the development of the students' own views. Given this premise, in Chapter 14 Frank C. Cronin suggests sets of questions for Salinger's *Catcher in the Rye.* The questions, keyed to issues to which students frequently react, are designed to trigger personal relationships with the characters and events and to consider emerging understandings. Cronin intersperses among the questions interpretations by literary critics. He suggests broaching these in a tentative fashion because their purpose is to excite speculation or open up a new avenue of thought rather than to provide definitive answers. Samples of students' responses to some of the questions illustrate the processing role that the teacher assumes.

In Chapter 15, Duane Roen proposes writing-to-learn strategies as a procedure for responding to literature, strategies that encourage the use of writing as a tool for making sense of the world. He argues that such techniques allow readers to respond individually and privately before public response, thus giving every student the opportunity for self-reflective thought. Roen demonstrates the use of the biopoem, the unsent letter, and the journal/learning log in the teaching of *Antigone*. He notes how these writings can be enhanced by dialogue, leading to broadened interpretations. He also offers a list of topics for classroom discussion and critical essays that correlate with the writing-to-learn model.

CHAPTER 10

Writing from, of, and about Literature

Robert E. Probst

We have, in much of our teaching of literature, emphasized explanatory knowing—
knowing that takes the form of propositions and demonstrations, generalizations and
evidence, and thus we have privileged the expository, analytical paper in many of our
courses. Keith Fort objected to this dogmatism in the English class many years ago:

> If teachers today were to insist that students reach only conclusions that were acceptable
> to our political establishment, violent protests would erupt. But when students are forced
> to use only one form, there is little rebellion although this formal tyranny may result in a
> more basic conformity than content tyranny. (629)

He suggested that insisting on argumentative essays amounts to

> demanding a particular kind of relation between a reader and a work being studied. In
> broad terms the connection is between understander and thing-to-be-understood; more
> particularly it is between thesis hunter and source of thesis. In other words, if the only
> form in which a writer can express himself on literature is one that requires a thesis, then
> he has to look at literature as a source of theses. (633)

There is, of course, nothing *wrong* with such writing—Fort argued simply that there
may be something wrong with the academic bias that imposes on students one form, and
one form only, for the literary essay. Such limitations may be unnecessarily confining,
restricting students inappropriately, dictating to them the stance they will take to the texts
they read, when other stances might also be productive or satisfying. The traditional
critical essay, valuable though it may be, isn't the only form, or necessarily the most
appropriate form, for every student with every text.

The work of the past twenty years or so in composition has suggested that broadening the range of discourse may be beneficial in the classroom. Britton and colleagues, Graves, Murray, Elbow, and others all have argued for a more balanced attention to the various modes. They call especially for more emphasis on expressive writing—writing that explores the perceptions, feelings, attitudes, and values of the students, in an effort to define who they are.

Similarly, literary theory has recently begun to show more interest in the uniqueness of the reader, suggesting that it would be reasonable to respect individuality, to pay attention to what the reader brings to the text and how each reader goes about making sense of it. [See especially Bleich (1978), Eco (1979), Holland (1975), Iser (1978), Kintgen (1983), Rosenblatt (1983, 1978), Slatoff (1970), and Tompkins (1980).] Many theorists argue that more is involved in reading literature than analysis of texts. Literary experience includes—or might include, if the schools do not discourage it too strongly— recalling previous experience, expressing and exploring emotions and associations evoked by a text, reflecting on the human issues addressed or suggested. It might, in other words, lead to intellectual activity other than analysis, the making and demonstrating of propositions, and thus to writing in forms other than the argumentative critical essay.

Considered together, the work in composition and in literary theory suggest that we should invite students to engage in those other ways of experiencing literature and in those other modes of writing. The making of meaning can be undertaken in a variety of forms or genres.

WRITING "FROM" LITERATURE

We might, for instance, find that our students are interested in dealing with some issue or event that seems only peripherally related to the text. The reading may awaken a memory or provoke reflections on some issue, question, or problem that seems more significant to the reader at that moment than anything within the literary work itself. Despite its tenuous connection with the text, despite our natural suspicion that it is off the point, a distraction from the work at hand, writing about those reflections might be extremely valuable. It might, first of all, be highly motivated writing, arising as it does from the student's own life history. And it might intimately connect the literary experience with other experiences, giving the student a broader base from which to forge understandings of self and world—and potentially of the text itself.

Consider several examples. In one class, a teacher, Anne Turner, working in a high school class with *A Separate Peace* by John Knowles, pointed out the passage describing Gene's inability or unwillingness to tell Finny that he considers Finny his best friend (Graham and Probst 30–46). Gene reflects that he should have told him; that he almost did; but that something stopped him. Inviting students to reflect on moments when they, too, had wanted to speak but did not, she led them into writing about those remembered incidents. One student wrote beautifully about his grandfather who had died several years—or perhaps it was many years—ago, and in the writing resolved for himself some of the difficult feelings that persist long after someone loved has died unexpectedly or too soon.

It could be argued that his writing was not about the literature, not about *A Separate Peace*, and of course we must grant that it was not about the *text*. It did not analyze the friendship between Gene and Finny, or Gene's inability to express it; it did not discuss Knowles's vision or style; it did not explain anything about the work itself. But it did, clearly, deal with the *reader's experience* with the text. Iser comments on the meaning of literary experience:

> The significance of the work, then, does not lie in the meaning sealed within the text, but in the fact that that meaning brings out what had previously been sealed within us. (157)

Presumably, those memories of his grandfather, and those unresolved issues, whatever they were, had been sealed within that reader until coaxed into the open by the book and Ms. Turner's skillful questioning. The discussion and subsequent writing gave him an opportunity to deal with the "significance of the work," which was, if we accept Iser's vision of literary experience, that meaning sealed within him.

The student writing of his grandfather chose the form of the personal narrative. He had been reassured that his thoughts and feelings, personal as they may be, were relevant, and he knew that he did not have to suppress them in order to produce a five-paragraph theme or a traditional critical essay. Another student—an adult in another class—also recognized and accepted the formal freedom his teacher allowed him, and chose the letter as the appropriate genre for his concerns; he wrote to his brother, from whom he had been estranged for about twenty years. The same points could be made about his writing—it was not about the text, but it was about the *meaning* of the literary experience for him. And, again, it would be difficult to argue that the experiences of reading and writing were not significant for him.

In both of these instances the students were writing, not "about" the literature, but "from" it. The literary work was the catalyst or prompt, but the students, as they pursued their own thoughts, departed from the literary work, writing about their own lives. Clearly, they were not being "responsible to the text" in any New Critical way. They were not making and defending propositions about the work. They had no literary thesis to offer and support. They were not purely objective, rational, detached. On the contrary, they were involved, committed, deeply concerned with the statements they had to make. They had assimilated the literary work and the task of writing into the fabric of their lives so that they could understand better their own experience. It would be difficult to argue that they would profit more by writing an analytical/critical/expository essay on some aspect of the text.

Other examples of this involvement with, and subsequent departure from, the text are easy to come by. In "As Best She Could," a short poem by Donald Jones (57), an old woman is turned down for welfare support because she lacks the proper documentation. One student who read the poem spoke passionately about her own experiences as a child in a family that survived *only* because of welfare support. The text had evoked a bittersweet memory of pain and comfort, and she, too, was more concerned with that memory than with the diction, the imagery, the tone, the movement of Jones's poem.

Students, in yet another class, after reading "So Much Unfairness of Things" (Bryan 342–67), a short story about a young man expelled from a prep school for cheating on a Latin examination, expressed great concern about the pressures on them to achieve, and the temptation to cheat that faced them all. They, too, might productively have written "from" the literature, had their teacher not directed them conscientiously back to the techniques of characterization employed by the writer. Required to think "about," and not allowed to think "from," the literature, they had to forego its potential meaning for them in favor of exercises in analysis.

Consider the potential of writing "from," rather than "about," the literary experience offered by the following poem:

"THE GOODNIGHT"

He stood still by her bed
Watching his daughter breathe,
The dark and silver head,
The fingers curled beneath,
And thought: Though she may have
Intelligence and charm
And luck, they will not save
Her Life from every harm.

The lives of children are
Dangerous to their parents
With fire, water, air,
And other accidents;
And some, for a child's sake,
Anticipating doom,
Empty the world to make
The world safe as a room.

Who could endure the pain
That was Laocoön's?
Twisting, he saw again
In the same coil his sons.

Plumed in his father's skill,
Young Icarus flew higher
Toward the sun, until
He fell in rings of fire.

A man who cannot stand
Children's perilous play,
With lifted voice and hand
Drives the children away.
Out of sight, out of reach,
The tumbling children pass;
He sits on an empty bench,
Holding an empty glass.

Who said that tenderness
Will turn the heart to stone?
May I endure her weakness
As I endure my own.
Better to say goodnight
To breathing flesh and blood
Each night as though the night
Were always only good.
                    —*Louis Simpson* Dream *85–86*

What associations, memories, issues might it draw to the surface? To whom might letters be addressed; what might journal entries deal with? If you were to write, not *about* this text, but rather, *from* it, what would you write? Who might your audience be? In what genre or form would you write?

The same questions might be raised about your students—where would their writing take them? What might the reading draw to the surface for them? About what might they write? Obviously, much will depend on who they are, and where they are in the course of their lives. Readers who have children of their own—and that includes many college students, a fair number of high school students, and some junior high students—may react differently from those who cannot imagine themselves as parents. How students read the poem may depend on whether they see themselves as the one fearing, or the one feared for.

How might we encourage students to write "from" this poem? We might ask such questions as the following, both for discussion and writing, to encourage them to attend to their own feelings and thoughts as they read:

As you read this poem, what thoughts or feelings did it awaken in you? Try to recapture them, and jot them down.

Perhaps your mind wandered far afield as you read the poem—if so, forget the poem and job down those digressive thoughts. When you've done so, look closely at them—are there any connections you can see between the text and your own thoughts?

If you were to be asked to write about your reading of this text, upon what would you focus? Would you write about some association or memory, about some aspect of the text itself, about the author, or about some other matter?

As you discussed this poem with others in your group, what did you observe about them?

We might also explain, and perhaps demonstrate, various modes appropriate for dealing with the issues likely to arise. We might encourage, for example, brief written responses, hastily prepared for the sake of focussing and stimulating discussion. Such writing is clearly exploratory, not intended to pass as a finished, publishable product. Its purpose is to help students find and articulate the personal significance in the literary experience.

Those brief responses might be extended in the form of journal entries, either brief notes or the more demanding writing of structured journals or commonplace books, which ask for longer, more elaborate discussion of responses (see Price; Progoff; Rainer). It is possible to structure entire papers around responses to the literary work, and the exchange and reading of such essays can sustain much productive discussion in the classroom (Bleich).

Writing "from" literature leads the student toward two kinds of knowledge: knowledge of self and knowledge of others. It demonstrates to the student the significance of introspection and reflection on one's own values and beliefs, one's own place in the culture, and one's relationships with others. It seems that a responsible and demanding literature curriculum could be designed to value, and to invite and encourage such exploration. In such a curriculum, literature would not only allow us to learn about ourselves, but it would also serve a socializing function. It would allow students to write about others—friends, family, classmates and thus enable them to understand the culture or writers of particular texts. Such writing might focus attention on one's self—feelings, associations and memories, thoughts and conceptions, and judgments. It would invite the student to reflect on and write about issues and ideas, ethical questions, and visions of human possibilities. The curriculum should respect the significance of that sort of learning.

WRITING "OF" LITERATURE

It's also possible that a happy experience with a literary work might lead students to writing imaginative literature of their own. Rosenblatt suggests that there may be value in that endeavor not yet examined:

> The potential role of the production of such artifacts in the education of the student of literature or art is another of the many implications of the transactional theory to be explored. (128)

It seems reasonable to assume that some benefit might accrue from efforts to produce, as well as receive, literary works. If we wish students to understand the structural complexities of literary forms, then efforts to create in those forms should be instructive. More important, the attempt to write literature might teach students something about the mind of the writer, helping them to see how the writer of poetry or fiction sees and thinks.

The task of writing imaginative literature—poems, stories, plays—is, after all, different from that of writing an analytical essay, possibly requiring a different focus for the writer's energy. Whereas the writer of the critical essay is analytical and rational, the writer of the poem is intuitive and receptive. Where the critic seeks to articulate and clarify the structures of a text, poets or story writers attempt to cultivate a sensitivity to patterns, connections, and links, that they may not fully see or understand. The different genres demand different labors. Little has been done with teaching students to write imaginative literature, although there are several good texts (Cassill; Gardner; Grossman; Jerome; Mearns; Mirrielees; Rehder; Riccio; Rilke; Ueland) that might be helpful to those who are interested.

Examples of instruction in the writing "of" literature are harder to come by, restricted as teachers are by curricula that fail to acknowledge the value of imaginative writing. Some teachers do, however, find ways of luring their students into writing imaginative literature. Dixie Bowden's students, for example, have written brilliant parodies and imitations of Shakespeare's sonnets, and of speeches in his plays. Given the form or the pattern, many students who might otherwise consider poetry beyond their ability have succeeded in producing satisfying poems. Imitation and parody are especially accessible, because they are light, burlesque, and exaggerated, and so excesses and other lapses of judgment are more easily accepted. Excesses in more solemn pieces may turn them into ridiculous caricatures, but excesses in pieces that are already caricatures, may simply add to the humor.

Some readers do, however, attempt more serious pieces, and often successfully. A reader of Louis Simpson's "My Father in the Night Commanding No," (*Collected Poems* 152–153) dashed off, within minutes of finishing the reading, a poem of his own addressed to his son. For him, the reading awakened matters that he needed to deal with, and could deal with best in poetry. To have demanded that he write a critical essay at a time when poetry was surely the more appropriate mode, would have been damaging.

Consider how the following poem might be used to encourage writing poetry, or stories, of one's own. We must keep in mind, of course, that the writing "of" literature may not be appropriate for all students in response to all texts, but we should be alert to the possibilities. What sort of experiences might this poem call to mind that would appropriately be dealt with in poetic form, and how might we invite students to pursue them?

SIGN FOR MY FATHER, WHO STRESSED THE BUNT

On the rough diamond,
the hand-cut field below the dog lot and barn,
we rehearsed the strict technique
of bunting. I watched from the infield,
the mound, the backstop
as your left hand climbed the bat, your legs

and shoulders squared toward the pitcher.
You could drop it like a seed
down either base line. I admired your style,
but not enough to take my eyes off the bank
that served as our center-field fence.

Years passed, three leagues of organized ball,
no few lives. I could homer
into the garden beyond the bank,
into the left-field lot Carmichael Motors,
and still you stressed the same technique,
the crouch and spring, the lead arm absorbing
just enough impact. That whole tiresome pitch
about basics never changing,
and I never learned what you were laying down.

Like a hand brushed across the bill of a cap,
let this be the sign
I'm getting a grip on the sacrifice.

—David Bottoms 22

What questions could we ask of students to encourage the sort of reflection that might lead to imaginative writing of their own? We might ask them to focus on visual images:

> What did you see as you read the poem? Describe the scene briefly. Don't worry about accurately reproducing the scene described in the text if what you saw in your imagination was something else. Perhaps you envisioned some scene in your own past—if so, write about it.

If students are able to recall a powerful image, as this poem about a father and son playing ball together might well evoke, then they might be encouraged to transform it into poetry. They could be asked to get it as clearly as possible in the mind's eye and then to record the details, trying to convey through the picture painted the feelings they recall.

Incidents powerful enough to be remembered for a long time are often the stuff of poetry. Students might be asked, not just for a visual image, but for associations or memories of whatever kind:

> Did the poem call to mind any memory—of people, places, events, sights, smells—or perhaps something more ambiguous, a feeling or attitude? If so, write briefly about it.

Poems are, of course, not the only genre suitable for students to explore. They may be led as well toward personal narratives, invented stories, dialogues (that might become short plays) on issues between real or imagined characters. The point is to make students aware of the possibility that the meaning they create in response to a literary work might take a variety of forms. They should remain open to all of the possibilities, and not assume that the argumentative essay is the only approved, acceptable genre in which to deal with literary experience.

The writing "of" literature might help lead the student toward knowledge of self and others, and possibly also toward more sophisticated knowledge of texts. It may well teach more about how texts work than any other approach we might consider. We wouldn't teach music without sooner or later asking students to try singing or playing an instrument, and we assume that it is everyone's unquestioned right to sing along, if only in the shower. But we often teach literature as if it is virtually unapproachable, something that can be produced only by an artistic elite. That may be hurting us, suggesting as it does that literature is for scholars only, and not for people. Students invited to try their hands at the literary forms might learn to see the writing of poetry or fiction as ways of thinking about the world, accessible to all, just as music is accessible to all.

Although it is an untested assumption, it seems reasonable to expect that writing poems and stories may enable us to read those genres with more sympathy and insight. We might begin to see and analyze the vision offered by other works with greater clarity and understanding. If so, it would ultimately make us more skillful at the traditional tasks of the student of literature: examining assumptions and perspectives, evaluating the implications of accepting visions, conceptions, and values offered by works, analyzing how texts work. It might yield sharpened understanding of the potential, limitations, and methods of various genres.

The writing "of" literature might also yield greater knowledge of contexts, as well as texts. Literature is written and read in a social and cultural context, and much of literary scholarship is devoted to exploring the effects of that context. Students should be able to examine its shaping effects. Observing how their own works are influenced by their experiences and their surroundings may help them see how the works they study are similarly shaped. They may come to see literature as part of a cultural fabric, both a product and a producer of that culture. Ideally, they would come to see the role of imaginative literature in forming conceptions of human possibilities.

WRITING "ABOUT" LITERATURE

Finally, there is writing "about" literature, the traditionally emphasized approach. Much that has preceded might, unfortunately, be taken as a rejection of writing in the traditional modes—explicating texts; analyzing structure, movement, diction; speculating about the author's values or assumptions; tracing the influences that might have shaped the author's work. The expository essay remains, however, an extremely important tool, and it would be foolish for the literature or composition program to ignore it.

Students need to learn something of the processes of making meaning, and the writing of critical essays might lead toward that goal. They should develop an awareness of the strategies of critical thinking, the influence on thought of personal associations and feelings, the processes of negotiation within a social or academic group, the importance of open-mindedness and flexibility in exploring ideas, and the criteria by which evidence is judged. They need to become aware of the difference between statements about themselves (their feelings and values) and assertions—factual or inferential—about texts and authors, realizing that different kinds of statements require different kinds of evidence or argument. It is also important, however, not to pretend to an unattainable objectivity or purity of reading. Even in the most rigorous analysis, the uniqueness of the reader is apparent, and shapes the reading.

What questions might a teacher raise to invite realistic and valuable writing "about" literary works? Those questions should not imply, as they often do, that there is a right answer, or a single correct interpretation lurking somewhere in the literary woods waiting to be hunted down and shot. They should instead respect the integrity of individual readers, allowing them to work without embarrassment from the limitations of their own perspective.

We might direct the reader to the analysis of texts through such questions and prompts as these:

As you read the text, what word, phrase, image, or idea struck you most powerfully—why? What seems to you to be the most important word or phrase in the text?

What is there in the text or in your reading that you have the most trouble understanding? Did your first reaction to the text raise questions for you that led you to analyze and interpret? How did those first responses guide your thinking?

What sort of person do you imagine the author of this text to be? Imagine the author commenting on or explaining the text to you—what would he/she say?

What beliefs does the author seem to hold? How do those views differ from your own, or how are they similar?

How did your reading of the text differ from the readings of those with whom you discussed it? Do you have vastly different understandings of it, or do you see it in much the same way? What similarities were there in your readings?

Do you think the text is a good one—why, or why not?

The writing students undertake "about" literary works should, of course, give them practice in inferential reasoning, in the building of demonstrations and arguments. Though it should not ignore response, it should move students from response toward analysis of both readings and texts. Structured assignment sequences, involving a series of questions each building on the one preceding, may help students learn to build more and more complex arguments.

The focus of this sort of writing might fall on any of a number of topics: the characters' attitudes and values; the ethical positions represented in the text; dilemmas in the plot—the character's problems and choices; stylistic or linguistic elements; the demands, possibilities, and rewards of the various genres; the pleasures in sound, image, and emotion; intellectual challenge; the author's ideas or assumptions, character, and values; the influences on the author's work; and the author's influence on others.

CONCLUSION

We should not ignore that in all of this work, a broad objective subsuming all others is pleasure. The literary experience, as all other intellectual and aesthetic experiences, should provide pleasure, whether it is the pleasure of self-expression, as in the personal narrative or the letter, the pleasure of artistic creation, as in the writing of poetry or fiction, or the pleasure of intellectual accomplishment or problem solving, as in the writing of the critical essay.

The purpose of broadening the range of discourse forms students might choose in responding to literary experience is to give them access to all of these pleasures and to enable them to realize their own potential for understanding and shaping themselves and their worlds.

REFERENCES

Bleich, David. *Readings and Feelings: An Introduction to Subjective Criticism.* Urbana, IL: National Council of Teachers of English, 1975.

———. *Subjective Criticism.* Baltimore: Johns Hopkins University Press, 1978.

Bottoms, David. "Sign for My Father, Who Stressed the Bunt." *In a U-Haul North of Damascus.* New York: William Morrow & Company, 1983. 22.

Britton, James, Tony Burgess, Nancy Martin, Alex McLeod, and Harold Rosen. *The Development of Writing Abilities (11–18).* London: Macmillan, 1975.

Bryan, C. D. B. "So Much Unfairness of Things." In *Literature and Life,* Ed. Helen McDonnell et. al. Glenview, IL: Scott, Foresman, 1979. 342–67.

Cassill, R. V. *Writing Fiction.* 2d ed. Englewood Cliffs, NJ: Prentice-Hall, 1975.

Elbow, Peter. *Writing Without Teachers.* New York: Oxford University Press, 1973.

Fort, Keith. "Form, Authority, and the Critical Essay." *College English* 32.6 (March 1971): 629–39.

Gardner, John. *The Art of Fiction: Notes on Craft for Young Writers.* New York: Vintage, 1983.

Graham, Joan, and Robert E. Probst. "Eliciting Response to Literature." *Kentucky English Bulletin* 32, (Fall 1982): 30–46.

Graves, Donald H. *Writing: Teachers and Children at Work.* London: Heinemann, 1983.

Grossman, Florence, *Writing from Here to There: Writing and Reading Poetry.* Portsmouth, NH: Boynton/Cook, 1982.

Iser, Wolfgang. *The Act of Reading: A Theory of Aesthetic Response.* Baltimore: Johns Hopkins University Press, 1978.

Jerome, Judson. *The Poet's Handbook.* Cincinnati, OH: Writer's Digest, 1980.

Jones, Donald. "As Best She Could." In *Man in the Poetic Mode,* vol. 6, Ed. Joy Zweigler. Evanston, IL: McDougal, Littell, 1970. 57.

Knowles, John. *A Separate Peace.* New York: Bantam, 1979.

Mearns, Hughes. *Creative Power: The Education of Youth in the Creative Arts.* New York: Dover, 1958.

Mirrielees, Edith Ronald. *Story Writing.* New York: Viking, 1962.

Murray, Donald. *A Writer Teaches Writing.* 2d ed. Boston: Houghton Mifflin, 1985.

Price, Gayle B. "A Case for a Modern Commonplace Book." *College Composition and Communication* 31.2 (May 1980): 175–82.

Progoff, Ira. *At A Journal Workshop.* New York: Dialogue House Library, 1975.

Rainer, Tristine. *The New Diary.* Los Angeles, CA: J. P. Tarcher, 1978.

Rehder, Jessie. *The Young Writer at Work.* New York: Odyssey, 1962.

Riccio, Ottone M. *The Intimate Art of Writing Poetry.* Englewood Cliffs, N.J.: Prentice-Hall, 1980.

Rilke, Rainer Maria. *Letters to a Young Poet.* New York: W. W. Norton, 1954.

Rosenblatt, Louise M. "The Aesthetic Transaction." *Journal of Aesthetic Education* 20.4 (Winter 1986): 122–28.

Simpson, Louis. "The Goodnight." In *A Dream of Governors*. Middletown, CT: Wesleyan University Press, 1959. 85–86.

———. "My Father in the Night Commanding No." In *Collected Poems*. New York: Paragon Press, 1988. 152–53.

Ueland, Brenda. *If You Want to Write: A Book About Art, Independence and Spirit*. St. Paul, MN: Greywolf, 1987.

CHAPTER 11

Teaching Eudora Welty's "Petrified Man":
Expanding Preliminary Insights

Marshall Toman

Eudora Welty sets her 1939 story "Petrified Man" in Leota's western Mississippi beauty parlor. As the story opens, Leota is speaking highly of a new friend, a Mrs. Pike. Mrs. Fletcher, a customer, is irritated to learn that Mrs. Pike is so sharp that she detected from a casual glimpse that Mrs. Fletcher is pregnant. Since the community now knows about the pregnancy through the gossiping of the newcomer, Mrs. Fletcher will certainly have to have the child. Leota, ignoring Mrs. Fletcher's irritation, goes on to tell about her friendship with Mrs. Pike: Leota and her husband Fred have rented rooms to Mr. and Mrs. Pike, Fred and Mr. Pike go fishing together, and Leota and Mrs. Pike have gone to a travelling freak show together. Among other things, they viewed a man whose joints have supposedly been slowly turning into stone.

One week later, when Mrs. Fletcher returns for her regular appointment, Leota's attitude toward Mrs. Pike has changed. While reading an old copy of *Startling G-Man Tales* that Leota had prettified her lodgers' room with, Mrs. Pike recognized that the petrified man was really Mr. Petrie, a neighbor of the Pikes from New Orleans, and she discovered that there was a $500 reward for information leading to his arrest for raping four women. The Pikes receive the reward and prepare to move out of Leota's rooms. The story ends with Mrs. Fletcher grabbing and holding and Leota vigorously spanking Billy Boy, Mrs. Pike's three-year-old, whom Leota had agreed to watch during business hours so Mrs. Pike could work at Fay's Millinery.

One of my most enlightening pedagogical experiences was witnessing my growth with respect to this story. My encounters with it underwent several revolutions; consequently, the stages were clearly marked. But I think my encounter(s) with "Petrified Man" recapitulates in an obvious way what I experience in any rereading. Being aware of one's own changing responses to a text helps a teacher effectively anticipate and organize various responses of students. Here, then, let me briefly recapitulate my experience.

MY READING EXPERIENCES OF "PETRIFIED MAN"

In one way, an ideal response to a text, from a pedagogical standpoint, may at first be inadequate. Such a response is likely to reproduce the less expert readings of students. I believe my own first reading of "Petrified Man" was circumscribed. In attempting to capture this first response to the story while my students were once writing down theirs, I came up with the following:

> The description was very realistic and slanted toward the dirty and dingy and morally corrupt (Leota flicking ashes into wet towels). I disliked ~~nearly~~ all the characters. Did Welty want us to dislike them? If so, why? What is the point of the story? There is very little I can relate to here except (as always with Eudora Welty) her portrayal of the small-town life and small-town mind.

I responded to Welty's portrayal and uncharacteristically biting satire of the small-town mind. Let me call this reading the small-town satire perspective.

The first change in my response to the story occurred when it was read and discussed in a graduate seminar on southern women writers. In this discussion the unpleasant characteristics of the men in the story were stressed. Where actions of the women were unworthy, the students tended to excuse them by the circumstances within which the women operated and over which the even more unworthy men shed their unsupportive influence. This interpretation I label the feminist perspective because it was put forward in the context of exploring the aesthetic and political sensibilities manifest in the story as they could be accounted for by the author's gender.

A second revolution in my experience of the story came with the reading of the critical literature, particularly the discussions by Ruth Vande Kieft and William M. Jones. In her study of Welty for the Twayne series, Vande Kieft takes almost an antifeminist stance. In my teaching of the story, I introduce one of her statements as the response of yet another reader to whom the class may respond. The statement, quoted later, encourages students to retrace their steps to a third and more complex response. Jones, in a brief but incisive *Explicator* article, argues for the fruitfulness of viewing the story from what I call the humanist perspective. The women, according to Jones,

> are smart enough to dominate the men; but money, the final indication of worldly success, is not theirs. Perhaps these women would be slightly smarter if they could train their men toward independent action rather than toward petrified servility. The men are useless as they are now, and so are the women. Each group is less than it ought to be. The result is a misery that finds release in beauty-parlor viciousness for the women and in drugged loafing for the men. (Item 21)

Examining Jones's position after having considered two other comparatively reductive responses permits a coherent ordering of a wide spectrum of student responses.

As if following the spiral of a gyre, I started at the bottom point of the satirist reading and circled 180 degrees around and upward to the feminist reading. The 180-degree oppositional positioning of these two readings represents my seeing the story's ridicule initially as directed at both genders and secondly as directed at only one. The height difference in this metaphor of a coil represents an increased awareness of the story's complexities. With another 180-degree upward turn, I was repositioned by my third reading, also universalist in applying to both sexes, directly over my first but at yet a higher lever. Going directly from the first to the third points would have had a linear effect of a standard teaching strategy: presenting a less and more sophisticated response. Travelling through all three points added a three-dimensionality that I could use to better accommodate a range of readers' responses when I taught the story.

These reading revolutions are the background that I bring into the classroom with me. While an individual's reading experience is a transaction between text and reader, what happens in a class, since class time is not spent reading the text, is a transaction between the interpretations of various readers. The participants' interpretations react off one another to produce a reading—a collective, consensus reading specific to that class and that day. How, then, do I allow my reading experiences to mesh with those of other, presumably first-time, readers? I cannot pretend that I do not have the background. I therefore acknowledge it, first of all; second, and most important, I use it to help students organize their responses. Thus I use my three readings of the story (the satirist, the feminist, and the humanist interpretations) to provide a preliminary, tentative organizational pattern for the discussion.

KEEPING DISCUSSION TRANSACTIONAL

But before I show how my own background operates on the teaching of the story, one caveat. Pains need to be taken to prevent the teacher's reading from becoming *the* reading. Ordinarily, teachers are the dominant readers, and given their usual greater experience and preparation, there is nothing overly authoritarian about this situation. It is helpful for teachers to be secure in their "final," that is, pre-class, interpretation. Acknowledging, however, that their own interpretations were formed through previous interactions with other readings of the story (perhaps, as in the case just sketched, in the context of informal discussions, or graduate seminars or undergraduate or high school classes, or by reading interpretations by other critics) provides an openness to the discussion. Avoidance of presenting an interpretation as though it were both obvious and cast in stone will also permit the possibility that a teacher's own "final" configuration, which could itself be limited, may be modified by student insight.

As with any two-way process, both parties should be changed, and often I find myself reassessing the story. One interesting way of viewing the petrifaction in the story was proposed by a student named Nicole. According to her interpretation, the men are socially petrified and the women are emotionally petrified. The women are cold, as though they are stone. The men, such as Mr. Pike, still acknowledge feeling. The women are able to control the men only because the men care about their wives. But socially the men are kept in straight jackets by their lack of ambition and will. The women, on the other hand, are socially free, out and about, talking, employed, engaged in a more communal entertainment than the solitude of fishing. Nicole's view can be assimilated into the third part of my paradigm, the humanist perspective that argues that both the men and the women in the story are morally stunted. Her fresh light on the story, however, will help me to integrate other students' comments when they fall along these lines. Being open to fresh insights and either assimilating them or using them as alternative patterns will keep the classroom transactional.

TEACHING "PETRIFIED MAN"

With this as background, let me describe the class on "Petrified Man." Before the discussion of the story begins, I survey students' ability to remember the story's title. This survey initiates a pedagogical "trick" that both makes use of student misreading and fixes the results of a day's discussion of "Petrified Man" in students' minds. Let me defer a complete discussion of the reason behind this survey. Administering it takes about three minutes. I ask students to write down the story's title as they remember it (the usual candidates are "The Petrified Man," "A Petrified Man," and "Petrified Man"). That's all. Whatever else the exercise does it generates some suspense.

Although it is crucial for students to see that a more experienced reader has deepened his response to the text, it is equally crucial that students begin their deepening encounter with a text from their own responses. In *Literature as Exploration,* Louise Rosenblatt offers a number of suggestions for getting students comfortable with their own tentative responses (70–71); one that I use is having students write brief responses to the simple question, "What did you relate to positively in the story and what negatively?" or, even more simply, "What did you like and what did you dislike?" Coming immediately after the students have indulged their instructor's bewildering whim and recorded the story's title to the best of their memory, this request, too, to many students is odd; many teachers of literature consider soliciting the reactions of inexpert readers a waste of time, so students are unlikely to have had much experience of teachers' insisting on the primacy of student responses. Nevertheless, I collect and silently read these responses as the students finish writing, and sort each response into groups, making notes that will later guide my use of their reactions in the class.

I ask them to take "about ten minutes." As I am reading and sorting the first responses, other students are finishing their paragraphs, adding to them, so that reading these longer paragraphs takes more time. In a class of about twenty students, the writing and my first reading of the reactions takes a little over twenty minutes. After these initial procedures, the discussion proper can begin.

A "SMALL-TOWN SATIRE" RESPONSE

I read aloud either a part of every reaction or else representative examples. As students hear different responses (liking/disliking the story; liking/disliking one of the characters), they begin discussing the differences, or if they don't, I clarify a discrepancy in responses and call on individual students to take a side. Students are uncomfortable with the contradictions and hope to see the story from a unified perspective.[1] I stake out zones on the blackboard and, as they arise, transcribe the students' ideas about the story. Some ideas that I can anticipate from past discussions are notions about the story's small-townishness, gossip, physical harshness and dirtiness, and moral turpitude. I also ask for some textual support for each notion.

From teaching the story over the course of eight years, I have found many students' written responses to be like my own first response to the story as small-town satire (I have preserved the students' comments typographically intact):

> In petrified man I found I related to the small-town atmosphere as well as the portrayal of these small-town women in their proper characters—not of lawyers and doctors, but of the uneducated, uncultured person in smalltown '40s. (Larry, May 1989)

In the classroom, I reread or call to mind some of the written responses that fit this small-town satire model. I mention that my own first reading of the story was similar, and I describe some of the personal background that led to my "small-town satire" reading, having spent my summers in a small town and having experienced beauty parlors there. If any student expresses an inability to empathize with any character in the story, I acknowledge that such a response can make the story more difficult to read but that that response may be one that Welty, as a satirist, wished to evoke.

Students have identified one of their responses as a reaction to the portrayal of small-town life, so I ask a question to get them to identify some of the story elements that may have led to this response: "If this story is a satire on small-town life, then the major elements in it that you have identified must be associated with the small-town. Is this so?" Students will have responded readily to the element of gossip.

> I can relate to *Petrified Man* in a couple ways. The way the ladies gossiped in Leona's hair salon reminds me of several people I know who have a habit of gossiping. (Christoper; May 1989)
>
> My thoughts on the story were that of hearing two people gossiping. But that doesn't mean the whole story was like that. That was what first popped into my mind in the beginning. (Bob; May 1989)
>
> I didn't like the gossip-like basis. . . . (Barb, May 1989)

Can the element of gossip be correlated with the small town?

Many of the student responses made the correlation.

> This story reminded myself of two things in which I could relate this too. The first being my small home town and the people in it. That story did an excellent job on describing what really goes on in beauty parlor. Beauty parlors are not a place for women to get their hair done, its the home base of all gossip that goes on in town. (Rex, May 1989)
>
> In *Petrified Man* I can relate to the unbelievable amount of gossip throughout the entire story. Being from Ellsworth, a town of less than 2000 people, gossip is spread like wild fire. (Angela, May 1989)

Thus, students feel a connection between small-townishness and the major element of gossip, but because some of the comments tend to view the gossiping as a universal predicament, I ask what textual evidence can be adduced and what arguments constructed to link the gossip to small-town life. A question I use to initiate thinking about this subject is "Is there more gossip in small-towns than in large cities, and if so, why?" I wait for students to arrive at various responses. One obvious response points out that the story is set in a small town, and in a small-town community people naturally are more interested in the affairs of their neighbors. This interest develops because it is possible; you know everyone else. This is not true in the city, where the instinct for self-preservation often leads city dwellers to close themselves off from the intimacy of shared knowledge frequently present in a small town.

Students from rural backgrounds are sensitive to the lack of opportunity in the story and may suggest that it is related to the gossiping. There is some evidence that the male characters are innately lazy (Leota believes her husband dreams of floating down the Yazoo river in a houseboat), yet when Leota demands that he seek a job in Vicksburg, Fred doesn't complain that there are jobs closer to home. The inference is that there are no jobs closer to home. Without jobs and many of the opportunities for relaxation supported by jobs, talk becomes a prime means of entertainment.

Lack of education can also be seen as a cause for gossip. Leota's superstitious belief in the fortune teller suggests a small-town lack of education. As one student put it:

> If she puts all that faith in something as abstract as fortune telling, she really can't be all that educated or sophisticated. (Bob; May 1989)

If a lack of education leads to a paucity of ideas and vocabulary to discuss them, it is often acquaintances' personal lives that take up the slack. Thus, causal connections and hierarchies can be generated as the separate ideas on the board begin to be ordered. I use outlining, titling, or drawing of arrows to keep track of these relations. For instance, one class might generate "Three Small-Town Causes for the Gossiping Presented in the Story."

When gossip has been linked to Welty's satire of the small-town mentality, I ask the class to evaluate other elements that emerge from the written or oral responses that need to be evaluated as specifically small-townish or not. By asking students about these elements, they generate textual details that led to their responses. A certain uncouthness is one such element. If students did respond to the uncouthness in the story, then I ask what actions of Leota led to this response. My students have been eager to offer some of the following details. Strong red-nailed fingers press into Mrs. Fletcher's scalp, she is yanked up by the back locks and she is choked until "she paddled her hands in the air" (24). Sometimes students mention that cold fluids trickle down Mrs. Fletcher's neck or that the beautician flicks cigarette ashes into a basket of dirty towels. I can assimilate these details into the pattern of the discussion so far by noting that Leota's inattention to customer amenities and her uncouthness are actions in a business establishment that are more likely to exist in a place where there is less competition than in Manhattan.

At this point I introduce pertinent background materials from Welty's life. Mentioning aspects of an author's life, no matter how pertinent, will usually be remembered better after readers have become engaged with the story. By this point in the discussion of "Petrified Man," students are prepared to hear that despite having lived in Jackson, Mississippi, and having attended Columbia and the University of Wisconsin, Welty was thoroughly familiar with small-town ways. Her first job, which was working for the Works Progress Administration (WPA), involved traveling the backroads of Mississippi during the Depression. I use her photographs of rural Mississippi life, published in *One Time, One Place: Mississippi in the Depression, A Snapshot Album,* to add visual vividness to her credentials as a small-town satirist.

Finally, a central, though off-stage, element of the story is the freak show. Both the show and Leota and Mrs. Pike's interest in it strike many readers as small-townish. I conclude the discussion of small-town life in the story by ending with (or coming back to) a mention of the freak show. It provides a capping example and a transition to a second way of viewing the story, a perspective that will help organize the responses of students whose reading insights have not been addressed adequately by the small-town satire discussion. A rhetorical question I use to initiate the transition is, "But, do you want to leave it at a story about small-town life, about the meanness connected with it and about people who visit freak shows?" More specifically, "Are there important elements that this view of the story leaves out?" One element that is not specific to small-town life is the element of the battle of the sexes. With these questions we begin to move toward this second perspective.

A "FEMINIST" RESPONSE

The class so far has accomplished a validation of many readers' responses to the story. Other readers, however, have noticed that the men in this story are rather "petrified," and these readers' perceptions need to be addressed. A question I ask to get the class thinking about this petrifaction of the males in the story is "What do the fetuses, the pygmies, and the petrified man have in common?" If this question proves too puzzling, I break it into its parts.

"What are pygmies?" Notions of what pygmies are circle around the idea that they are people whom we tend to consider as not having reached "normal" height.

"What do you think about fetuses?" The story's fetuses never mature.

"What do we know about what is supposedly wrong with the Petrified Man? Why is he a freak?" The Petrified Man is supposedly petrifying in his limbs instead of naturally replenishing his vitality.

"What, then, do these three things share?" These story details are united by the notion that each has its natural growth checked. Once students see how many elements in the story literally share this trait—suggesting that this is probably not coincidental on the part of the author—their interpretive strategies are usually developed to the point of their searching for figuratively portrayed stunted growth. I ask "Who else in the story has his growth stunted?" Using the masculine pronoun usually means that the men are scrutinized first. When female characters are suggested, I begin a second list on the board (along with, naturally, the textual evidence that the character is indeed stunted).

At this point, I return briefly—before we actually again look at the story closely and begin a list of males who are stunted—to those written reactions that indicate a sense of stunted growth. Such a return to student responses reminds them that some of them had experienced this element in the story.

I can relate to the way the ladies referred to their husbands as "Petrified Men." Leona says that her husband Fred just lays around the house all day. (Christopher, May 1989)

To me, it seemed as if Leota & Mrs. Fletcher felt their husbands were "above" the petrified man, but they both seemed kind of petrified to me. (Linda, May 1989)

Once the students see the men as petrified, I ask the class about the women: "If the men are unstereotypically passive and weak, are the women unstereotypically active and strong?"

Many of the following aspects of women being in charge will come out in discussion. Mrs. Fletcher claims that Mr. Fletcher "can't do a thing with me. . . . I'll have one of my sick headaches, and then I'm just not fit to live with" (19). She makes him take bending exercises. She pretends to include him in important decisions, but does not tell him of her pregnancy. She only asks his advice about when to get her hair done, and even then, he can only encourage her to do what she wants anyway. Mrs. Mountjoy is another person with whom her husband cannot do a thing; he waits nervously in the car while his wife insists on having her hair done before continuing to the hospital to have her baby. Mr. Pike cannot persuade Mrs. Pike to forego turning over Mr. Petrie to the police. Leota can demand that her husband look for work in Vicksburg. Billy Boy is bossed around by such demands as "mustn't bother nice ladies" (19). Billy Boy is even spanked for his independent action of eating peanuts, as Jones notes, and the women in the beauty parlor gather round to watch.

A "HUMANIST" RESPONSE

Having considered this feminist reading ("feminist," really, only in the sense of the sex-role reversals), further questions can prepare the ground for a humanist perspective. A rhetorical question parallel to the previous one about small-town satire can initiate the discussion of the next perspective: "But, do you want to leave it at a story about women who gain something in our society because they, uncharacteristically, can dominate the men in their lives?" Genuine questions for the class to ponder include "Should the women be in charge?" "How do the women use their domination?" and "What results from the women's efforts?"

A number of readers side with the women. They see admirable traits in Mrs. Pike (her acuity of observation), Mrs. Fletcher (her stubborn striving for dominance), and Leota.

> I felt that Leota was a very talented beautician. (Being able to carry on her duties at the same time as telling dramatic stories to entice Mrs. Fletcher.) (Linda, May 1989)
> Their attitude of independence is admirable. (Barb, May 1989)

Those who admire the women have a more difficult time maintaining their admiration in the face of the text; consequently, I try to insure that the characters of the story's women are thoroughly looked at for their positive traits. If we can accomplish this positive look, I then ask those supporting the "feminist" perspective to consider Vande Kieft's reaction to Mr. Petrie. I read Vande Kieft's statement out loud, asking the class to ponder whether it is just the men in the story who are petrified: "One is amused at the comically grotesque turn of events, and gratified that at least one man—Mr. Petrie—turned violently, if only briefly, against the collective monstrosity of female sexual action with a comparable male monstrosity of action" (74). If the feminist perspective has been given a thorough hearing, Vande Kieft's response, even if from an established critic, should not be enough to univocally turn the tide. Those students who responded to the story on the feminist level need not feel that they must abandon it. Nevertheless, the quotation is a thorn to deal with from that perspective, a thorn that can modify the feminist reading.

Naturally, other readers disapprove of the women.

> I didn't care for the women's attitudes toward their husbands (Leota esp.) or their pending motherhood (Mrs. Fletcher) although I suppose it is more true to life than anyone cares to admit. . . . Leota didn't seem to truly care about her husband and her life must be pretty dull for all the faith she puts in her fortune teller. The women in the story need to get a life and not worry so much about nothing. They seemed to have nothing better to do than worry what other people think and go to freak shows. (Barb, May 1989—the same student who also acknowledged that there was something admirable about the women's independence)
>
> She [Leota] seemed to have something to say about everything and everybody but where did it get her? (Margarete, July 1989)

Students can explore in an articulated way the story's being anti-woman as much as anti-man. The women possess a number of character traits that are not flattering. Leota's quick friendship with Mrs. Pike and her equally quick change of loyalties, Mrs. Mountjoy's ill-timed permanent, and Mrs. Fletcher's belief that only public opinion would hamper her getting an abortion indicate a superficiality. They are back-sniping, referring to another customer as "Old Horse Face" (18). With little true substance to their characters, Leota and Mrs. Fletcher engage in a petty one-upwomanship in regard to what their husbands' heights are (Leota wins) and where they met their husbands (Mrs. Fletcher wins, a library to a rumble seat).

Some students are concerned with what seem to be loose ends in the story, the presence of Billy Boy being one of the most puzzling.

> Some parts of the story didn't seem to need to be present such as the boy in the Saloon. (Erich, May 1989)
>
> What I did not relate to was the use of the little boy in the story—what force was he to represent, so many riddles that one can not help but search for meaning in it all. (Larry, May 1989)

The structure of readings advocated here, particularly the return to a notion of the universality of the satire, can give an answer to the question of Billy Boy's presence. The story closes with the women spanking Billy Boy for insufficient cause. I ask my students "Why?" Some students are good at articulating a reason:

> At the end of 'Petrified Man', the little boy questions why the women aren't rich if they are so smart. Billy Boy was in the beauty parlor the whole day absorbing every conversation that was going on. He finally deduced that instead of talking about everyone else and chastising them, they could constructively take a careful look at themselves. I get the feeling that when people find problems with everyone else, they often don't find the problems with themselves. I think this was described nicely. (Susan, July 1989)

One student's comment shows that, whether or not one can articulate a reason for Billy Boy's presence, his last words *affect* readers along the lines suggested:

> She (Leota) should not have taken her jealousy out on the little kid but he had the last laugh by
> saying if you are so smart how come you aren't rich. When he said that, it made me smile.
> (Bob, May 1989)

Students can discuss the idea that Leota and Mrs. Fletcher are taking their frustrations out on the nearest available male. But this male has the last words, literally the last words in the story, and that position grants them a privileged status. His "If you're so smart why ain't you rich" points out that for all the women's domination, their tactics get them no place they really want to go. Billy Boy serves not only to highlight the repression of male assertion (he is continually told to stop some one of his actions) but also and more important to underscore the women's error, that their tactics are self-defeating.

This third perspective on the story returns us to a satirical reading similar to the satire-on-small-town-life initial reading. However, the process of getting here—via consideration of a second level of the story—like the *process* (rather than the result) *of reading* itself, makes the crucial difference. Viewing the story as a satire *after* discussing the relationship of the sexes is a different, fuller viewpoint than simply understanding the story as a satire, because the third response encompasses the earlier two. The characters are satirized, but the issue is not just small-town mentality. Rather, we can see the issue as the battle of the sexes where both genders are culpable.

"MISREADINGS" CAN CAPTURE ESSENTIAL ASPECTS OF A TEXT

With these three readings in mind, I refer back to the "titles." I write three titles on the board ("The Petrified Man," "A Petrified Man," and "Petrified Man") and give the number of students who chose each title. I have not kept a record of results for every time I teach the story, but an instructor who asks students for the title is almost assured of two responses, the first and the last.

We discuss the specificity of "The Petrified Man" and the generality of the actual title, with the occasionally misremembered "A Petrified Man" falling between. Students who remembered "The Petrified Man" as the story's title are focusing on the story's literal level of the one side-show freak, *the* petrified man. Such a title suggests a realistic portrayal of small-town people, those who are interested in the minimal entertainments of freak shows and gossiping (hence, one can argue, rural-background students, who tend to remember this title, are especially attuned to the portrayal of small-town life).

Students who chose "A Petrified Man"—and even if none do, that hypothetical title can be discussed—encapsulate the theme of the story at a more general level. "A petrified man" can refer to Mr. Petrie, but the phrase is also potentially more generally applicable to a number of "petrified" men, such as the lazy, dominated Mr. Pike or Mr. Fletcher. Such a title would easily mesh with the battle-of-the-sexes reading.

Welty's actual title, of course, is the most universal. The ambiguity of "Man" can still refer back to the males in the story, but in the sense of "mankind," humankind, it can apply to the women as well as the men. I believe that the way students remember the title may reflect their experience of the story, which may be the result of focusing their response on one of the story's levels. Pedagogically, at least, a student's remembering an incorrect title can actually be used as a badge of capturing a portion of the story—all, after all, that any reader can be expected to do.

LEADING A TRANSACTIONAL DISCUSSION

A main problem in leading a transactional discussion of literature, implied but not addressed in the foregoing outline of my approach, is processing the different responses. Let me categorize, generally, potential responses in two ways: first, intellectually, as plausible (that is, within the realm of responses that the author probably had hoped to generate) or implausible (outside that realm) and, second, emotionally, as positive about the text or as expressing a negative reaction to some feature. I make these distinctions in order to illustrate general strategies for dealing with student responses when the discussion in the classroom begins.

First, though, what does plausible mean in a transactional context? Every response produced by the student's confrontation with the text is "accurate" in the sense that a student voices a feeling or an idea engendered by the transaction. The more experienced reader, however, understands some responses as not reasonably within the realm of responses that the author had hoped to arouse. The teacher, while valuing open expression of reactions, seeks to insure that responses are rooted in the text. Three criteria guide a teacher:

1. *There should be evidence in the text for the reader's contention.* If a teacher sets up the early expectation of some citation of evidence for every expression of reaction, students acquire early the habit of finding some. A general rule should be established stating that an unsupported reaction, although very possibly plausible, cannot count in the arena of the classroom until it is supported.
2. *There should be no evidence that contradicts the reader's contention.* If contradictory evidence obviously exists, the teacher can ask what others think about the proposed idea. When another student offers the contradictory evidence, I turn back to the original student in an effort to get the discussion to by-pass me as the teacher. The original student can, disappointingly, simply back down or, on more positive notes, either propose counter evidence or modify the original view. If no one comes up with the contradictory evidence, the teacher can offer it and ask the student what he or she thinks in its light.
3. Finally, *the reader must have taken cognizance of the major elements of the text in their reasonable interpretations.*

POSITIVE AND PLAUSIBLE RESPONSES

The easiest types of responses to process are those that are positive and plausible, particularly those that a teacher can anticipate from previous classroom experience. Although a positive comment may fulfill the three criteria for plausibility, only an agile teacher will recognize it as plausible if, practically speaking, the comment doesn't also fit with the teacher's already organized responses. Granted my structuring of the story, an example of a positive, plausible comment on "Petrified Man" was given in Rex's comment:

> This story reminded myself of two things in which I could relate this too. The first being my small home town and the people in it. That story did an excellent job on describing what really goes on in beauty parlor. Beauty parlors are not a place for woman to get their hair done, its the home base of all gossip that goes on in town. (Rex, May, 1989)

For me, this comment gets at two basic elements of the story: the satire of small-town life and the gossip. With positive, plausible comments, I sometimes have to remind myself to ask for—if the student forgets to give—supporting evidence. I separate long comments into components (in this case, gossip and small-town life) and put shorthand titles of these components on the board and list the elicited supporting evidence underneath. This charting of comments on a blackboard will allow for an overall patterning of responses to emerge clearly at the end of the discussion.

Other positive, plausible comments tend to express admiration for Welty's realistic depiction of setting

> I got comfortable with the setting. (Susan, July 1989)

and humorous dialogue/precise dialect

> I liked the characters and their dialogue the best. Welty has a way of making them funny people. (Erin, July 1989)

During discussion of the story, these positive reactions to Welty's setting and characterization can be set against the main negative (though plausible) reaction: frustration over the lack of plot.

NEGATIVE AND PLAUSIBLE RESPONSES

The dominating negative reaction that nonetheless seems a legitimate response to the story is one of frustration.

> I started this story late at night, and by the time I was three-quarters through it, I threw the book across the room. (Dawn; July 1990)

Often there are nods of agreement when a comment like this one is read. A teacher can label such comments with a general expression that will cover many individually phrased responses, and here I point to the "frustration" that Dawn and others experienced. With any negative comment, I probe into its cause by simply asking "Why?"—"Why were you frustrated?" Responses generally split along two lines: the already mentioned intellectual dissatisfaction with the apparent lack of plot ("The story didn't seem to be going anywhere" [Dawn; July 1990]) or an empathetic reaction against the unlikability of most of the characters ("I did not really like the story. . . . The characters—the two women in the hair dressers—did not seem good or humane and I guess just dislikeable" [Meena;

July 1989]). Once these types of negative reactions are clarified for the class, they can be dealt with by two techniques suggested in *Literature as Exploration:* discussion and presentation of background material.

The plot structure is not that of an O. Henry nor even a Henry James, but discussion can help readers deal with their frustration over this element. Admission that a certain lack of plot is evident in the story can itself be very relieving to insecure readers. From that starting point, two rejoinders are possible: the author was more concerned with other things than with plot; or there exists a type of plot that is latent, and detection of this unobvious thread permits a reader to follow at least a plotlike trail. With respect to the first rejoinder, I can remind students of the positive reactions to the setting and characteriza- tion. Sometimes readers must grant an author her chosen emphases. Also, however, there is a plotlike element to the story involving the one-ups(wo)manship that carries through the narrative. This aspect of a submerged plot will probably best be treated toward the end of discussion when all the story's elements begin to coalesce.

For those readers who are frustrated because they cannot like any of the characters, presentation of the nature of the genre of satire can help. Some readers have a grasp on the story's genre. Meena, quoted earlier, starts out her comment on "Petrified Man" with "I did not really like the story" because the characters were not good or humane, but continues in the same sentence: "and I thought maybe that was the author's intention" (July 1989). If we think of "Petrified Man" as, at least to some degree, a satire, readers are quite correct to dislike the main characters, the objects of the satire. The story's blurring of the boundaries of satire (it also reads like a realistic slice of life) can be offered as a reason for students' not immediately picking up on the conventions that the piece invokes. Discussion here can take several directions, but its most important effect is in allaying the frustration of some readers: frustration, rightly understood, is part of the point, and feeling it is a response encouraged by the text.

It is important to note that such negative comments, as much as positive comments, help elucidate the text and should be equally encouraged. With "Petrified Man," students who would be lost to further discussion because of frustration have a chance to put aside their negative reactions, at least temporarily, in order to more fully participate in the text.

NEGATIVE AND IMPLAUSIBLE RESPONSES

But every teacher knows that merely positive and negative comments are not the only ones to deal with; are implausible comments helpful to elucidating the text? Implausible com- ments can derail discussion whose fruitfulness under most educational systems is subject to time constraints. Such comments, however, must be dealt with tactfully and, ideally, productively if the openness of discussion that is essential to a transactional pedagogical approach is to be maintained.

The *implausibility* of hostile comments can be used to clarify aspects of the text. If someone so egregiously misread/misremembered the story as to state that Mrs. Fletcher turned the Petrified Man in or that Fred had raped four women, these statements can be corrected. (Quite often, in order to encourage absolutely free discussion, I put inaccurate comments on the board—for cogitation—with a question mark appended or, later, an actual erasure, depending on discussion.) In addition, such clarification offers a springboard to exploring real tensions within the story by turning the error and clarification into a question. By asking why it is important that Mrs. Pike and not Mrs. Fletcher turned the Petrified Man over to the authorities, obviously intended textual impressions (Mrs. Fletcher's relative fecklessness; Mrs. Pike's sharpness, untrustworthiness, selfishness) can be elicited. By asking why Fred would never have raped four women, his laziness and passiveness can be brought out and the irony of the "Petrified" Man's *action* explored.

The *hostility* of implausible comments are the least pedagogically useful and from a transactional perspective tend to indicate the student's not giving a text a fair chance. An appropriate response, when assimilation to another of the techniques mentioned seems unworkable, is to suggest that the student hold his hostility in abeyance until after the discussion in order to see whether others' comments make a difference. (And then really do come back to hostile students at the end.)

POSITIVE AND IMPLAUSIBLE RESPONSES

Lastly, enthusiastic but implausible comments are sometimes the most disheartening to address because a teacher's intellectual obligation to the text and his supportive role of the student come in conflict. A positive reaction to "Petrified Man" on the grounds of its evoking the peacefulness of hunting season is stupefying. Nevertheless, the transactional approach obligates the teacher, who is essentially a co-explorer, to attempt to trace the origins of such a response. Hypothetically, these origins may lay in the story's having been encountered in October, and the reader may have had a positive, elaborate imagining of the story's men on their fishing expedition. If the genesis of the response can be traced, a teacher can separate the personal (reading the story in October, which reminded the student of hunting) from the text (the fishing). Then the connotations of the text can be explored. In this case, the teacher could ask what hunting means to the student, perhaps attempting to elicit the plausible responses of peacefulness and escape. Then the text could be returned to in order to see whether the same connotations applied to fishing. They, of course, do—to an even greater extent than hunting with its connotations of brutality. Finally, the question of how fishing relates to the men in the story would bring out story elements that would put the discussion back on a track that is firmly laid on the text. Perhaps this technique elaborately coddles a shoddy reader, but the same reader may be encouraged (rather than discouraged) to read, and read carefully, and later may offer fruitful insights rather than becoming silent.

CONCLUSION

In summary, this approach to "Petrified Man" illustrates four aspects of a transactional approach. The first is the teachers' awareness of their own responses. The second is the enlargement of the teachers' initial response through participation in "discussions" by other readers so as to prepare teachers to accommodate agilely and suggest helpful organizing patterns for the many responses they will encounter in the classroom. In the case of my experience with "Petrified Man," my initial response was enlarged both through actual discussions and through reading the critical literature.[2] The third is the organization of the teacher's own responses into a pattern that will help students make sense of their own reactions. Last is the allowance of free discussion, both in terms of what is encouraged and when responses are recorded: a teacher can allow discussion responses to come as they come, using separate spaces on the board to organize them. Such a procedure begins as it only can in reality, with readers' responses; it values those (usually divergent) responses; yet it achieves at its conclusion the (tentative) wholeness and coherence of the aesthetic experience.

A last student comment on the story illustrates, I believe, how stories, given that they are intended to generate affective responses, are most objectively appreciated when those responses are identified. And Linda's comment also provides an insight into how the form of "Petrified Man" works to implicate the reader in its theme.

> I enjoyed this short story for the most part. It was amusing to me to 'listen in' on the conversations between Mrs. Fletcher and Leota the beautician. The gossip that took place struck me funny in that it was so absurd and seemed very trivial.

The comment points to the eavesdropping that, enjoyed, consequently implicates the readers and casts them as an object of the satire on gossip. The third perspective on this story is thus truly operating here, its satire applying to every reader who enjoys the story.

NOTES

1. In *The Act of Reading*, Wolfgang Iser discussed this desire for a consistent interpretation, a unified perspective, in his typically sound and cogent fashion (16–19). Since consistency is fundamental for achieving comprehension, when teachers encounter resistance to one of their readings of a story, they may do so because students feel that their accustomed interpretive strategies for building consistency have been disregarded. Until these strategies can be either absorbed into a class interpretation or persuasively shown to be less appropriate to the story at hand than other interpretive strategies, students will continue to feel cheated, stupid, or misguided. An enthusiastic feminist reading of Charlotte Perkins Gilman's "The Yellow Wall-Paper" may afford an example of an approach that could encounter unnecessary resistance if relatively less comprehensive readings of the story as a Poe-esque tale of madness (after all, the traditional interpretation of the story for decades) are not aired *first*. The process outlined here is designed to allow such readings into the debate in order for students to reach the more encompassing interpretation on their own.
2. For the short story, accessing the criticism has been made relatively easy by a number of bibliographic aids. These include the Modern Language Association's annual bibliography; Jarvis A. Thurston's *Short Fiction Criticism;* and Warren S. Walker's *Twentieth-Century Short Story Explication* and its supplements.

REFERENCES

Iser, Wolfgang. *The Act of Reading: A Theory of Aesthetic Response.* Baltimore: Johns Hopkins University Press, 1978.
Jones, William. M. "Welty's 'Petrified Man.'" *The Explicator* 15.4 (Jan. 1957): item 21.

MLA International Bibliography of Books and Articles on the Modern Languages and Literatures. New York: Modern Language Association.

Rosenblatt, Louise M. *Literature as Exploration.* 3d ed. New York: Noble and Noble, 1976.

Thurston, Jarvis A. et al. *Short Fiction Criticism: A Checklist of Interpretations Since 1925 of Stories and Novelettes (American, British, Continental, 1800–1958).* Denver: Swallow, 1958.

Vande Kieft, Ruth. *Eudora Welty.* Boston: Twayne, 1962.

Walker, Warren S. *Twentieth-Century Short Story Explication: Interpretations, 1900–1966 Inclusive, of Short Fiction Since 1800.* 2d ed. Hamden, CT: Shoe String Press, 1968.

Welty, Eudora. *One Time, One Place: Mississippi in the Depression, A Snapshot Album.* New York: Random House, 1971.

———. "Petrified Man." In *The Collected Stories of Eudora Welty.* New York: Harvest, 1982. 17–28.

.PTER **12**

Hill-Climbing with Thoreau:
Creating Meaningful Carryover

Mary Jo Schaars

PERIOD 7

Studying Walden—a weaving back and forth from preteaching, personalizing, associat-
ing, intellectualizing (the nitty-gritty). I like a class period shaped like a hill—a gentle hill
is best. The student's job is to move over it in the course of 50 minutes. A relaxed
beginning—some chatter, role taking. "Attention, please," my signal to get ready: first
step up the gentle slope and walking easy, still fresh.

We had been talking about Thoreau's idea that we complicate our lives with material
things. On the news this morning I had heard that 79 percent of the affluent Americans
interviewed "could not get along without" their microwaves; 49 percent, their VCRs; and
42 percent, their home computers.

Making Thoreau meaningful begins here. Rosenblatt remarks that "understanding of
even one word demands a framework of ideas about man, nature, and society" (113). I
believe my students have such a framework that I can tap. And then Rosenblatt suggests
that nothing has much value unless the student "feels the need of it" (123). As a teacher, I
am in tune to that.

"What do you suppose most rich people said they couldn't get along without?" I ask.

Responses include "a big house, fancy car, limo, butler, maid"—maybe fifteen or
more are offered before they guess "microwave." Then a bit of surprise. "We don't even
have a microwave."

"How many don't have microwaves?" I ask. Only two raise their hands.

"And I'm darn proud of it," Sarah states. (Wouldn't Thoreau be pleased, I gloat.)

Yesterday we had figured out what kind of crop Thoreau wanted from the Hollowell
farm, and why he went to Walden in the first place. Today we talk about morning, shams
and delusions, the railroad "that rides on us," and grapple with "Time is but a stream I go

afishing in." We center on the text now and talk about what Thoreau means in 130-plus-word sentences—the difference between morning as A.M. and morning as an attitude. We round off the top of the hill.

We each hunker down with the text. For a while all is quiet, everyone concentrating, working to meet the challenge Thoreau and I set for us. Five minutes are left. Now, the hilltop is behind us and the coast down gentle—not a thrill, just a sorting out.

"He's packed too much in the last paragraph. I can't get it." Greg slides the text away.

I smile with empathy. "I don't quite know either," I confess.

I know Greg won't go back to look now. We're done with the top of the hill for this period. Tomorrow we'll talk it over. About half the class asks for handouts on this excerpt from *Walden* to take home. Bus announcements burst forth from the PA, the bell rings, and my students go forth. I look at the empty room and take a moment to muse. I wonder if anyone will think about anything that has to do with today's discussion of Thoreau between this moment and tomorrow class time. I'll have to ask.

A question has been recurring to me lately: How do we measure what the student goes away with? Rosenblatt comments that "the individual needs to build for himself a mental and emotional base from which to meet the fluctuating currents about him" (170). Surely, studying what Thoreau has to say should help; but of course, it won't unless there is some carry-over. I decide to try a simple approach.

The following day, period seven, we begin to climb the hill. "Attention, class." (pause) "Did any of you spend even one minute since class yesterday thinking about what we talked about?" I wince, expecting someone to say, "What did we do yesterday?" Instead . . .

"I was looking around in the Sentry Theater last night—soft seats and everything. I mean, do we really need all that?" (Jeanine)

"I was just walking to my locker last period thinking about materialism. . . ." (Sarah)

"I work at Piggly Wiggly, and I always have to ask 'paper or plastic.' I hate that. Sometimes I just use paper. Last night I bagged (groceries) for someone who not only wanted plastic but bought only junk food besides." (Matt)

"I got up without an alarm clock. It was still dark . . . and I took time to eat a big breakfast." (Steve)

"My family and I talked about all the conveniences we have last night at the dinner table." (Vicki)

"Time is but the stream I go afishin in" (Thoreau, "Where" 193). The human intellect—we do what we can to tap the capacity of our minds.

THE PLAN: SETTING UP CAMP

In reality, the teacher is just a "fellow seeker of truth and knowledge" (Macrorie 50). How natural this is when students willingly find commitment. We begin by developing mutual trust—a satisfying balance. Students trust me to provide the text. (My responsibility is assumed and natural. They know I would not bring to them something meaningless.) I trust them to read, think, and talk—together and with me.

We look at the text, associate and personalize until the threads get properly woven into a pattern of understanding; and that understanding needs to deepen, hold, create something new for each individual. The teacher's job is a coming around again, making sure there is pattern or design that will carry over. Thoreau says, "When any real progress is made, we unlearn and learn what we thought we knew before" (qtd in Macrorie, 188). And we can only let go and build anew if we have confidence. Comradery helps.

Teaching from *Walden* without personal, intellectual, social connections? Impossible. Imagine an objective test: How much did Thoreau pay for his cabin in the woods? What years did he live there? How old was he? Thoreau did/did not purchase the Hollowell farm. Fill in the blank: "We do not ride on the _____, it rides upon us." All kinds of facts like these lie on the surface—that's automatic. Creating meaningful carry-over must lie elsewhere, perhaps in the discovered ideas we drive into a corner (as Thoreau suggests life must be) and examine for "meanness" or prove "sublime."

Where does the intellectual path of Thoreau intersect mine/theirs? That's what we seek every hill-climbing day. By juxtaposing scenes from our past, our perception of the text's words, listening and understanding from others' experiences, we climb to larger, more pervasive meanings.

Carry-over. We create carry-over with journaling, grappling with our own ideas, and then comparing them with Thoreau's. We take a nature walk, meet Henry in central Wisconsin at the age of seventeen, and then we leave him when we've acquired what we can understand here and now—knowing we will meet him again in school, while reading a newspaper, while attempting to give meaning to living somewhere, sometime when it is important to stop and consider.

CONSIDERING THE OBSTACLES

Creating carry-over is, in fact, the major job of the teacher. First, students need a focus, something personally and intellectually meaningful on their level. The responsibility of the teacher is not to make sure the students understand *Walden,* but to be sure that they can relate to it, incorporate whatever of Thoreau's ideas they are ready for, recognize a bit of the essence of Thoreau when they rub up against a future quote, reference, or event. Ideally, the careful juggling of the teacher will enable each student to become confidently curious rather than turned off and frustrated. The teacher's objective must be to increase the odds that a student meeting Thoreau again might try again, "climb" again. That is ultimate carry-over.

Look at this sentence from *Walden:*

Let us settle ourselves, and work and wedge our feet downward through the mud and slush of opinion, and prejudice, and tradition and delusion, and appearance, that alluvion which covers the globe, through Paris and London, through New York and Boston and Concord, through Church and State, through poetry and philosophy and religion, til we come to a hard bottom and rocks in place, which we can call *reality,* and say, This is, and no mistake; and then begin, having a *point d'appui,* below freshet and frost and fire, a place where you might found a wall or a state, or set a lamppost safely, or perhaps a gauge, not a Nilometer, but a Realometer, that future ages might know how deep a freshet of shams and appearances had gathered from time to time. (Thoreau, "Where" 193)

Unless one is a masochist, struggling to decipher the meaning by oneself, age seventeen, in America, today, would certainly make Thoreau's "Realometer" a Deadometer.

FITTING OUT

Thus, a couple of class periods hill-climbing with Thoreau really starts on the level—learning some connections. In my class, students never catch a glimpse of *Walden* before they find out how they feel about materialism, moral commitment, goals, lifestyle, and so forth. Each student fills out a questionnaire and then we talk about the answers:

1. If you didn't have to worry about making a lot of money what occupation would you choose? Why?
2. What do you like best about autumn (spring)?
3. Are clothes and your appearance important to you?
4. What do you consider your highest achievement so far?
5. What do you consider your greatest failure?
6. Do you ever just take a walk with no destination in mind?
7. When, during a routine day, do you find yourself happiest? Most bored?
8. Do you believe you have too many, just enough, too few conveniences in your life? Explain, if necessary.
9. Would you go to jail rather than conform to a law that went against your conscience? Explain, if necessary.
10. Check one: (Explain, if necessary.)
    a. Money can buy most things I want in life.
    b. Money can buy few things I want in life.
11. Do you express your opinions even when they aren't popular? Explain. Circle "A" if you agree with the statement and "D" if you disagree. Explain your answers if you feel it's necessary.
    A   D   Every person is basically good.
    A   D   I try to depend on myself and be independent.
    A   D   I want to simplify my life.
    A   D   It is possible to have a life filled with both material things and spiritual ideas.

Next we talk about transcendentalism, briefly exploring some terms: self-reliance, divine spark, intuition, reason, and others. Then we get away from the teacher-centered. If the weather cooperates, we take a class period to get "A Breath of Nature"—tone up the senses. Students take a brief walk paying close attention to the smells inside and outside the building; they examine closely a small plot of ground and then a larger landscape. All their responses are written as journal entries. The following are excerpts that show a variety of honest observations:

> My patch of earth is beautiful. Within, it contains three sun stripes, where a tree holds back the nurturing rays. There are two yellow flowers, each with a group of tooth edged weeds around them. One is glowing as the light shines on it. The other is shaded behind the tree. . . .
> Cars go by and I hear the rumble of their engines, the sound of their jolts as they hit a bump.

I suddenly hear a sharp, sawing sound, then a radio playing in the distance. I hear my classmates quietly talking as a handyman stands on a ladder and hammers on a roof panel of some sort. The trees are all different colors now. . . . They are starting to look lonely and bleak—getting ready for the white fluffs to submerge them. (Steph)

A Patch of Ground Develops a Philosophical Parallel
Sunlight makes brown grass seem almost golden. . . . Sun, like divine spark, when covered by society's shams and delusions (clouds), we (grass) become dull and lifeless. (Jennifer)

Here, the Thinking Clusters and Branches. Thoreau Would Like That
One foot of ground—. . . . The grass, once green is now dry, tan and matted together. A large green dandelion plant flattened and tinted red intertwines with the wild grass. One large yellow leaf, long fallen from a summer home, is slowly finding its way to the underground sleep of winter. . . .

A second glance takes me out of my fall-clouded head. Many green mountains exist on the backdrop of a far away cloud, arching down out of sight. Black silhouettes also lay against the sky . . . so still . . . they seem totally unreal when I look down . . . at the street where the cars scurry by. Where to? Even stiller yet are the buildings who never say a word, not a whisper. The only sound beyond the wind on my ears is a roar of a machine; where it comes from I can't place it—it is all around me. (Lorelei)

Around school real nature is foiled by man, but that's *truth;* Thoreau would have to deal with that if he were writing today. The sounds of trucks and cars and ventilator fans and the smell of grease wafting toward us from the burger joints a quarter of a mile away make us realize how tenacious nature must be to survive man's environment. Thus Thoreau's lessons are updated and realized.

PSYCHING UP

Then, taking a step "closer" to *Walden,* we read two essays: "Death of a Pine" by Thoreau and "Seeing" by Annie Dillard. The resulting journal entries center on the literary for "Death of a Pine" and on the personal for "Seeing." In "Death of a Pine," Thoreau laments the destruction of "a noble pine," a fallen "warrior," by two men with a saw and an axe, who are described as "beavers or insects gnawing." I ask students to identify similes and metaphors and then to indicate what ideas they come away with. Most students grasp Thoreau's inferences:

Thoreau is presenting the idea that although the tree is a home for the fish hawk and hen hawk and the squirrel, nobody in town considers the tree coming down a disaster even though if two houses were ruined it would be. He also wants to point out to us that once the squirrel and hawks are accustomed to the new tree the woodcutters will ruin that house, too. One final thought: I think Thoreau is trying to present that other living things have to suffer so we can have luxuries. The lumber will be used to make luxurious, expensive (things) that aren't a necessity in life. (Jenny)

In "Seeing" Annie Dilland recounts a childhood experience where she would hide a penny on a stretch of sidewalk, then make arrows and labels, "Surprise ahead," (47) for bypassers. She hopes that finding a penny will literally "make someone's day." She goes on to compare pennies to "a healthy poverty and simplicity" and to events, easily missed, in nature, like sighting a fish, a deer, a flock of red-winged blackbirds.

After reading, students write about pennies either found or overlooked in their own lives. The excerpts reveal that students are capable of personalizing in ways that will help them to understand when they come to read *Walden*. Shelley and Trina had no concept of Thoreau's "fabulous realities" when they wrote these:

> Finding pennies in my life would be something simple like when I was taking pictures for photography I was photographing my aunt's geese and one of the geese reached over and started smoothing another one's feathers. Almost like they were helping each other get ready for the photograph. Another one would be when I was at work I would take the food out to the table and they say, "Gosh, that was fast!" It makes you feel appreciated. . . .
>
> One of my favorite "pennies" would be when one night I was getting ready to go out and I was doing my hair, and in the mirror I saw my little sister trying to copy what I was doing.
>
> My "pennies" are just something that kind of makes you want to smile! (Shelley)

> I remember once when I was walking around in the woods, across from the creek behind my grandfather's house, I found two sheets of scrap iron. I was only about six, but every year I'd go back there to visit the scrap iron. I'd sit on the iron, because the two sheets were huge, and wonder how long they'd been there and who put them there.
>
> Anyway, about two summers ago when I was visiting my grandfather, I heard him and my dad talking about two pieces of scrap iron. My grandpa said he didn't know where he put them, but he knew he'd left two pieces of scrap iron out in the woods about 25 years ago. There was the answer to my questions. . . . But since they didn't know I'd over heard their conversation—I just went on my merry way. Those two pieces of metal are my place to go when I'm visiting my grandparents; no one else knows where they are. Those two pieces of rusted iron buried under leaves and pine needles have been mine since I was six and I wasn't about to tell them where they were. (Trina)

THE CLIMB

And Walden is next. We read an excerpt, "Where I Lived, and What I Lived For." Here I ask students to look at six topics: the Hollowell farm (described in the beginning), why Thoreau went to the woods to live, why he considers morning the best time of day, his objections to the ways people live, what he means by "shams and delusions are esteemed for soundest truths, while reality is fabulous," and what point we can make from the last paragraph, "Time is but the stream I go a-fishing in. . . . My head is hands and feet (to) burrow my way through these hills."

Often we read a good part of this essay out loud and talk about it as we go. I see no sense assigning this as homework. While we read together we can associate and personalize; students can announce they are bewildered and get immediate relief. My purpose is to climb gentle hills, not make mountains.

How do my students respond? They seldom respond the same way; each class reflects its own individuality—particularly because Thoreau elicits such personal reactions. Take, for example, our challenge to understand what Thoreau is talking about as he describes his experience of attempting to buy the Hollowell farm, then feeling a sense of relief when the deal falls through. It seems he reaped his rewards simply by wandering about and observing the farm, talking and thinking about it: "I found thus that I had been a rich man without any damage to my poverty" (186). Then he advises that we should "live free and uncommitted. It makes but little difference whether you are committed to a farm or the county jail" (186).

For discussion I set up the classroom beforehand by placing all the tables and chairs in a large circle so that everyone is face to face. I am part of the circle on a level with the students. The discussion goal is for the students to grasp whatever-it-is they are ready and able to understand from the passage. Such a general approach, at first glance, may seem an easy-out for the teacher who need not "prepare" ahead of time. However it does, in fact, require much discipline (and occasionally a bit of anxiety) on my part. First, I must not allow myself too many expectations, for then I will tend to dominate and lead the talk. Second, I must realize that having no "script" will make the discussion roundabout rather than focused and direct. Therefore, I need to exercise patience and restraint. Third, I know something about my students that enters in: Many have found safety in not responding and have become, instead, passive observers; in many cases their "tuneout" encompasses not only failure to enter class discussions, but failure to "think" as well. It is only when I ask the class, "Where should we begin?" and all is silent for a few moments that students realize: "She means it. We're going to sit here until somebody says something!" At that point the more conscientious will relook at the text and someone will inevitably bring up an idea or ask a question. As much as possible I promote students talking to students. One recent group response went like this:

> KARI: It's funny. Thoreau got what he wanted by *not* buying the farm. That way he didn't have any commitment, and that's the way he wanted to live.
>
> CHUCK: Well, people always have dreams though, and goals.
>
> SEAN: Yeah, but sometimes the dreams are better than the goals.
>
> CHUCK: Maybe people ought to have a series of goals. When they reach one, then they can reach for another, and after that another.
>
> SEAN: Man is never satisfied.
>
> LYNN: What do you think Thoreau means when he says, "As long as possible live free and uncommitted. It makes but little difference whether you are committed to a farm or the county jail" (p. 186)?
>
> KARI: That's what I said. Any kind of commitment was bad to him. I mean he wasn't married, he didn't want anything.
>
> JENNIFER: Just think, he wouldn't have family get-togethers and birthday parties for young children. . . .
>
> AMY: . . . or girlfriends.
>
> NATE: No job.
>
> SEAN: But he *was* committed to nature.
>
> KARI: He said, "As long as possible. . . ." And anyway, I don't think being committed to nature is the same as what he's talking about.
>
> JENNIFER: I think commitment to other people is important. Like husbands and wives.
>
> KARI: Oh, I don't! look at all the divorces taking place today.
>
> JENNIFER: But that doesn't mean it's not important.
>
> KARI: Well our commitments sure aren't *forever* like it says in the marriage ceremony! I think people are much more committed to their children than to their husbands and wives.
>
> JENNIFER: Yes, you can't just leave your kids. . . .

KARI: Sometimes in a bad divorce the parents use the kids to get back at each other in custody fights.

JENNIFER: Sure, you can always turn commitment into something bad, I suppose.

SEAN: Maybe you've got to just enjoy the trip—not set any goals.

JAMIE: Well, I think he's just a wierdo. He'd probably be a nerd. . . .

LORI: No. He'd probably commit suicide if he came back today and saw all the destruction of nature and the pollution and stuff.

JENNIFER: I still think you have to consider friends and the family. That's what my "Hollowell farm" would be.

CHUCK: I guess right now I'm committed to getting good grades and I want a good job in the future.

LYNN: What does he mean about Atlas?

SEAN: Oh. He (Atlas) did a lot of work and didn't get any pay. I guess maybe he liked what he was doing. Evidently Thoreau did too.

LYNN: This is pretty hard. How long ago did you say he lived?

In a similar discussion in another class, one student attempted to describe the place she envisioned where she would eventually live. Her description of a pristine, country manor moved us far away from "dilapidated fences" and "lichen-covered apple trees" (p. 185). However, her sincerity sparked interest until nearly all the students had proposed their dream house. During a very animated exchange, students grappled with ideas on simplicity rather than grandeur, dreams, or reality. And although they were much more concerned with materialism than Thoreau would have wished, they were united in seeking a place to live that "fit" them individually, in which they could be relaxed and at peace; they had garnered something important to take away with them. As Rosenblatt explains:

> The teacher realistically concerned with helping his [her] students to develop a vital sense of literature cannot, then, keep his [her] eyes focused only on the literary materials he [she] is seeking to make available. He [she] must also understand the personalities who are to experience this literature. He [she] must be ready to face the fact that the student's reactions will inevitably be in terms of his [her] own temperament and background. . . . No matter how imperfect or mistaken, this will constitute the present meaning of the work for him [her], rather than anything he [she] docilely repeats about it. . . . The nature of the student's rudimentary response is, perforce, part of our teaching materials. (51)

Most students jot down notes to answer discussion questions. We read and talk for two days. Then, it seems as though we have absorbed what we can, and it is time to move on. When Thoreau left Walden Pond he recounts, "It seems to me that I had several more lives to live and could not spare any more time for that one" (184). So, too, when one is climbing through over 300 years of American literature in one semester (90 hours).

THE DESCENT

We do, however, take a little time and thought about leaving before we pack up and go. Carry-over continues when students are asked to reread that questionnaire they filled out before they knew Walden was anything but a bookstore in the mall. Now, after two days intellectualizing and developing analogies to grasp concepts, we take some time to turn inward with our new ideas. The task is to compare ourselves with Thoreau on three or four topics to discover to what extent we agree or disagree.

On the initial questionnaire, students have expressed how they feel about making money, about the importance of clothes and appearance, their achievements and failures, about being self-reliant and speaking out, and about being in nature. Now, when I ask students to return to themselves, they choose a diversity of topics to consider, though most center on appearance, the simple versus complex life, and being in nature. There are as wide a variety of approaches to these topics as there are personalities, but in each case the individual associations with Thoreau's ideas can be seen—each student's fund of knowledge about the philosophy we have just been pursuing.

The Simple Versus Complex Life

I want to somewhat simplify my life, but not too much. It (would) become too dull and repetitious. . . . I also think that if you go and live all alone you limit the amount you can learn. Yes, more about yourself—the type of person you are, and also about the beauty of nature. But I think you learn from everyone. No matter if it's good or bad. There's always more to learn and the best way is through people. When you're alone, you think in one perspective and never get anyone else's opinions, just yours. (Steph)

Too many conveniences in life—Thoreau and I think alike on this subject. Perhaps he is more against material items than I, but human beings are spoiled. We share that thought. He puts his frustration toward material items into his writings, while I have not found an outlet for these feelings. Perhaps I will choose a similar situation such as the Peace Corps or some other humanity organization. (Sarah)

Just enough conveniences. Thoreau would strongly disagree with me on this point. Compared to him, I live a life of absolute ease. My family has a microwave, vcr, a large house, and an alarm clock that listens. Thoreau would tell me that these "conveniences" are poisoning my soul. They are keeping me away from inner peace and happiness. They take up too much of my time and become distractions. They make my life simply too complex. Ultimately, I should give up these tools of Satan and gain a life of simplicity in the wilderness. (John)

On Nature

Walking is very important to me; it matters not where or when, only why. And why is to clear my head and just think good or challenging thoughts. Destination only clutters things up, and when one gets to a certain place and it feels right, you'll turn around and go home. It's funny when your mind is free the things you can pick up on. Transcendentalism again. Thoreau would agree. . . . Freedom of the mind is very important; until one exposes oneself to it, you don't really know what you're missing. . . . I could make a pretty good transcendentalist; maybe it's just my nature, maybe it's my Mom. (Rob)

On Clothes and Appearance

I guess most teenage girls are pretty fashion conscious. I mean I'd be lying if I said I wasn't. You would have to be a pretty big person to dress in an orange polka-dot shirt and plaid bell-bottoms because you wanted to. Thoreau would say clothes don't matter and everyone could go bucknaked for all he cared. . . . If you've got the money and you want to look good, who cares what Thoreau thinks. You can still be an intellectual and wear Esprit. Clothing is often a way of expressing yourself. (Gretchen)

Our last experience with Thoreau tends toward the personal too, although the res
are published for the class. As "teacher" my duty is to administer a test, and I choose to
follow the established design, even though evaluation is very subjective. As a result,
grades, based on creativity and logical and complete support, tend to be As and Bs—
deservedly, I think. The test is an essay question, the idea originating in *Clearing the Way*
by Tom Romano (156–157).

> Through the miracle of 1980s technology, young Henry David Thoreau (same character,
> personality and principles) has been transported to the present. He is seventeen years old and
> living in Central Wisconsin. In an essay *describe six things he possesses* that reflect his
> personality, character, and concerns. Explain what each possession reveals about him. (Be
> sure to show an understanding of the man and his philosophy from our talking and reading.)

Students may use any notes or sources they wish as they write the answer during one
class period. Following is a representative sample of selected possessions along with two
excerpts of student answers. (As you can see, some of these are almost impossible to
defend. The numbers refer to the frequency of selection of these items.)

Thoreau's Possessions

5 fishing gear/line and hook	antibiotics
5 sets of (3) chairs	a criminal record
8 hiking boots	1973 Pinto
16 notebook, journal or diary	generic food
2 watch/alarm clock	2 Walkman/stereo
2 magnifying glass	gas mask
10 bike	Polaroid
9 binoculars	backpack
5 camera/telephoto lens	dog
Walden & *Civil Disobedience*	bland wardrobe (assorted items)
6 selection of books	2 snow shoes
2 walking shoes/tennis shoes	4 computer/typewriter
5 pencils and pens	1 cassette/tape recorder
3 canoe	2 camcorder/video camera
3 pen and paper	bird feeder
match	hang glider
2 axe/Swiss army knife	wool blanket
bracelet of worn leather	2 sketchbook & pencil
tent/one-room shack	his own inventions

Essay Excerpts on Thoreau

And last, Thoreau would possess a boat. He could see more on a large scale in a boat. He
could paddle out to the middle of a pond, lay on his back and see the birds, clouds. From the
boat he could view the shores and see the trees and land animals come to drink. Since Thoreau
likes the idea of the circle, I think he would really enjoy this because everything would revolve
around the water. Its underground springs reach the tree's root and animals drink out of it.
(Kim)

Thoreau would probably have a journal or diary to write down his daily events . . . what his inspirations were or what things were important. . . . It would tell people in the future (whoever found it) what Thoreau was thinking and what kind of person he was. It would let us know that he believed nature was a soul-searching place. "Now" should be what we're thinking of. Life should be simple and easy. We shouldn't get messed up in the hassles of bargain hunting or coupon clipping because money isn't everything. Thoreau would own a diary to write down his feelings about the hussle and bussle of today's society. (Jennifer)

RECOLLECTIONS

Finally, after returning graded tests, we talk and question and hypothesize on what "things" students have selected (each student receives the list), then file the papers in notebooks and prepare for *The Crucible, The Scarlet Letter,* for *A Separate Peace* and *Go Tell It On a Mountain,* where that "spark of goodness" and life's values must be questioned time and again. Carry-over can't end with a test on Friday.

One final question remains, the idea I grappled with in the beginning. What about the ultimate: literature's life-long carry-over? Rosenblatt writes, "The criterion for judging the success of any educational process must be its effect on the actual life of the student; its ultimate value depends on its assimilation into the very marrow of personality" (182). From my classroom hill climbing to Rosenblatt's pristine summit seems of immeasurable distance. Only a leap of faith allows me to think I might possibly influence my students to such a degree. It is best, I tell myself, to approach one hill at a time, giving each student the opportunity to "function at his [her] fullest emotional and intellectual capacity" (Rosenblatt 173).

Occasionally there are moments: Stu, working in the produce department at the IGA said, "Do you still teach Mark Twain's essay on Fenimore Cooper? I loved it. Could I get a copy?"

Next time I'm buying oranges I'll have to ask him about Thoreau.

REFERENCES

Dillard, Annie. "Seeing." *Literary Cavalcade* 34 (1982): 47.
Macrorie, Ken. *Uptaught.* New York: Hayden Book Company, Inc., 1970.
Romano, Tom. *Clearing the Way.* Portsmouth, NH: Heinemann, 1987.
Rosenblatt, Louise M. *Literature as Exploration.* 3d ed. New York: Noble and Noble, 1976.
Thoreau, Henry David. "Death of a Pine." *Literary Cavalcade* 34 (1982): 46.
———. "Where I Lived and What I Lived For." In *Adventures in American Literature.* Ed. James Early. Classic ed. New York: Harcourt, 1973. 183–193.

CHAPTER 13

Intensifying Transactions through Multiple Text Exploration

Elizabeth Ann Poe

As a literature teacher, I welcome Louise Rosenblatt's theory of reader response, particularly her emphasis on the importance of a rich, satisfying transaction between reader and text. I want my students to read a novel that is interesting, holds their attention, and builds on their individual backgrounds. I want them to read a novel not just because they are required to read it, but because it speaks to them personally and aesthetically. I want them to read a novel that offers an appropriate reading challenge: one that draws them in, enables them to identify with characters or situations, and inspires them to learn about and from these connections. I want them to read a text that will make them appreciate that particular book and want to read more because this experience was enjoyable, thought provoking, and gratifying. These components comprise a rich and satisfying transaction with a text.

But it is difficult to find one book that will offer this rich literary experience to every class member. Therefore, to provide students with increased possibilities for satisfying transactions, I present literary choices and opportunities for individual responses whenever possible. In a high school sophomore English course, I allowed students to select their reading materials from a group of thematically intertwined novels that offer an appropriate range of reading levels, a wide variety of characters, a number of different situations, and several diverse geographical settings. I hope the differences in the novels will allow students to find a book to which they can initially relate. At the same time, the books are all set in the United States during World War II and have teenage protagonists who are affected by the war. This similarity makes it possible for students to read different novels concurrently and respond to them individually as well as explore them both in small groups and as a whole class.

PRELIMINARY JOURNAL EXPLORATIONS

To begin this exploration, students write in their journals about war in general, describing their thoughts, feelings, and associations with the concept. Then they write specifically about World War II, including all they know about this event, whatever thoughts or feelings it brings to mind, and questions they might have. I collect, read, and respond to these informal pieces of writing immediately. They help me gauge students' concepts of war and ascertain their familiarity with World War II. Sometimes students include personal information, perhaps about a relative lost or disabled in war or stories about their parents or grandparents' activities during wartime. These personal disclosures sensitize me toward students for whom the unit may be particularly painful as well as toward those who may serve as future resources. I also use these entries at the end of the unit to enable students to compare and contrast their pre-reading and post-reading thoughts. In my responses, I try to communicate that I am interested in what students have to say and sympathetic toward painful associations they may reveal.

SELECTING TEXTS

Following this preliminary activity, I introduce the six novels from which they may choose. The students understand I hope each of them will select a personally engaging book that will provide an appropriate challenge. Being careful not to give them too much information or color their perceptions with my own opinions, I give a brief booktalk about each of the texts.

A *Separate Peace,* written by John Knowles, tells the story of two teenage boys who room together at a New England boarding school. One of the boys is an exceptional athlete and the other is an excellent student. Although they are best of friends, there is a dark side to their relationship. *Jacob Have I Loved,* written by Katherine Paterson, is the story of twin sisters who live on Rass Island, in Chesapeake Bay. Even though they are twins, Caroline and Louise do not get along. Louise is miserable because Caroline gets all the attention. *The Chosen,* by Chaim Potok, is about two teenage boys in New York who become friends despite the fact that Reuven comes from a more liberal religious background than does Danny, making it necessary for them to attend different types of Jewish schools. They have fascinating philosophical discussions about religion and politics.

Bette Green's *Summer of My German Soldier* is the story of Patti, a Jewish girl in Arkansas, who hides an escaped German prisoner of war. This is a particularly risky undertaking because her father is already ill-disposed toward Patti and beats her at the slightest provocation. In *Red Sky at Morning,* written by Richard Bradford, teenage Joshua moves with his mother from Mobile, Alabama to a secluded mountain village in New Mexico because his father is serving on a battleship. In New Mexico, Joshua becomes friends with white, Chicano, and Indian teenagers with whom he shares several exciting adventures. *Los Alamos Light,* by Larry Bograd, is the story of Maggie who moves with her parents to Los Alamos, New Mexico, so her father can work with a group of scientists who are secretly developing the atom bomb. Maggie forms friendships with some of the other teenagers living there, but she must come to her own conclusions about the morality of what her father did.

The booktalks and passing the books around usually enable students to self-select books that are appropriately challenging and potentially engaging. Better readers generally select *The Chosen* or *A Separate Peace* and less able readers seem relieved to choose *Summer of My German Soldier* or *Jacob Have I Loved.* Middle-level readers often prefer *Red Sky at Morning* or *Los Alamos Light.* This match between reader and reading level of the text is crucial if readers are to feel equal to the task of reading the book.

I encourage students to change books if they do not like their original selection. Sometimes they change because a book is too difficult, or not challenging enough, or seems uninteresting. Sometimes they decide to read the same book a friend has chosen. I have never had it happen, but if a parent objected to a particular book, the student could easily switch to another book offered as part of the unit.

Once students settle on their texts, we form book groups based on the chosen texts. If more than five students in one class are reading the same book, we make two groups for that book, rather than have a group too large for effective collaboration. If only one student selects a certain book, that student may choose to work alone, change books, or try to persuade someone else to change books; no one is ever forced to read a book just for the sake of group structure, but students selecting a book no one else chose have always opted to create or join a group. I think they realize the advantages of sharing their responses with other class members.

EXPLORING PERSONAL RESPONSES TO TEXTS

I tell the class we will be reading these books for exploration. I would like to leave it there, for the sake of purity, but of course they want further elaboration. So I explain that when they read these novels, I want them to explore their own response to the book. This might include responses to what happens in the story, what the characters are like, what the situations or people remind them of, questions they may formulate about the time period, geographical setting, religious ideas, or any other thoughts or feelings the story evokes.

Their exploration might include other people's responses to the book or extend to reference resources or other literary works. They will record their responses in spiral notebooks, called *response journals,* which I will read. They will also be given opportunities to share their thoughts with members of their small group. I stress that there are no right or wrong responses, but they should aim at responses that fully articulate thoughts and feelings and explore why they responded as they did. Through the exploration of their responses, readers reflect about themselves and their connection with the text. Such introspection leads to self-awareness and understanding, the foundation of personal growth and empathy for others.

Students respond in their journals following the completion of each chapter or group of chapters if they read more than one in a sitting. They submit their journals whenever they want my feedback, which I try to provide by the following day.

As I read their entries, I make comments intended to show I have read the entry and understand its content. I compliment thoughtful entries and indicate when my own response coincides with the student's. When students respond in a manner different from my own, I thank them for providing a new perspective. If remarks indicate students are way off track, I ask questions designed to help them take a second look at the text. If students ask questions about the storyline or characters, I answer them. However, if they just say "I don't understand," I ask them to be more specific, so I can help them, or I direct them to group members who may be able to clarify the confusion. For example, a student named Lisa wrote: "The characters [in *The Chosen*] use so many Jewish terms that it is hard for me to understand because I don't know the vocabulary." I wrote back: "Which terms don't you understand? Maybe someone in your group can help you figure them out. If that doesn't work, come talk to me about them." If a student's response is vague, I ask questions like: "What do you mean by this?" or "Why do you say this?" I try to help them expand and deepen their transactions with the text by inviting them to tell me more and provide specific instances or details.

When students make personal associations with the text or provide autobiographical information, I encourage them to explore the connections they have discovered. Sometimes I try to draw out these personal connections as when Lisa wrote:

> I was very upset with Danny's father when he did not allow Danny and Reuven to remain friends. I just wanted to yell and scream at him. He seemed to be ruining Danny's life because he would never talk to him, except about Talmud. And that wasn't talking. Reuven was Danny's only friend, and now that was taken away. I admired Reuven's father for helping him in understanding Danny and his family. It seemed like he could always count on his father for help whenever he was confused or needed an opinion.

Here's my response:

> I know what you mean about the two fathers. They certainly treated their sons differently. Does either of them remind you of anyone you know?

Students sometimes respond to my comments or answer my questions on the page where I asked them or in subsequent entries. I don't require them to do this, but they seem to have a natural desire to communicate their thoughts and discoveries. Lisa, for example, wrote back:

> I guess each of these two fathers reminds me a bit of my own father. He's not as stern as Danny's father, but we don't talk as much as I would like. He's supportive of me, but not as much as Reuven's father is of him. I wish he was more like Reuven's father, but I'm glad he's not as bad as Danny's father. I couldn't take that.

My response to her was "I understand," and that was the end of our correspondence on this matter. I enjoy reading and responding to journals because I can give students personal attention. It also keeps me informed as to their progress with and insights into the novels.

My responses vary in length according to the content of the entry. Often I write a brief phrase, like "thoughtful response," or "interesting reaction," or "good question." Other times I comment more extensively, especially when students express confusion or deep personal involvement. But whether my comments are brief or extensive, it does take time to read and respond to each entry. When colleagues ask me about this, I explain that I can do this because I am not spending time preparing lectures about the historical period, the author's life, or literary criticism. Nor am I using my time to create and grade quizzes, tests, and study guides. By not grading each entry, but giving each journal a holistic grade, based on whether the student responded to each section, the thoroughness of the responses, and the overall effort involved in the exploration, I optimize time as well as shift the focus from grades to quality of responses. Although the final journal grade is admittedly somewhat subjective, my students understand it is based on many years of experience reading response journals.

DEVELOPING RESPONSES:
SMALL-GROUP INTERACTIONS

During the weeks when students are reading the novels, they discuss them periodically in small groups. Each group determines which days will be reading days and which will be discussion days. Some days there are six small groups scattered throughout the classroom, all discussing different books. I ask each group to tell me when they plan to discuss, and I try to join them, at least for part of each discussion. I do this for three reasons. First, I want to hear what the students have to say about their chosen texts. As students soon discover, I love to talk about literature and find the exchange of responses exhilarating and enlightening. I join the group as another reader-responder, listening to group members as they explain their responses and sharing my responses.

Second, I want to help group members expand on their responses and try to understand why they and others in their group reacted as they did. For example, a student in a group who had read *A Separate Peace* said he identified with Gene Forrester. When I asked him why, we were able to discover that he had been jealous of a friend and hoped he would fail a chemistry test. This insight elicited similar confessions from several other group members. I think we all understood Gene a little better and our human weaknesses after this discussion. In another instance, a student who had read *Jacob Have I Loved* told her group she did not like the novel. As we explored her response, it became clear that she was confused by all the crabbing terminology. Other group members were experiencing similar frustration. They decided to work on this together and devoted a good bit of time trying to decipher the language of the waterfront.

In both these instances I served as a facilitator. I do this by asking what the students thought about the book so far. Then I gently probe their initial responses, which are usually "I like it" or "I don't like it," by asking them why. I ask them to specify characters or incidents or passages that cause them to like or dislike the novel. I ask them if anything in the book reminds them of themselves or people they know. I ask them what they can learn about themselves and others by reading the book. And when they respond, I usually ask them why they responded that way. I think I am successful at this because the students sense I am genuinely interested in them and their exploration of the text. In addition, the fact that I share my own responses, and do not treat these as the only acceptable or "right" responses, demonstrates I truly respect my students as readers with unique transactions with the text. They know I respect the texts because I frequently suggest they return to the book to clarify a point or find a detail that will help explain their responses.

I also facilitate their exploration of the text when I use the reader-response technique of asking them to identify a word or passage they particularly liked and explain its appeal.

The passages they select usually concern content, such as an idea expressed by a character, but sometimes they are descriptions of a character or place. I often select passages because I like the flow of the words or an image created or a literary allusion and then invite students to do the same. Our discussion of these passages enhances students' understanding of the novel as well as their appreciation for it as a source of aesthetic enjoyment.

My third reason for joining small-group discussions is so I can evaluate students' participation in this important aspect of the unit. They know they receive a group participation grade, which is based on effort and attention to the task at hand, not the quality of the discussions.

As students finish their books, they write their response to the work as a whole. These whole-book responses give students an opportunity to synthesize their thoughts and feelings about the book, reflect on their experience with it, and assess what they have gained from reading it. These responses often represent some of the students' clearest, most focused writing because they have been so intensely involved with the literary work.

From my point of view, these whole-book responses are important not only because they provide insight into the students' transactions with the books, but also because they function as a reality check and help me determine the appropriateness of the array of books offered for the unit. Comments like "I enjoyed this book even though I never would have picked it up on my own because I usually hate anything that has to do with war," "I learned a lot about my beliefs about war," "This was the first book I ever enjoyed reading," and "Thanks for letting us choose our books; I finally got to read a book I cared about," indicate students have had satisfying literary transactions.

EXTENDING RESPONSES:
WHOLE-CLASS DISCUSSIONS

When all the groups have finished their books and whole-book responses entries, we are ready for whole-class discussions. To begin this, each group presents a panel discussion focusing on group members' responses to the book. In order for other class members to understand these responses, each group provides information about the book's plot, characters, literary style, or other necessary details. Then panel members basically answer the question, "What did you think about your book and why?" When the groups have finished their presentations, I ask the class if they noticed any common aspects in the novels. Eager to respond, they mention teenage friendships, jealous feelings, religious concepts, World War II. The way these topics recur in the different novels forms the basis for several days' worth of lively and provocative discussions in which students frequently make comments such as, "That's a lot like my novel because. . . ."

The theme of friendship figures in each novel and is of particular interest to most teenagers, and therefore elicits involved discussions. Whether parents should forbid friendships, as Danny's father did in *The Chosen,* is an example of a question that produces emotional discussions heavily laden with personal experiences. Students in *The Chosen* group have already shared their thoughts on this topic; now they have a larger group of peers with whom to discuss this issue. Examples of Louise's (*Jacob Have I*

Loved) friendship with the elderly Captain, Patti's (*Summer of My German Soldier*) illegal relationship with Anton the POW, and Joshua's (*Red Sky at Morning*) and Maggie's (*Los Alamos Light*) friendships with teens from different racial and cultural backgrounds evoke frank discussions about benefits and potential problems when friends differ in age and personal backgrounds.

When I ask how hearing about the other books affects their exploration of their own books, students often comment that their perceptions about common themes are broadened and intensified by hearing other students' remarks. Although many of the themes are recurring, war, specifically World War II, is common to all six novels; therefore, we decide to focus our class discussion on war.

We discuss World War II and, through the various perspectives provided in each novel, we piece together information about this time period. For example, readers of *Jacob Have I Loved* tell of the sisters listening to the radio and hearing of the Japanese bombing of Pearl Harbor. Those who read *A Separate Peace* explain about sixteen-year-old boys preparing to enlist in the service. *Red Sky at Morning* readers recount how Joshua's father was killed in the war. Readers of *The Chosen* add information about Hitler and Zionism. Those who read *Summer of My German Soldier* inform us about German prisoners of war incarcerated in the United States. And students who read *Los Alamos Light* discuss the top-secret work of scientists who developed the atomic bomb that ended the war.

Much of what happened is difficult for students to comprehend beyond an informational level, so I ask how the war changed the daily lives of the characters in the books and how they, as readers, feel about these changes. Readers of *A Separate Peace* explain that sixteen-year-old Gene and Finny attended summer school so they can graduate early and join the war. But the war came to them even before they left Devon School when older students participated in prewar physical training and school buildings were used as sewing stations for military supplies. Many conversations among boys at Devon School focused on the war, the progress of the Allied powers being of major importance to them. Most of my students are the same age as Gene and Finny and are firm believers that these are the best years of their lives. To think that these joyful years could be cut short and overshadowed by a war that is so far away appalls them.

In a similar vein, the war caused Louise in *Jacob Have I Loved* to work even harder and make more sacrifices for Caroline's music lessons. Louise's friend Call left Rass Island to join the Marines. Due to the war most young men could not go to college, and it became possible for Louise to enter medical school. Louise's experience raises the issue of education for women. Class members do not have to have read this novel to have opinions on this subject. Some feel Louise benefitted from the circumstances and others feel she was shortchanged when she had to settle for a career as a midwife instead of a doctor. Students can get rather emotional about women's rights, and I may need to remind them of the importance of listening to each other and respecting differing points of view.

Danny and Reuven in *The Chosen* spend much of their time in long philosophical discussions about the war, the Jewish people in Europe, and the state of Israel. Patti in *Summer of My German Soldier* risked the wrath of her father to harbor Anton, the German POW, and ended up being sent to reform school for it. In *Red Sky at Morning*, not only did Joshua have to move from his home to New Mexico, but his father is killed in battle, changing Joshua's life forever. Maggie, in *Los Alamos Light,* spends much of her time wondering about the secret work of her father and his colleagues. When they test the bomb, she realizes the terrible destructive force they have created.

As the stories of these characters are told, students are horrified by the far-reaching effects of the war. They sympathize with the characters and sometimes disclose personal stories about family members during the war. They also philosophize about the bomb and the effect it has on us all. Once students understand I am interested in their thoughts on these issues, they are usually eager to discuss them. If they are hesitant or do not offer their opinions, I gently urge them by first mentioning a topic they have referred to and then asking what they think about it.

Tapping the personal level, I ask the class if the teenagers in these novels are much like them. Students generally have kindred feelings toward the teens in the novels, identifying with their desire for friendships, their problems with parents and teachers, and their questions and plans concerning the future. The students do not strongly identify with the plight of these teens during wartime (the United States was not at war when we had this discussion) but they understand how a war can make teenagers grow up faster and change their lives forever. Had we read these novels during wartime, students would undoubtedly recognize close connections with their teenage counterparts during World War II.

CULMINATING PROJECTS

The next step in our exploration of the novels entails personal response projects. Their purpose is to intensify each reader's transaction with the text. Students select a character with whom they identify, an idea that intrigues them, an image that haunts them, a scene that appeals to them, or another aspect of the text to explore in depth. They then create a project that appropriately expresses their responses to or exploration of this aspect of the novel. Students share their project with the class, explaining the relationship between the project, the novel, and their transaction with the text.

Examples of projects include charcoal drawings of characters from *Red Sky at Morning,* a board game based on *Summer of My German Soldier,* background music for *Jacob Have I Loved,* a report on Jewish religious customs by a reader of *The Chosen,* and entries from the long lost diary of Maggie from *Los Alamos Light.* Students sometimes choose to collaborate and have created such projects as a videotaped interview with characters from *A Separate Peace* discussing their feelings about competition; a panel discussion about the war involving Danny, Reuven, and their fathers from *The Chosen;* and a visit from a student's grandfather, a World War II naval captain, who discussed what Joshua's father in *Red Sky at Morning* might have experienced aboard the battleship. These projects represent emotional and intellectual responses, many of which are artistically expressed. Research for the projects involves close reading of the text and utilizing human and library resources.

Students generally seem to have fun presenting their projects and enjoy experiencing their classmates' creations. I ask them to write a response to the response project, and most of them say it helped them understand some part of the novel more fully. Those who did research projects on topics of personal interest, such as sibling rivalry and child abuse, say they learned not only about the characters in *Jacob Have I Loved* and *Summer of My German Soldier,* but about themselves and their families as well. Those who chose to write poetry, short stories, or sequels based on their novels often indicate they came to a closer understanding of the characters and their personal and/or historical situations. Many of the artistic responses are expressions of a reader's emotional reaction to the text. Some of the projects, like the board games, stay rather close to the storyline, but they may include knowledge or interpretation of characters' motivations. Although they do not use the terminology, the students almost unanimously indicate the project has enriched their transaction with the text. Additionally, the quality of their projects and the pride the students take in them enable me to see their extended involvement with the novel and the development of their responses.

We conclude the unit by writing formal essays. Drawing from response journal entries, small-group and class discussions and new thoughts generated by the assignment, students write an essay based on their chosen novel. Although they are free to write on any aspect of their novel they like, many students choose to continue the exploration of one of the themes already identified and analyze the personal meaning this theme holds for them. It is a natural transition for book groups to become writing groups and provide peer responses and editing for each other's essays during this final stage in the exploration of the novel.

When the polished drafts of the essays are submitted, students write a final response journal entry on what they have gained through the unit. Although many students find the unit provocative and intend to further explore ideas generated by the novels or our discussions, I'll never forget the comment of one bright, but heretofore disinterested student. She said that reading *The Chosen* had inspired her to read more books by Chaim Potok and to further explore her Jewish heritage.

Comments like hers are reasons why I use reader-response techniques whenever I facilitate literature study, be it in elementary, secondary, undergraduate, or graduate classes. Offering choices in reading materials and providing multiple means for exploring personal responses make it possible for readers to have the rich, satisfying transactions that keep them reading and exploring literature.

REFERENCES

Bograd, Larry. *Los Alamos Light.* New York: Farrar Straus Giroux, 1983.
Bradford, Richard. *Red Sky at Morning.* New York: Lippincott, 1968.
Greene, Bette. *Summer of My German Soldier.* New York: Dial, 1973.
Knowles, John. *A Separate Peace.* New York: Macmillan, 1959.
Paterson, Katherine. *Jacob Have I Loved.* New York: Thomas Y. Crowell, 1980.
Potok, Chaim, *The Chosen.* New York: Ballantine, 1967.

CHAPTER 14

A Reader-Response Approach to *The Catcher in the Rye:*
Key Issues/Developmental Questions

Frank C. Cronin

Louise Rosenblatt was many years ahead of her time in 1938 when she wrote that the student's literary experience "must be phrased as a *transaction* between the reader and the text" (34–35, modified version, 4th ed., 1983). Elsewhere she wrote that "much of even the best teaching is analogous to typical American 'spectator sports.' The students sit on the sidelines watching the instructor or professor react to works of art" (60).

Even when there is lots of discussion, that discussion usually revolves around material to be mastered for a test, official interpretations and opinions, and student guesses about what the teacher already knows. Serious students may read "literary histories and biographies, criticism, introductions to editions, so-called study guides, *and then, if there is time, they read the works*" (63, italics mine). The end result of an emphasis on content to be "taught and tested" rather than literary experience is that students "seem shut off from the personal nourishment that literature can give" (63).

The teacher "may never glimpse the student's personal sense of the work discussed" that is essential to understanding and appreciating the work. If we teachers do not take personal, emotional responses to the work into account in some way, then we are leading our students "to consider literature as something academic, remote from his [her] own present concerns and needs" (61–62). From the point of view of the student, the text becomes nothing more than a document in the author's biography, a monument to be studied, and "a means of displaying analytic virtuosity" (63).

To put the problem another way, Rosenblatt observes that students function on two distinct planes in some English classes: "On one plane, he [she] learns the ideas about literature that the teacher or literary critic presents to him [her] as traditional and accepted by educated people; on the other plane, he [she] reads the literature and reacts to it personally, perhaps never expressing that reaction or paying much attention to it" (63).

But "the student's primary experience of the work will have meaning for him [her] in these personal terms and no others" (97).

If there is an authentic personal transaction between the student and the text through reading, discussion, and writing, then the literature may not be left behind when the examination is over—to gather dust with old class notes. Instead, when our students turn back to "the various problems and satisfactions" of their lives, they are more likely to resume the transaction with literature, "finding new meanings that grow out of the new and changing circumstances" (35).

As Robert E. Probst writes,

> Patterns of instruction have, for a long time, deluded students into thinking that there was an objective reality to literary knowledge—that it was demonstrable and verifiable, primarily through reference to the text. To allow them to stray to the opposite pole, where they may insist that there is nothing beyond their own perceptions, their own assertions, would, of course, be equally deceitful and damaging. They need instead to learn that the knowledge emerging from the act of reading is like the shape of the river and its banks— neither the river nor the shore determines, in and of itself, what that shape will be. (14)

J. D. Salinger's *The Catcher in the Rye* is a particularly appropriate text for a reader-response approach with adolescent and young adult students. They easily relate to this perennially popular classic in terms of their own experience. Furthermore, a successful class study of Salinger's book can provide the momentum for the study of more remote classics.

It is difficult for teachers to resist the temptation to lecture. But if students rely only on us for an official interpretation of the book, then their own personal interpretations may never develop. Consequently, teachers should avoid giving definitive interpretations that students can merely copy into their notebooks and memorize for a test. Lots of questions, lots of discussion, small discussion groups, and journal entries provide students with the opportunity to develop their own views.

Students are enabled to process the text for themselves through class discussion. Most of the time, teachers may choose to wait until students have expressed their initial reactions to the text before introducing interpretations and arguments made by literary critics. These views should be introduced in a tentative fashion together with teacher comments such as: "What do you make of these critics' opinions?" "Do they help you go develop your own sense of the text or not?" And, subsequently, "Can you give me reasons for your own viewpoints on the critics and the text?" (Contradictory statements by prominent critics are especially helpful in triggering further student thought.)

Critics hold such contradictory views—as they regularly do in the discussion of good books—because the text alone does not yield final answers, as everyone thought in the New Critical era. Nowadays, specialists realize that the literary work exists somewhere between the text and each individual reader's experience. Students should be brought to understand this revolution that has transformed English literary criticism so that they will feel confident in expressing their own personal interpretations. However, we must continue to insist that they keep coming back to read the text carefully and avoid a "criticism" in which the text, read superficially, becomes merely a springboard for autobiographical rambling.

Background material and statements by critics provided in this chapter are not intended to encourage lectures, especially lectures that provide the kind of definitive answers that close off discussion. Such teacher pronouncements destroy reader-response teaching by reducing "discussion" and writing to guessing what the teacher is thinking—the "official" interpretation.

TEACHER BACKGROUND: CENSORSHIP OF THE BOOK

At the beginning I try to give enough background to arouse interest without closing off areas for discussion. Interesting background material, like the censorship story, can raise questions and encourage further thought. Students are interested to hear that *The Catcher in the Rye* has been the object of intense censorship attacks that continue to this day. In the years after the book's 1951 publication, teachers were fired for using it in the classroom, and the book was banned from some high school and even college classrooms. In 1961, Edward P. J. Corbett responded to the censors' principal charges against the book, charges that he organized under three generalizations: (a) "The language of the book is crude, profane, obscene"; (b) "some of the episodes in the book are scandalous"; and (c) "Holden, constantly protesting against phonies, is a phony himself" (442–43).

Most student responses to the censorship express astonishment. For example:

> JOHN: This whole censorship business is absurd. This kind of Victorian prudery does not even deserve a response.

> INSTRUCTOR: Don't discount the process of rapid cultural change that has occurred in the intervening years. For better or for worse; the sexual revolution of the 70s has profoundly changed our whole culture.

> TONY: I'm not sure all the changes are for the better. Film makers exploit sexual curiosity under the protection of the First Amendment. The institution of marriage is disintegrating while AIDS and other diseases are becoming an epidemic among young adults. Why does our culture have to be so sex-drenched?

> SUSAN: But, wait a minute. Holden doesn't do anything sinister; he is pretty innocent and naive. His sexual curiosity is normal. Those attacks against the book are hypocritical.

KEY QUESTIONS ABOUT THE WHOLE BOOK

Some critics see Holden as an immature, spoiled rich boy. Others see him as a compassionate saint who refuses to play a part in a dishonest world. The latter group of critics argue that even though Holden is a neglected adolescent himself, he always sympathizes with the plight of the exploited, like Jane, and the outcasts like Ackley. The former group of critics point out that he is an impulsive, cliche-babbling adolescent who can afford pity, a child of wealth and privilege who often reveals an admixture of New York fastidiousness and snobbishness.

Many critics have observed that Holden's sensitivity and suffering are typical of young people your age. Consider the following questions:

1. How much do you agree with this observation?
2. Why have so many young adults identified so strongly with this book over the years?
3. The theme set in the first lines of the book is one of truthful confidentiality, but Holden tells a lot of lies throughout the book. How can we make sense of this seeming contradiction?
4. To what degree is Holden's compassion a projection of his own loneliness?

MARGARET: Holden really does have to put up with problems like ours. It's humiliating to hear his favorite history teacher scold him on the things he has heard many times over.

EDWARDO: Yes. Holden was deeply hurt by having his test paper with all its flaws read back to him. He writes about exactly what interests him. That's the way education should be. He's a bright kid. Why should he be forced to do nothing more than regurgitate Spencer's lectures?

BILL: Ancient history is irrelevant to his life anyway. We have to study and memorize so many things that are irrelevant to our lives.

KATE: He was hurt by Stradlater's response to his essay on the baseball mitt. Like his interest in the Egyptians, the mitt story really meant something to him personally. That's what teachers should encourage us to write about—things that move us personally.

TONY: Adolescence *is* a very painful time—even though our parents and teachers tells us otherwise. They just remember the good things.

JACK: Yes—parents forget how hard it was for them. They were just as lonely.

MELISSA: Everyone's growing up is unique—and no other person can ever understand what it was really like.

MARGARET: Holden's lies are a way of getting back at a world that doesn't care about him. The scene with Mrs. Morrow is one of the funniest in the book. Ernest has a good build as a defense mechanism. Holden only has his smarts and the cleverness to pull it off.

CATHY: Holden pulls things into perspective for the average student. We are benefiting from his experience. It's vicarious experience.

Responses to such questions will often be quite contradictory because students bring their unique personal experiences to the encounter with literature. Clearly, the "whole truth" is not within the depths of the art work; this structuralist dogma has been completely demythologized. For example, consider student responses to the question: Is Holden relevant or too dated?

MIKE: I don't think that Holden has an awful lot to do with our generation because we don't live with the restrictions that young people in the 50s had. Our parents seem to be a lot more lax. It's more live and let live today.

ANDREA: Well, first of all, I don't agree with a thing you said. All modern education is like leading cattle through the gates. High school does nothing but prepare you for college, and college does nothing but prepare you for a career; and if you have any creative juices in you at all, you're considered an oddball. If anything, today's society needs more people like Holden Caulfield. He's sensitive, sure, but I think the world could use a few more sensitive people like him.

BILL: I agree with most of what you said; most people of this generation are not unfeeling robots. I think Holden should become a hero for our generation because he honestly struggles with the kind of problems that face us. He speaks the humanitarian truth. I'm not saying he's a saint, but Holden knows a lot about human nature as well as the problems of youth.

INSTRUCTOR: You talk about Holden speaking the truth. Is there much truth in what he is saying from your point of view? Is he only an abandoned, rich boy of the fifties entangled in unique and outdated personal problems? Aren't there some aspects of his experience and points of view that you can identify with?

KATE: Yes, his problems are also very real for us today. He personifies many of the problems of discouraged youth, the disenchantment with friends and teachers and human nature in general.

JOHN: I don't see it that way. All I keep thinking is what is this guy's problem? He just *refuses* to go with the flow, even once in a while. Everywhere he went, he had some high and mighty soap box to stand on. Maybe if he simply tried to apply himself every once in a while, he might do better in school. Instead, he always has some personal vendetta against something or someone; he needs to bite the bullet. I do.

MELISSA: But he has no visible parents or any real home. Allie is gone, and life has no real purpose without people you love and who love you.

Through such exchanges and further reflections on the text, students will share insights and be able to define more precisely their agreements and disagreements, both in class discussion and writing. After having heard each others' reasoning, they will respectfully agree to disagree on many points. This is an important lesson for life. Neither scientists nor humanists ever agree fully, and the good poststructuralist teacher does not impose a phony coherence.

However, the disagreements should serve as a creative trigger for further critical thinking. The instructor can say: "Let's go on to look at particular parts of the text more carefully. Write your observations and arguments in your journals. In your journals and short papers you will get credit for original insights and careful reasoning from the text. By sharing our views and incubating our own and other people's insights, we will arrive at greater insight into Holden, the book, into ourselves, and we may come to a greater consensus among ourselves."

TEACHER BACKGROUND: PENCY PREP EPISODES

Some students will quickly perceive that the story is set in a brief frame tale and skip ahead to the last chapter to see that a California psychiatrist is the recipient of Holden's confidences. This discovery further encourages students to look beneath the surface of the plot to discover what makes Holden "tick." Stradlater and Ackley seem to serve as antithetical foils to Holden's character. Holden is so upset about what Stradlater might have done to Jane that he attacks the powerfully built boy, who reluctantly injures him. The puzzled and somewhat regretful Stradlater has no idea that he has blundered into what critics call Holden's secret world. That world seems to revolve around Holden's dead brother, Allie, the subject of his essay, and Jane Gallagher, who may have had to fend off the advances of an alcoholic stepfather and who keeps her kings in the back row in a seeming gesture of sexual defensiveness.

Reader-Response Questions
1. Do we and our friends have secret worlds like Holden?
2. How is Pency like and unlike your own high school or college?
3. Do you sympathize more with Holden or Stradlater. Explain why?
4. Do you know people like Ackley, Stradlater, James Castle, Holden, or Jane?
5. Do you understand Holden's anxiety about Jane?

THE ALIENATED HERO

Students will be interested to learn that Holden is one of many outcast heroes in American literature. Critics compare Holden to Huck Finn and Natty Bumpo. Holden flees from what he perceives to be the dishonesty and hypocrisy of society, represented by such satirical portraits as Ossenberger, the rich, preachy undertaker; the snobbish headmaster of his last school who studiously ignored poor parents; the speech teacher who encouraged his class to humiliate Richard Kinsalla; and the clique that harassed James Castle to the point of suicide. Holden's visit with Mr. Spencer seems a failed attempt by the lonely boy to communicate with a paternal figure.

Response and Discussion
1. Why do you think so many heroes in American literature are alienated heroes?
2. You have lots of insight into snobbishness, school cliques, and class victims— what are your responses to these observations by the critics?
3. Why does the well-meaning history teacher humiliate Holden?
4. To what degree is this a failure of communication a result of the understanding gap between youth and age?
5. Do you know many older people who can really communicate with and understand young people?
6. What age groups can and cannot talk to each other?

A SECRET WORLD IN THE MIDST OF A UNIVERSE OF "PHONIES"

Holden's frequently used word, "phony," can be the focal point for discussing the characters and caricatures who represent the world that he rejects. Later on, students can be asked if the word acquires new meanings in their own rereading after the discussions. Holden uses the word throughout the book to describe many people he encounters like the wealthy children of New York who affect a superficial sophistication in imitation of their parents. The New York snobs like D. B.'s former girlfriend, the preppies at Ernie's club and Carl Luce represent an affluent, Ivy League world of growing up that repels Holden. Though students may be unfamiliar with Eastern snobbishness, they may have a lot to say about analogous situations in their own lives.

The night after Allie dies, Holden hurts himself smashing the car windows and sleeps in the garage. Immediately afterward, his parents pack him off to a series of boarding schools. The subject of missing or marginal parents is a delicate one nowadays, but it is central to this book, and therefore, ought to be talked about. Do people regularly create secret worlds as a means of dealing with the lack of parents and family in their lives—or the loss of family? As Carl F. Strauch observes, "In Holden's maturing, there is no repudiation of childhood or even the secret world" (26).

More Discussion Questions
1. What do the "phonies" of the book have in common?
2. How do you understand Holden's observations on phonies in terms of your own experience?
3. Don't we all have our own secret worlds?
4. How is Holden's secret world different from our own?

LOST IN NEW YORK

Once the lonely boy arrives in New York, he hides from his parents in an East Side hotel. There he experiences the desire to communicate by phone fifteen times but can only complete four calls. His messages do not really get through to anyone except Phoebe. He fantasizes about running away from society and living the life of a romantic recluse at the very same time that he feels lonely, depressed, and painfully isolated. Holden even proposes a Wordsworthian elopement to Sally Hayes. Students may wish to discuss Holden's motives for his contradictory behavior in terms of their own experience.

More Discussion Questions
1. Can you make any coherent sense out of Holden's feelings and behavior toward Sally? Why does he insult her? Why does he act in such a frantic and thoughtless manner? Why does he date her? Why does he call her up later when he is drunk?
2. What does Holden reveal about himself in his other encounters? (e.g., with Mrs. Morrow, the nuns, D. B.'s old girlfriend, etc.). How do those encounters echo experiences in your world and those of your friends?
3. Some critics think that Holden is trapped between childhood and adulthood. What do you make of this observation?
4. Does this book suggest to you any thoughts about the subject of insecurity and adjustment in high school or college (e.g., freshman, sophomore years, etc.)?
5. How would a more maternal and sensitive prostitute have made a difference?
6. How would a less self-centered and more sensitive Carl Luce have been able to help Holden?

As Warren French notes, Sally's own adjustment is still too precarious for her to be able to help Holden (112). Do French's observations make sense from the point of view of your own world? How do you interpret his critical observations?

EDWARDO: Sally has been taught to accept what is going on around her. She is threatened because Holden questions fundamentals of a world in which she is just beginning to find her way.

CATHY: She may have many of the same doubts as Holden does—it's too scary for her.

MIKE: We are taught to go along with what teachers and parents tell us. But we know that they are often wrong. But Sally isn't as personally affronted by these dishonesties as Holden—who is so sensitive.

SEXUAL CURIOSITY

The lonely adolescent's search for companionship through New York is intermingled with a considerable measure of sexual curiosity. Holden drives away the Wooten sexual guru, Carl Luce, with impertinent questions and manages to find his way into a hotel "full of perverts and morons." Students should discuss Holden's encounters, especially with Maurice and Sonny in terms of self-deception and unconscious motivation.

THE UNCHANGING WORLD OF CHILDHOOD

Throughout his erratic New York odyssey, sixteen-year-old Holden is sustained by the hope of being able to talk with Phoebe and by memories of Allie. Some critics point to the Indian Room at the Museum of Natural History as a symbol of the unchanging world of childhood to which Holden would like to cling, but which is an Eden that is gone forever. During their adolescence, our students are making similar transitions during which they are sustained by affection for memories of places and events that often date back to their early years. Through discussing Holden's experience, students can talk about and reflect on their own.

More Discussion Questions
1. Is Holden's enthusiasm for a childhood world, free of sordidness and sex, also a kind of death wish, as some critics have suggested? (The Indians are immutable, but long dead. Allie is forever a lovable child, frozen in time by death; Holden is thinking about Egyptian mummies from early on in the book, etc.)
2. Why is Holden drawn to the nuns, Phoebe, Allie, and other children?
3. What do you make of the "Catcher" fantasy?
4. Would you say that his idealization of Allie helps to save him or contributes to his failures?
5. To what degree do you identify with some of Holden's feelings?

MOVIE FANTASIES

Holden also finds refuge in movie fantasies, even though he expresses a sophisticated disdain for popular movies such as the one he sees at Radio City Music Hall. He also expresses a currently fashionable adult viewpoint when he tells the reader that D. B. has "prostituted" himself by going to Hollywood as a writer. But when he is bored or troubled, he slips into a movie fantasy (e.g., when Stradlater is shaving and he is worried about Jane). After he is cruelly beaten by Maurice, Holden escapes into a movie fantasy of himself as a dying gangster. Later, this "bullet in the gut" fantasy recurs late at night in a bar when he is very drunk, lonely, and depressed. The next day, thoughts of James Castle's escape through suicide lead him to imagine a movie version of his own funeral. As students are discussing the contradictions in Holden's relationship to movies, they may also wish to discuss the question of whether TV and movie fantasies contribute to arrested development or simply constitute another dimension of healthy adolescent fantasy life.

THE ANTOLINI EPISODE

Holden's emotional collapse seems to follow quickly after the ambiguous Antolini episode. The exhausted Holden scarcely seemed to understand the advice offered by his favorite English teacher. He needs help and a safe refuge far more than advice. But, the father figure who could save him turns out to be just another shabby adult, and seemingly, a sexually threatening adult. Ironically, as William Wiegand observes, "Mr. Antolini has represented the last bastion of moral conscience" (12).

More Questions
1. Does Mr. Antolini give Holden any advice that you would consider good or useful, in terms of your own experience?
2. How accurate is his analysis of Holden's plight?
3. What clues does Salinger give the reader to foreshadow the petting incident?
4. Isn't the discovery that some respected adults have feet of clay a normal part of the process of growing up?

SUSAN: Our teachers have failings, but not many are like Antolini.

CATHY: But what about all we are hearing these days about child abuse by trusted adults—and the victims keep silent?

JACK: The point is that a trusted friend who is also a teacher does something that is the last straw in shattering his world. Mr. Antolini is the one person who always did the right thing in the past—like covering James Castle.

BILL: I guess he *was* a last bastion. It's all downhill for Holden after this.

MARGARET: But the whole event could have been innocent on Antolini's part. He is so drunk! And Holden is so paranoid and spaced out. Maybe Antolini thought he was patting his dog's head.

PHOEBE AND HOLDEN'S SALVATION?

Holden has retreated so fully into his childhood memories that he goes to his beloved park late in the winter night in a drunken, unsuccessful search for the ducks of summer. As the water in his hair freezes and the "Shirley Bean" record falls and shatters, the park appears to be a strange and forbidding place.

This theme of secret fantasy worlds of childhood versus reality is further developed in the closely related scene at the apartment with Phoebe. As Holden shares his fantasy of Wordsworthian escape with Phoebe, she begins to change his thinking by trying to join him. She sits like a Buddha in the middle of her bed and shares some adult common sense with her brother. "Allie is dead," she tells him. Also, the story of the mercy killing, "Daddy will kill you" and Phoebe's covering her head with a pillow, are clearly symbolic. Students will want to make sense of them in their own way. Little Phoebe seems to be able to do for Holden what Mr. Antolini or any other adult could not. This little mother listens as he pours out his troubles and then reasons with him. She also gives him her Christmas money, prescribes aspirin and takes the blame for his smoking. Students should be encouraged to analyze the changes in Holden that occur during these two closely related and climatic scenes: at home and the final scene in the park—and at the carousel.

More Questions
1. What is the best therapy that friends and family members can offer a young person trapped in emotional involvements that are history?
2. How much do we all live in our own past, real, fantasy, or idealized?
3. Is this both healthy and normal or does it impede emotional growth?

Here are some typical student responses to what the critics have said about Phoebe's role:

EDWARDO: I think she simply took the place of Allie. Holden and his younger brother were so close that I think when Allie died and Phoebe was no longer a baby, he focused his fantasies on her instead.

MELISSA: I think you're right; Holden's problem is that he lives in the past with the memories of Allie and refuses to get on with his life. Just because some people aren't as perfect as his dream of Allie, he has to crucify them. Holden is nothing but a spoiled kid in some respects.

INSTRUCTOR: You're saying Holden is immature mentally and that is why he looks to Phoebe?

JOHN: Yeah, I guess that's what I mean. Although he sometimes relates to adults well.

INSTRUCTOR: So he's only immature in some ways?

TONY: Yeah.

BILL: I can't buy all this immature garbage. Holden sees in Phoebe what seems to be lacking in the rest of the people he knows, a certain sense for the personal and the emotional, and Holden respects that. This lacking is the reason he got into a fight with Stradlater. Stradlater is supposed to be mature, but he didn't care about Jane as a person.

INSTRUCTOR: Why did Holden care so much about where the ducks went in the wintertime? What did that have to do with anything else in the book?

MIKE: That goes back to what I said before; he is ultra-sensitive to people and things. Why does he care about those ducks? Well, they are a part of life and Holden feels that if he cannot be concerned about them, who will be?

KATE: Yes, but Holden has a problem there because the ducks don't matter to most people.

CATHY: Yeah, but they do to him just as the forgotten people do.

As this excerpt suggests, teacher responses and questions must go with the flow of student thinking. Otherwise, students will begin to assume that the teacher is trying to fit them into a preconceived set of teacher solutions. If students begin to suspect that this is the case, then they will feel that we are not interested in their personal creative insights, that our reader-response discussion is fraudulent and they are really back to playing the same old depressing game of trying to read the teacher's mind. Consensus, and respectful dissent can only emerge from the exchange of really free discussion.

Final analyses of the book that are coherent for each individual student will have to take into account Holden's and the individual student's concept of phoniness—in the book and in life. Final questions might include: Holden's philosophy does contain a lot about what is phony and what is real. To what degree do you agree with him?

BILL: He refuses to accept societal norms as genuine and questions them. He doesn't believe you should put on a show or a mask to try and impress someone, which is the way it should be. People should accept you for what you are. I agree with him.

MELISSA: I admit that he is trying to live up to an ideal. He wants a perfect, safe world. But he doesn't understand that people have flaws and how to find his way in the world.

ANDREA: I don't necessarily believe in that quote that Mr. Antolini gave him and I don't think Salinger buys it all that much either. It's too easy.

INSTRUCTOR: You're referring to the Wilhelm Stekel quote, "The mark of the immature man is that he wants to die nobly for a cause, while the mark of the mature man is that he wants to live humbly for one"?

JOHN: Yeah. That's too conservative a message. And plus if Salinger wanted us to take that to heart, he wouldn't have had Holden become so disillusioned with Mr. Antolini.

MIKE: But maybe Salinger is showing us that in youth we don't listen, but have to learn on our own.

MARGARET: But at the end of the book does Holden say, "You know, I think I'm going to live humbly for a cause"? No. He looks at his sister and realizes that he cannot live for every cause or for every person. And remember, he is telling this story in retrospect.

INSTRUCTOR: Is Holden being too critical?

SUSAN: I think so. There are times when you need to bend a little. He has to grow up and learn to live with other people's limitations or he cannot survive and be happy in the world.

EDWARDO: I admit that he is a pretty extreme case, but he is simply developing a philosophy and refuses to bend on what he feels is the right thing to do. This causes his collapse.

JOHN: I think he's gifted with insight into people. He is a creative and very sensitive kid who needs to learn that everyone is not as perceptive as he is. Holden will still fight for his opinions. I feel that he will get important things done without compromising his principles.

Conflicting student viewpoints will often go beyond the text and into the realm of speculation. In reader-response criticism, this is legitimate if it is integral to the individual student's achievement of a coherent perspective on the book by taking into account what is indeterminate in the text.

CONCLUSION

In the summaries I have attempted to emphasize the ambiguous and often contradictory nature of the textual evidence and the critical commentary. These ambiguities, inconsistencies, and contradictions enable individual students to deconstruct the text for themselves and then construct their own unique reader responses. Thus, reader-response discussion and writing can go in many directions. At the same time, students' common convictions and similar backgrounds provide a basis for building a considerable degree of class consensus in the readings of particular texts and for the whole book. Such discussion, argument and eventual agreements are a great deal more creative and interesting for both teacher and students than the old, "canned" New Critical mode of "teaching" official interpretations, which students merely memorized for tests. Original journal entries, essays, and class arguments from the text, seen in the light of personal experience, now reveal how deeply a particular student has read and thought.

REFERENCES

Corbett, Edward P. J. "Raise High the Barriers, Censors." *America* civ. (January 7, 1961): 441–443.

French, Warren. *J. D. Salinger*. Twayne Series, Revised. Riverside, NJ: G. K. Hall, 1976.

Probst, Robert E. "Response and Analysis in the Teaching of Literature." In *Passages to Literature*. Ed. Joseph Milner and Lucy Milner. Urbana, IL: National Council of Teachers of English, 1989. 3–16.

Rosenblatt, Louise M. *Literature as Exploration* 4th ed. New York: Modern Language Association, 1983.

Salinger, J. D. *The Catcher in the Rye*. New York: Bantam Books, 1964.

Strauch, Carl F. "King in the Back Row: Meaning Through Structure, A Reading of Salinger's *The Catcher in the Rye*," Wisconsin Studies in Contemporary Literature II (Winter 1961): 5–30.

Weigand, William. "J. D. Salinger's Seventy-Eight Bananas." *Chicago Review XI* (Winter 1958): 3–19.

CHAPTER 15

A Writing-to-Learn/Reader-Response Approach to Teaching *Antigone*

Duane H. Roen

I must begin with a confession. When I was a senior in Clair Stein's humanities class at Baldwin-Woodville High School, Wisconsin, in the spring of 1967, we studied Sophocles' *Antigone*. By the time I had finished reading the play, I fantasized that I could save Antigone from her cursed fate if I were to marry her. Since then, every time I have read or seen or taught the play, I have had flashbacks to those romantic adolescent dreams. I also have them every time I drive by the Antigone Bookstore at the intersection of Fifth Street and Fourth Avenue in Tucson—something that happens several times each week.

I've chosen to write about *Antigone* in this chapter because my own experiences with the play suggest that it, more than most works of literature, evokes strong emotional responses in those who read or see it—responses that can serve as foundations for in-depth study of the work.

I also have chosen to offer a writing-to-learn approach (WTL), as described by Anne Ruggles Gere in *Roots in the Sawdust: Writing to Learn Across the Disciplines* and by Stuart Brown, Robert Mittan, and Duane Roen in *Becoming Expert: Writing and Learning in the Disciplines*. In a nutshell writing-to-learn approaches, as I demonstrate throughout this chapter, encourage people to use writing as a tool for learning—for making sense of the world. The focus is on learning, not on learning to write as it is in composition classrooms. Learning to write may be a by-product of writing to learn, but it is not the primary goal.

Writing-to-learn strategies work especially well in conjunction with the kinds of reader-response strategies that Louise Rosenblatt offers in *Literature as Exploration* and *The Reader, the Text, the Poem* because they encourage readers to respond individually

I must thank Robert Mittan and Nicholas Karolides for their comments on earlier draft versions of this chapter. I also thank Louise Rosenblatt for offering the profession, decades before anyone else did, wonderfully useful strategies for making literature come alive. We are all indebted to her.

and privately *before* choosing how to respond publicly, particularly in a classroom filled with peers.

BIOPOEMS

I begin with the *biopoem,* one of the most effective and versatile of the many writing-to-learn activities available. This activity has been a mainstay at National Writing Project sites since at least 1981, but it was formally institutionalized by Gere (222) and later by Brown, Mittan, and Roen (46–50). The form looks like this:

Line 1: First name

Line 2: Four traits that describe character

Line 3: Relative of _____

Line 4: Lover of _____ (list several people or things)

Line 5: Who feels _____ (several things)

Line 6: Who needs _____ (several things)

Line 7: Who fears _____ (several things)

Line 8: Who gives _____ (several things)

Line 9: Who would like to see _____ (several things)

Line 10: Resident of _____

Line 11: Last name

When I use the biopoem, I first use it as an autobiographical poem to give students a chance to introduce themselves to everyone in the class. Of course, as I introduce the form to them, I write one about myself on the board for several reasons: (a) so they can see their teacher modeling the activity; (b) so they can get to know and feel comfortable with their teacher early in the course; and (c) so they can see their teacher struggle to produce a draft of something. The last reason is important because students often hold the myth that English teachers always write perfectly formed, complete discourse on the first attempt. My completed autobiographical poem might look like this:

Duane,
a Norwegian, a nerd, a romantic, an optimist
father of Nicholas James and Hanna Elizabeth
who loves playing shortstop, listening to *A Prairie Home
    Companion,* and restoring antique furniture
who feels sometimes overworked, often tired, but usually
    optimistic
who needs more time to work, to parent, and to recreate
who fears that he will outlive his children, that true
    success will elude him, and that the world's problems
    will persist
who gives lots of time to his students, too little to his
    children, and his best whenever he can

who would like to see all of his ancestors, an end to all suffering
   in the world, and a happy ending to the Oedipus Cycle
resident of one of the warmest cities in the United States,
Roen

Notice that I have used this opportunity to show students that I'm a lot like them; I'm not without frailties and have a full range of emotions. I've also noted that I have a particular emotional stake in *Antigone,* the play that we will soon study. On the day that we do these autobiographical poems, as many students as possible and who are willing, will read their autobiographical poems to the class. And, members of the class will respond using a procedure borrowed from Peter Elbow (76–99) and modified by others, including Richard Koch and Bill Lyons. It works this way. After you've read some of your writing to your readers (or they've read it themselves), ask them first to tell you two or three things they identified with in the writing. That is, have them tell you how their experiences relate to those described in the piece of writing. Second, ask them to tell you several features of the writing that they liked. Third, have them ask questions to clarify points from your writing. Fourth, encourage them to offer suggestions for improving the writing.

It may help your readers if you go so far as to give them part of the wording for responding:

- I identify with . . .
- I like . . .
- I have these questions: . . .
- I suggest . . .

This procedure works successfully for training readers because it accommodates the needs of both the writers and their readers so well. The first step in the procedure, identification, allows a reader to establish a sense of community with the writer. Writers need to feel confident that everyone in the room is concerned about their and everyone else's welfare. The second step, relating approval, gives a reader a chance to reinforce the writer's sense of self-worth. This is very important because too many inexperienced writers have endured a decade or more of abusive comments aimed at their writing. Once these first two procedures have made both writers and readers feel comfortable with the transaction, the third step, the questions, will work to show writers that they may not have quite met readers' needs. It helps writers see ways of translating what Carnegie Mellon University writing scholars Linda Flower and John Hayes call "writer-based prose" (writing that meets the *writer's* needs and/or that makes sense to the writer) into "reader-based prose" (writing that also meets *readers'* needs and/or that makes sense to readers). Answering these questions helps writers understand that although readers can read words on paper, readers cannot read the writers' mind. The fourth step, asking for suggestions, if it were not preceded by the first three, would be difficult for both writers and readers; it's not always easy to either offer or accept suggestions. But because it follows the first three steps, writers and their readers trust each other enough to feel comfortable with suggestions. Incidentally, I've found that carefully guiding readers through the first three steps makes the fourth step unnecessary, especially if readers are encouraged to ask a sufficient number of questions at step three.

I describe and explain this response procedure here because I think that it teaches students to respond to others' written and oral classroom work in a constructive, respectful way. As a result, I have found, students feel secure about offering ideas to the class. Of course, later responses are not limited to this four-step procedure, but I think that it is an important starting point for group discussion.

Once the class has begun to read *Antigone,* each student writes a biopoem for some character in the play. The poem might be biographical, or it might be autobiographical, with each student assuming the persona of a character. In either case, students usually choose the title character. A biopoem about Antigone might look like this:

Antigone,
resolved, brave, ill-fated
daughter of Oedipus and Jocasta
who loved her dead brothers, Polyneices and Eteocles,
     and who loves her sister, Ismene, and her betrothed
     Haemon
who feels loyalty to both of her brothers, contempt
     for her uncle Creon, and lots of sorrow
who needs a resolution to a paradoxical problem and
     greater reason
who fears the fate of the unburied Polyneices and the curse
     on her family
who gives her love freely and her life foolishly
who would like to see a family history free of curse
resident of Thebes in Greece
_____.

When this student reads this biopoem to her classmates, they can respond in all sorts of ways. They might, for example, use the aforementioned four-step procedure. Or, one of them might say something like, "My biopoem is a lot like yours. Let me read it now." Alternatively, someone might say, "My poem is a much different portrait of Antigone. Here's how I see her." In any event, it's easy to see how this writing-to-learn activity can lead to much discussion. What's best about this exercise, and other WTL activities as well, is the way it allows individual students to respond privately to Antigone or to Creon, Ismene, Polyneices, Eteocles, or Eurydice. In contrast, by responding to literature orally without benefit of writing about it first, some students never have an opportunity to voice much of a response—because of timidity or because someone else has already said it more eloquently.

The biopoem is particularly useful in Rosenblatt's terms because "the reader must remain faithful to the text. He [she] must be alert to the clues concerning character and motive present in the text" (*Literature* 11). When students read this or another biopoem to their classmates, they can respond by pointing out how they found and used other clues. Furthermore, when several students have read their biopoems about Antigone, more and more clues are offered for consideration. Students can then debate and perhaps come to a consensus about how to interpret various clues. Then, as Rosenblatt suggests, each student "will then be led to revise or broaden his initial tentative assumptions" (*Literature* 12); however, each original biopoem still exists as a partial record of each student's thinking.

UNSENT LETTERS

Another favorite WTL activity is the unsent letter, thoroughly described in Gere (227) and in Brown, Mittan, and Roen (54–56). The name of this activity tells much about it. Each student in the class writes a letter. Students may keep their own persona to write a letter to Antigone, for example. Other students may assume the persona of Oedipus, writing to his daughter from beyond the grave. Still other students, taking the persona of Ismene, may write to her sister to try to accomplish what she could not achieve in oral pleading. Yet another group of students, keeping their own persona, may write to Sophocles to urge him to change the ending of the play because they like happy endings. Each of these letters, of course, must remain unsent because the "receivers" of them are either dead or fictional. If I had known about unsent letters when I read *Antigone* in high school, I might have written the following letter:

February 14, 1967

Antigone
The Palace of Creon
Thebes, Greece 32200

Dearest Antigone,

I love you, Antigone. I have loved you since I first met you when I read the play that Sophocles wrote about you and your family. Since then, I have not been able to sleep or eat because of my great longing for you. I want to take you away from Creon and Thebes and Greece so that you can live in happiness—a happiness that your family's curse will not allow. If you will let me marry you and take you from that wretched place, I will find a way to bury your dear brother Polyneices. I will find a way. And if I should get caught burying your brother, I will gladly face the consequences, knowing that you will live, if not in happiness, then in peace.

    Please listen to me, Antigone, for I love you more than anyone else does or could—even Haemon, your betrothed. Together, you and I can put your life back in order.

With a longing heart,

Duane

    Of course, eighteen-year-old Duane, on an emotional binge, ignores some details from the play—especially that Antigone's fate, like the fate of every descendent of Oedipus, is a horrible one that can't be altered. Still, his emotional response to the work— one that he might risk because he is secure in the privacy of writing—is a strong place to begin working on other, more intellectual considerations of the work. Moreover, my teaching experience tells me that students who take such risks in writing are often willing to share that writing with classmates if the class has the kind of supportive atmosphere that I've been describing throughout this chapter.

Unsent letters also work well because the letter form encourages writers to consider audience more carefully as they write. The act of writing the salutation in a letter helps to focus attention on the addressee—and, in this case, a particular literary character. In addition, the salutation helps the writer adopt the persona of someone actually addressing that character. Characters seem more "alive."

One extension of this activity that uses letters more fully is to encourage students to exchange letters and write replies. For example, if my student Tim assumes the person of Haemon to write to Antigone, I will encourage Eileen, who has assumed the persona of the title character, to exchange letters with Tim. The exchanges can go on for some time, and they can lead to ever-deepening understanding of the character involved.

Of course, at times I will encourage students to share their letters and their exchanges of letters with the class; I may even duplicate some for the class. The resulting classroom discussions can be vigorous and engaging. Each "reader's contribution in the two-way, 'transactional' relationship with the text" (Rosenblatt, *Reader* ix) becomes obvious to everyone in the room because the letter form makes it so explicit. (For more on matters of audience, see Kirsch and Roen.)

JOURNAL/LEARNING LOG WRITINGS

In addition to the activities that I've already described, I have other favorite WTL activities designed to help students respond to literature in such a way that they begin to see literature as related to human experience. Recommended as journal/learning log writings, the following activities, like those already described, enable students to read more carefully and to understand characters, events, settings, and other features of literature more fully. Here's how I word them for students:

1. If a passage or scene strikes some chord in you, stop to freewrite about it. You might start with the emotional response that the passage or scene evokes.
2. Write a hypothetical conversation that you might have with a character. You might tell that character about another character's actions or thoughts. You might warn that character about upcoming events in the novel. You might counsel the character to act in a certain way. You might tell how the character misunderstands events or characters in the novel.
3. Write a hypothetical conversation between two characters.
4. List personality traits of each character.
5. Write a letter to the author telling what you like and dislike about the literary work.
6. Place a character in a setting not found in the literary work. Describe how the character would act in that new setting. Explain why the character would act that way.
7. Pretend that you will make a film from the literary work. How would you cast the film? Where would you shoot it? What sorts of shots (camera angle, distance, lens) would you use for some particular scene(s)?

8. List questions that occur to you as you read or after you have read. Bring those questions to class for discussion.
9. Does this literary work remind you of other works of literature? Or does some character or some issue remind you of others? If so, describe the similarities.
10. Write a dialogue in which you introduce a character to a friend of yours.
11. Take a special interest that you have—your major or a hobby, for example. Use some system of analysis from that special interest to analyze some feature of the literary work. This approach might easily lead directly to a critical essay, by the way.
12. Take on the persona of a character; write a diary entry.
13. Use metaphors to describe a character, setting, or conflict.
14. Retell the story to a child and/or an adult who hasn't read the literary work.
15. Make a time-line for the story.
16. Rewrite the story into a soap opera.

TOPICS FOR CLASSROOM DISCUSSION AND CRITICAL ESSAYS

To help teachers find ways to translate these pieces of writing into classroom discussion and, in some cases, critical essays, I offer the following strategies:

1. You might ask several students to read entries at the beginning of class. Those entries might serve as the basis for that day's discussion. Of course, you will need to plan to use specific kinds of entries to generate specific kinds of discussions.
2. You might ask students to do a specific kind of entry before they come to class. At the beginning of class, in large group, you will give students very specific instructions for using the entries in small groups.
3. You might respond in writing to certain entries to help students see how the entries can lead to their critical essays. Here, of course, you may use both comments and questions.
4. You might ask questions in students' logs to encourage them to do certain kinds of additional entries.
5. You might use the last five minutes of class to have students synthesize the day's discussion.
6. You might ask students to write log entries to summarize or synthesize the work they did in small groups on a particular day.
7. You might ask two students to exchange logs to respond to each other's entries.

CONCLUSION

As the teacher, I try to assume several roles in the vigorous and engaging discussions that result from these discussions. First, of course, I do what I can to establish and encourage a supportive atmosphere. That is, I must be as supportive as I can by showing my interest, by offering positive feedback, by making certain that everyone in the room knows the groundrules for the discussion, and by expecting everyone else to be supportive. I also demonstrate my support by doing whatever writing my students do—especially the writing that they do in class. My second role is to become one of the learners in the class when we discuss anything. In this second role, I ask questions and offer comments just as students do. My responses are no more or less valuable than anyone else's. Of course, I have to step out of this role once in a while when discussions go awry—because someone decides to be hurtful or because someone wants to dominate the conversation. I don't have to do this very often, though.

I am convinced that writing-to-learn activities do much to enhance "aesthetic" reading, in which, as Rosenblatt asserts, "the reader's primary concern is with what happens *during* (emphasis hers) the actual reading event" (*Reader* 24). These WTL activities encourage so much self-reflective thought that they help the reader ensure that his or her "*attention is centered directly on what he [she] is living through during his [her] relationship with that particular text*" (25, her italics)—in this case, *Antigone*. The reader "fixes his [her] attention on the actual experience he [she] is living through. This permits the whole range of responses generated by the text to enter into the center of awareness, and out of these materials he [she] selects and weaves what he [she] sees as the literary work of art" (*Reader* 26–27). Writing is a powerful tool for learning because it "involves an *active reconstruction* of the knowledge or skill that is presented" to the learner (Wells 118). In this model teachers find ways to encourage students to use writing for exploring and reflecting on course content—again, in this case, *Antigone*. Students become more responsible for their learning, and they must work more diligently and think more critically. The teachers does not need to practice all of the skills of a writing teacher—very few of them, in fact. The teacher also does not make curricular sacrifices. I believe, as the Soviet psychologist Lev Vygotsky did that "thought is not merely expressed in words; it comes into existence through them" (218).

Students who use their own written words to study *Antigone* and to prepare for class discussions of the play find that their thoughts about the dramatic work do come into existence through that writing. Furthermore, their written responses to the characters and events in *Antigone* give them a sense of ownership for their thoughts, for they are there, permanently, on the page, ready to be considered again and again and again.

REFERENCES

Brown, Stuart C., Robert K. Mittan, and Duane H. Roen. *Becoming Expert: Writing and Learning in the Disciplines.* Dubuque, IA: Kendall/Hunt, 1990.

Elbow, Peter. *Writing Without Teachers.* New York: Oxford University Press, 1973.

Flower, Linda, and John Hayes. "Plans That Guide the Composing Process." In *Writing: The Nature, Development, and Teaching of Written Communication: Vol. 2. Writing: Process, Development, and Communication.* Ed. C. H. Frederiksen and J. F. Dominic, Hillsdale, NJ: Lawrence Erlbaum, 1981. 39–58.

Gere, Anne Ruggles, ed. *Roots in the Sawdust: Writing to Learn Across the Disciplines.* Urbana, IL: National Council of Teachers of English, 1985.

Kirsch, Gesa, and Duane H. Roen, eds. *A Sense of Audience in Written Communication.* Newbury Park, CA: Sage, 1990.

Koch, Richard. "Syllogisms and Superstitions: The Current State of Responding to Writing." *Language Arts* 59 (1982): 464–471.

Lyons, Bill. "Well What Do You Like About My Paper." *Iowa English Newsletter* (Sept. 1978): 4–5.

Rosenblatt, Louise M. *Literature as Exploration.* 4th ed. New York: Modern Language Association, 1983.

———. *The Reader, the Text, the Poem: The Transactional Theory of the Literary Work.* Carbondale, IL: Southern Illinois University Press, 1978.

Sophocles. *Antigone. Oedipus the King and Antigone.* Trans. and Ed. Peter D. Arnott. New York: Appleton-Century-Crofts, 1960.

Vygotsky, Lev S. *Thought and Language.* 1934. Trans. Eugenia Hanfmann and Gertrude Vakar. Cambridge, MA: MIT Press, 1962.

Wells, Gordon. *The Meaning Makers: Children Learning Language and Using Language to Learn.* Portsmouth, NH: Heinemann, 1986.

PART IV

Exploring Differences: Gender, Race, and Culture

The dynamics of personal and cultural experiences as they affect readers' transactions are the focus of the chapters in this section. The authors examine the distancing effected by gender, race, and culture and exemplify strategies that open students to texts. These strategies include an exploration of the evoked responses, a reflection on the factors and processes that influenced the reading.

The process of exploring the evoked response is itself a learning experience. It cultivates a habit of mind that is provocatively thoughtful and democratic. Classroom dynamics stimulate the expression and recognition of multiple viewpoints and cause readers to further reconsider their own knowledge, ideas, and belief structures. In this context, bridges of understanding to characters and cultures are built.

Reader-response approaches are particularly well suited to teaching feminist and ethnic literature. Teachers, who themselves may be "outsiders," need not place themselves in a position of authority, expressing the "correct" interpretation. And, instead of being outsiders peering in, students may undertake to assume the persona of the character in the text. This allows those outside the gender or ethnic group depicted in the text to become momentary insiders and those inside the gender or ethnic group to validate their own experiences.

In Chapter 16, Laura Quinn expresses the nature of "gendered reading" and develops comprehension of the orientation of such female and male readings in response to Susan Glaspell's "feminist" drama *Trifles*. Through class interactions and journal writing she provides opportunities for the "evolution and elaboration" of these preliminary responses. Quinn identifies two intervention strategies she uses to help students understand the gendered nature of their responses and reflect on their implications. The description of the preliminary and the evolving responses demonstrates the progressive transaction with the text engendered by such class collaboration: the responses become "more complex and less closed in their understanding."

At the center of Chapter 17 is the concept of the reader as outsider. In order to help his students gain access to two native American novels, David Furniss asks them to identify problems and questions they face as readers in responding to experiences far removed from their own. His focus is on opening their reactions to the text and exploring these as a means of getting closer to the events and characters. He describes a reading journal strategy accomplished in class (and two other failed attempts) that generates personal reactions revealing the students' outsider perspective. He projects the discussion of these journal entries, highlighting the focus of the students' concerns and their wide divergence of opinions. He notes that the subsequent response to the novels was closer to characters and their world—"close enough to be able to talk to other outsiders *and* insiders about them in a way they might not have been able to before."

The monologue exercise that Ogle Duff processes in Chapter 18 helps students to experience literature through involvement. Aiming to create empathy and a deeper understanding of black–white relationships, she asks her students to visualize themselves, by role playing as Langston Hughes's African-American hobo hero of "On the Road." The range of their monologue responses—the degree that they can participate in the character's persona—is illustrated as is their assessment of the experience. The classroom procedure of reading the monologues aloud and the ensuing discussion reflects the students' willingness to talk about their perceptions of the character as well as their own ability to relate to him. Duff offers several warm-up activities to use with students at different levels to get them ready to engage with the experience of such texts.

In Chapter 19, Jean E. Brown and Louise Garcia Harrison illustrate the range of responses to Theodore Roethke's "My Papa's Waltz" and discuss the influence of personal and social contexts on the transactions of readers. Two methods of involving students are explained—an oral brainstorming approach and a written journal activity. The discussion that follows expresses the students' recognition of multiple perspectives as well as how and why there have been varied responses.

CHAPTER 16

Trifles as Treason:
Coming to Consciousness as a Gendered Reader

Laura Quinn

In *Literature as Exploration* Louise M. Rosenblatt described one of the aims of her reader-response approach to literature in the following manner:

> If the student's structure of attitudes and ideas is built on too narrow a base of experience, he [she] should be helped to gain broader and deeper insight through literature itself. That is why throughout this discussion the emphasis has been on the interaction between the reader and the text. When the reader becomes aware of the dynamic nature of that interaction, he [she] may gain some critical consciousness of the strengths or weaknesses of the emotional and intellectual equipment with which he [she] approaches literature (and life). Since he [she] interprets the book or poem in terms of his [her] fund of past experiences, it is equally possible and necessary that he [she] come to reinterpret his old sense of things in the light of this new literary experience, in the light of the new ways of thinking and feeling offered by the work of art. Only when this happens has there been a full interplay between book and reader, and hence a complete and rewarding literary experience. (107)

I find this statement of purpose to be of use to me, consistently and paradigmatically as I employ a reader-response approach in my literature classes. It is particularly applicable to the project of encouraging gendered reading—reading that acknowledges all of the cultural bases and biases of gender on the part of the reader—among students who have never consciously regarded themselves as gendered readers and may well resist doing so. One way to bring students to such consciousness is to begin a literature course with a discussion of the first statement in the previous Rosenblatt passage. Generally students "have no quarrel" with the statement and are often interested in naming, listing, writing about (in a journal assignment or an in-class impromptu) the elements of their past experience that they believe they bring to the reading of a literary text. The products of such an exercise, written or oral, will, of course, contain gendered components (as well as those marked by race, ethnicity, and class) that the students themselves can readily identify as categories under which their past experience can be organized. The process of situating themselves as readers sets the stage for the kind of self-conscious and reflective reading that a reader-response approach demands.

As Rosenblatt indicates in the passage quoted, however, the situating of oneself as a reader must be a dynamic process if learning is to take place. Indeed, the very purpose of identifying oneself as, for example, a white male middle-class reader with a strong work ethic and a Christian belief system, is to be enabled to "gain some critical consciousness of the strength and weaknesses of the emotional and intellectual equipment with which he approaches literature (and life)."

What I wish to achieve in the classroom when using a reader-response approach to a text is students' understanding of both the conditional nature of their response(s) to a text and the potential for evolution and elaboration of those responses as a result of interaction with the responses of others, intervention by the instructor, of time, reflection, and rereading. A text that I have found particularly valuable in achieving these ends is Susan Glaspell's 1916 play, *Trifles* (or its short story version "A Jury of Her Peers"). *Trifles* raises close-to-the-bone gender issues to which any student can respond, but it also raises those issues in a problematic way that discourages (eventually if not initially) reductive readings, simplistic analyses, and premature responsive closure. It is a short and accessible text, one that can be taught so as to produce the "full interplay between book and reader" celebrated by Louise Rosenblatt.

Judith Fetterley calls *Trifles* a story about reading in which "the theory of reading proposed in it is explicitly linked to the issue of gender" (147). It is because this text is "about" gendered reading that it can be used to get students to look at as well as to engage in gendered reading. Such reading (or the consciousness of such reading) will not take place without careful strategizing on the part of the teacher. Perhaps more than any other theoretical approach to texts, in my experience, the reader-response strategy works best in the classroom when it becomes both a highly permissive and a highly self-conscious approach—an approach that (initially) turns students loose on a text and admits almost any response as potentially interesting, while, at the same time, pulling back regularly and rigorously to examine variant responses, feel for their roots, and evaluate not their correctness or usefulness, but rather their relation to text, to classroom, to responder, and to a larger social context.

More concretely, when students claim at the start, for example, (as some, mostly male students do when I teach *Trifles*) that the play is a bore, it is important and productive to credit that response with some authenticity and plausibility by posing the question (which may not be answerable until much later in the discussion but can be posed at the time of the response) of why and to whom this particular text might seem initially boring. The text may bore more men than women, the text may bore dominant readers[1] (such readers are often bored by the texts they dominate), and, less obviously, the text may bore not only those who have been culturally programmed to resist it but also and especially those against whom the text's treason (to be discussed later) is committed. In short, boredom may be a logical defensive response that can be illuminated rather than trashed in class discussion and one that can, thus, enrich the class's experience of the text.

I have taught *Trifles* repeatedly in two quite different courses; one is an introductory college-level sophomore literature course on Tragedy as a literary tradition and the other is a lower-division, interdisciplinary team-taught Women's Studies course called Women and the Arts. In each case I have learned that student response will be marked by gender and my position as an unabashedly feminist woman teacher colors student discussion responses in a variety of ways, sometimes eliciting resistance or, alternatively, obedient party-line responses; sometimes creating inhibition; occasionally authorizing the exploration of new ideas. Of course, the fact that the Women and the Arts students are generally around 80 percent female while the Tragedy class tends to be evenly divided has an important impact on the group interaction to *Trifles* and on the way in which each group interaction brings about revision or revamping of a student's initial response to the text. It is important to note here that this approach to teaching this or other texts need not, indeed should not, be limited to the college classroom; at any level at which literature is taught, students have some sense of who they are in terms of gender identity and can be encouraged to see this as an ingredient in their reading strategies.

INITIAL RESPONSES TO THE TEXT

My early (pre-reader response) experience with teaching Glaspell's one-act play was less than successful, largely because I did not yet know how to move students beyond their initial response to the text. Often many male and female student readers first respond with comments that the text is obsolete, a period piece. The following reading journal reaction of a male student is typical:

> As for importance, I see nothing but a play about sex roles. This had its time and place, but things are to the point where such stressings are a bit outdated.

The "that was then and this is now" response often leads to discussions consisting of anecdotal evidence of the state of gender equality in the here and now or to extended arguments (often conducted along gender lines) as to whether women's experience "then" and "now" is appreciably different. Although such discussions are often heated and interesting, they do not serve the purpose of developing and refining students' response to the text. In fact they are, I believe, a way of avoiding some of the more disturbing implications of *Trifles*. Still, I needed to learn, as the teacher in a reader-response context, to let these discussions have some play, to let students work their way through them, rather than obeying my impulse to correct and abort such a focus.

The other typical initial response to *Trifles* (as recorded in reading journals or proffered in class discussion) and one that, again, is shared at least in emphasis by both male and female readers is a strong tendency to focus on the events that precede the play as what the play is "about." *Trifles* centers on solving a murder mystery—which isn't much of a mystery because all the characters believe (whether eagerly or reluctantly) that Minnie Wright killed her husband John by strangling him in bed in their isolated farmhouse. As official and officious male characters—the Sheriff and the County Attorney—search for significant clues to motive and to the larger picture of the crime, tag-along women—Mrs. Hale and Mrs. Peters—are assigned the task of gathering Minnie Wright's "things" to take to her in jail. The women, in their preoccupation with domestic trifles, discover the salient clues to Minnie Wright's guilt and motive (the erratic stitching of a quilt-piece, the strangled canary kept in a small ornate box) while the men, who don't look in the right places, are stymied. In an extraordinary act of sisterhood and solidarity, the two stolid and conventional women (Mrs. Peters, indeed, the wife of the Sheriff) *conceal* the clues they find, protecting Minnie and thwarting the investigation. What takes place within the play's boundaries is a self-discovery on the part of both Mrs. Peters and Mrs. Hale (at different rates and perhaps to different degrees)—a discovery of themselves as gendered subjects whose identification with Minnie Wright makes clear to each of them that they are implicated in her crime inasmuch as they, too, have experienced the kind of anger toward men that must have precipitated her violence. The further—and truly treasonous—realization that they concur in the *justice* of Minnie Wright's action is what enables them to conceal evidence from "their" men.

It is not surprising that students gravitate toward the murder itself (which takes place outside of and prior to the play) rather than to the collaborative aiding and abetting on the part of "normal" characters. For one thing, students are trained by the popular mystery genre to focus on "whodunit" as the interesting issue in a murder story; though Minnie Wright's guilt is never substantively questioned in the play, students often want to read the text in ways that will rewrite it, exonerating Minnie. Additionally, the particular scenario is not an unfamiliar one in our culture; the rightness or wrongness of a woman murdering a cruel and abusive husband is a burning and current legal and moral issue, and it is thus natural that students will find their way to this discussion. More important, I believe, is the possibility that the behavior of Mrs. Hale and Mrs. Peters in concealing the "trifles" (the dead bird, the erratic stitching) is potentially far more threatening and more "treasonous" to established gender relations than is the murder itself. Students understandably reduce the text to the murder plot to avoid the implications of the "other crime," the one that takes place within the text's boundaries.

EVOLUTION AND ELABORATION OF THE TEXT

There is, then, this challenge for the teacher of *Trifles:* how does one elicit a *fuller* response to the text, one that looks not only at the "other" crime but also at the gendered nature of that crime and the gendered nature of responses to it, resistance to it, and fear of it. I have learned as I have attempted to meet this challenge that a process must be undergone in the classroom, a process in which we must collaboratively circle in on the text's complexities.

Although class discussion is the main vehicle of this process, I have found two other strategies essential: teacher intervention that illuminates the process at certain key points (identified and elaborated later in the chapter) is necessary, and short, written journallike individual responses at several different stages of the process can both get it started and get it unstuck along the way. Asking students to stop discussing at any point and to write for five minutes about what they are thinking of the text and of the issues under discussion *at this point* has many benefits: it can provide quiet students with a way into the discussion if they are asked to read their written response; it can help students "discover" what they are thinking; and, importantly, it legitimizes the process of revising one's initial response and encourages further revision.

As the discussion leader or facilitator, I had to learn to allow the inevitable (and, for me, frustrating) discussions of both the text's obsolescence and its "whodunit" preliminaries to take place for a bit with minimal intervention on my part. When this happens astute students realize that the issues in the pre-text (what Minnie Wright's marriage was like and what made her murder John) undermine the claim of obsolescence. In other words, a text that leads us to argue whether spouse abuse should be a legitimate legal defense in a husband murder—an issue still not resolved in our culture—can hardly be obsolete. This realization—at which I often don't have to assist at all—forces some students to regroup, to reconsider their frontal response to *Trifles,* thereby setting an important precedent for reconsideration of other responses they may have had to the text. What is important for me as teacher to do at this point is to acknowledge and recognize the process of response *revision* and to validate not the revised response but the act of revision itself. I point out to the class here that secondary or tertiary responses are both authentic and valuable; a short writing exercise that asks the students to record their present reading of the text seems appropriate here.

The pre-text discussion—that of the rightness or wrongness of the murder, the options that Minnie Wright did or didn't have—needs to play itself out further in most classes. Many male students and some strongly male-identified female students hold the view that murder is against the law, that no excuses can be made for it, that John Wright's strangling of Minnie's canary does not justify her strangling of him; a man is worth more than a bird. The following prediscussion journal response is characteristic of this response:

> I sympathize with Mrs. Wright to the degree of her problem but not with the killing of her husband. I believe that was too extreme of a measure to carry out. She could've sought consolation from neighboring wives or might have gone back to her family.

The clearly opposite view (and one that appears more spontaneously in the Women and the Arts class) is most often evinced by female readers and may fall short of condoning the murder but sees the provocation as sufficient morally if not legally, as this female student's journal entry implies:

> The most important thing in *Trifles* is the portrayal of how women put up with a lot more than they should have to then they can't take it anymore and bust or lose control. Mrs. Wright had been pushed to the limit and she couldn't take it anymore especially when her husband killed the bird, the only thing in her life that she could identify with.

Once these two positions surface in class discussion, sharp and impatient debate can break out, producing some interesting mediating strategies on the part of (mostly) female students who are uncomfortable with conflict in general and with conflict along gender lines in particular. The three mediating strategies that I have observed repeatedly are these:

1. Students return to the period piece argument that the play reflects the attitudes of earlier, less egalitarian times: "Women seemed to not be valued or given credit for being smart, functioning parts of society [then]."

2. The mediators complain that we don't get Minnie Wright's viewpoint, only sec-ond-hand piecing together of her story: "The only information given about John Wright was through the other characters. They interpreted and gave their indi-vidual views; but who is to say that they made fair judgments?"

3. Finally, we get the argument that the community of women as represented by Mrs. Hale and Mrs. Peters failed Minnie Wright. This views comes almost exclusively from female readers: "The men were callous and logical and reason-ing and careless of Mrs. Wright's house or life, and though the women were upset by the men's carelessness and they respected Mrs. Wright's house, privacy, and life, they too were still intruders and 'after the fact.' They should have visited her before."

These three mitigating and mediating responses represent a progressive transaction with the text: The first anxiously moves back to the comforting claim of the text's obsolescence, overlooking earlier discussion that effectively finished off this point; these mediators are resisting the demands of the text's complexity. The second position is a critique of the playwright's formal choice; it asks for a different play than the one written by Glaspell, but it has the merit of moving the discussion to the issue of why Glaspell made the choice she did to focus on Mrs. Hale and Mrs. Peters rather than on Minnie Wright. It, more than the first mediating response, opens discussion rather than closing it off. The third mediating response moves us clearly toward the play's cruces; it leads to the acknowledgment of separate, gendered spheres of activity and attitude as social phe-nomena and, it importantly shifts the focus from Minnie Wright's guilt or innocence to the events and concerns within the play's boundaries. The student's have "come to" the text and are ready to begin interaction with its complexity. It is crucial, however, that they see for themselves that the third strategy "gets us farther"; at this point we must step back from the substance of the discussion and engage in a critical examination of the reading strategies that have emerged. Here I generally record on the blackboard the reading strategies that they have generated (asking them to help me label the strategies; we might call the second one described earlier the "different play" strategy, for instance) and ask, simply, which gives us the most to talk about. The act of evaluating their own readings, interventions, and mediations reinforces the process of ongoing response revision and, in a larger sense, includes students as members of an interpretative community from which traditional pedagogies sometimes exclude them.

INTERVENTION STRATEGIES

After this collaborative effort to see where we are and how far we have come seems clear and complete to all of us, I intervene and appropriate the class discussion for a bit. I do so because I wish to describe for them what I believe they have just accomplished as readers/responders (they have sorted through a variety of responses, they have debated the text's timeliness, they have grappled with the pre-text), and to go on to put what they have done into a larger context.

The first part of my intervention relates their discussion of *Trifles* to that of other works we've read in the term. In the Tragedy class I ask them to think about the legalistic/relativistic debate over Minnie Wright's crime in light of the argument in *Antigone* between Antigone and Creon over her crime of burying her brother; I also refer them to the conflict between Nora and Krogstad in *A Doll's House* over the legality and morality of her act of forgery. I give a journal assignment here that asks them to compare and contrast their responses to those three crimes and to those three debates. In the Women and the Arts class, *Trifles* appears in an altogether different literary context, one that includes such texts as Ntozake Shange's *For Colored Girls Who Have Considered Suicide When the Rainbow Is Enuf*, Marge Piercy's "For Inez Garcia," Ann Petry's "Like a Winding Sheet," and Alice Walker's *The Color Purple*. These female-authored texts clearly construct a supportive context for *Trifles*, one that enables the wronged woman's perspective to be foregrounded and validated. Here, too, I ask students to engage in journal writing that measures comparatively their responses to the legal and moral issues raised in those works. It is not to load the dice that I intertextualize *Trifles* in this manner; my goal is to nudge readers into consciousness of their readerly responses to (possibly) parallel texts and to get them to bring those responses to the surface, to look at them both critically and with interest.

With such an aim still in mind, I present the second part of my intervention strategy, which is to briefly and broadly describe to the class, Carol Gilligan's findings in *In a Different Voice: Psychological Theory and Women's Development*. Gilligan's findings, summarized briefly and generally, were that male responses tend to be legalistic, rule-governed, and clearly resolved in terms of a winner and a loser. Female responses in Gilligan's study tend to be fluid, contextual, relational, and directed at somewhat fuzzier everyone-wins kinds of resolutions. I present a few of Gilligan's experimental narratives and the variant male and female responses to the moral issues raised in those narratives (e.g., should the husband whose dying wife is suffering from pain and who can't afford pain medicine steal it from the pharmacy?). I have two goals in mind in introducing Gilligan; I want students to apply her general findings on gender-specific behavior and attitudes to the "story" in *Trifles*, and I want them to consider the extent to which the discussion they've been engaged in and the responses they have experienced individually and as a group illustrate Gilligan's observations.

An interesting phenomenon occurs every time I do this in class: neither male nor female students question or deny that they have just acted out Gilligan's principles of differing gendered voices; they see that most of the female students have responded in a relational way to Minnie Wright's dilemma, sympathizing with the suffering that John Wright's cold, silent nature and his cruel strangling of her pet bird have caused her; they can see, as well, that the legalistic position—the one that must condemn Minnie Wright because she has violated the law, because she has disrupted the social order—has been put forward mostly by male students.

Of course there are important exceptions to this positioning by gender, and these must not be ignored in class discussion. Granting that for some female students the legalistic position is paramount whereas some male students adopt a more relational stance, we can still raise the question of whether culturally and socially constructed roles are consistent with the differences described by Gilligan. It is also important here, I believe, to introduce some of the difficulties that other theorists of difference (including feminists) have with Gilligan's categories and research methods (such as her focus on white middle-class subjects). Students tend to naturalize assumptions about gender very readily, and a vigilant, ongoing strategy of destabilization of assumptions needs to be undertaken, both to help them resist oversimplification of the complexities of gender as a category and to inculcate the principle of self-conscious examination of the tools of criticism that they are acquiring, even at very rudimentary levels.

At this point I ask them if they see parallels between the acts of interpretation—of "reading" the text—that they have engaged in and the investigations (both the formal one undertaken by the men in *Trifles* and the informal one that Mrs. Hale and Mrs. Peters find forced on them) of the murder scene in the play. This (admittedly leading) question is designed to get us to an understanding of what gendered reading consists of, as illustrated in parallel manner by both the text and by students' own experience with it.

Students are prepared now to see their own responses to *Trifles* as marked by gender and to continue to "read" the play with this consciousness. I ask them at this point to write again, briefly and in class, about their responses to the play and to focus this time not on Minnie Wright and the murder but on Mrs. Hale and Mrs. Peters and their "crime." Generally speaking, these responses become more complex than the initial responses to the play. Of course, this complexity is overdetermined; the class discussion itself, my introduction of Gilligan and reference to other texts they have read, the factor of time, and second thoughts discovered through writing, all contribute to the complexity of the advanced set of responses. Here are fairly typical female and male responses to this later writing task:

> FEMALE: The women, supposedly so weak-minded and incapable of mental feats, pieced together the motives for the murder quite compactly. The men, with their rough ways and unseeing eyes, missed everything. They probably would have misunderstood the dead bird that the women barely were able to conceal. The story seems sad to me in that it shows how squashed women are in a man's world, but it also shows how women can band together, help each other, and love each other. Concealing the evidence may not have been a pure gesture of love, but it was an act that probably saved the murderer's life.

> MALE: The Sheriff and County Attorney strike me as very simplistic in their attitudes and thinking and don't appeal to me at all. Mrs. Hale and Mrs. Peters I sort of identify with in a small way. I can see their need to be protective of "their own kind." From the beginning they have this attitude and maintain it to the end. The play shows two different opposing forces in the sexes.

What seems important to me in each of these revised responses is not whether they are "politically correct" from a feminist standpoint or closer to my view of the play than some of the earlier responses were, but they are more complex and less closed in their understanding. The female response implies (obliquely) that there may be more than one motive for the concealment of the dead bird. The male response advances this by noting that the sense of separate camps—"their own kind"—that pervades the play is important and may help to explain the actions of the two women characters.

CONCLUSION

It is, I believe, exceedingly difficult for students at ages eighteen to twenty to acknowledge and examine the "otherness" of men and women, not to speak of the problem of seeing that asymmetry and inequality have accompanied that otherness throughout history.

(Or, as Louise Rosenblatt notes in the passage that opened this essay, "the student's structure of attitudes and ideas is built on too narrow a base of experience.") *Trifles*, taught in a manner that validates reader response but also sees response as a fluid, developing phenomenon, can illuminate the issue of otherness in a powerful and convincing manner and can help to make students aware of their need for a more mature and sophisticated sense of otherness than their "structure of attitudes and ideas" has allowed them. Because the play is about "reading," it can also serve as a vehicle for bringing the reader-response approach into the classroom as a tool that students can use individually and collectively to make meaning from a text and to make meaning of their own experience in the interactive manner that Rosenblatt introduced to the world of literary criticism fifty years ago.

Lest I be oversanguine, however, I must acknowledge a resistance to *Trifles* on the part of (mostly) male readers—one that is difficult to overcome in the classroom transaction and finally needs to be assessed analytically by the class and allowed, perhaps, to remain unresolved. (This resistance is considerably less intransigent in the Women's Studies class than in the Tragedy class.) In her essay "Reading About Reading," Judith Fetterley sheds some light on the problem in reading *Trifles*. She argues that the play is about a text, the text of Minnie Wright's life as reflected in her "trifles," her kitchen, her quilting. Mrs. Hale is able to read this text immediately; Mrs. Peters remains a resisting reader until the dead bird is found. The men in the story are not able to read Minnie Wright's text for two reasons: First, "they literally cannot recognize it as a text because they cannot imagine that women have stories" (147–48). (This recalls to me the male student who remarked in his first written response that "[he] was . . . surprised how almost the whole play circled around the two women, Mrs. Hale and Mrs. Peters." He does not account for his surprise, but we can speculate that he assumes that the "natural" protagonists of the play would be the official male characters, the Sheriff and the County Attorney.)

Second, even if the play's men could recognize the text of Minnie Wright's life, it remains that sometimes they will not read it (Fetterley 152), a conviction that Fetterley extends to current controversies over the literary canon (the literary works that are given authority by the academy and are considered "must reads" for every student of literature) and the place (or displacement) of women's texts in it. Fetterley also points out what constitutes the substantive treason in *Trifles*: men (in *Trifles* and reading *Trifles*) cannot afford to read Minnie Wright's text because it presents "a radical challenge to the premises of men's texts, premises that men rely upon to maintain the fictions of their own identity" (153). She argues that Minnie Wright's text is "nothing less than the story of men's systematic, institutionalized, and culturally approved violence toward women, and of women's potential for retaliatory violence against men" (153). The fact that this text is highly threatening to both male and female students makes it both difficult and imperative to teach. Only by teaching such treason can we hope to destabilize the cultural and political hegemony of maleness.

The most radical element in *Trifles* is its thoroughly female perspective—a perspective so female that it must be kept hidden from the men in the text and from the world. In fact, as Fetterley notes Mrs. Hale and Mrs. Peters "erase the text as they read it" (152), by correcting the wayward stitching, hiding the dead bird. What is easier to get to in the Women and the Arts class than in the Tragedy class is the way in which this erasure is a metaphor for what has happened to many women's stories throughout literary history. The fact that women erase a woman's text to save that woman is a comment on women's lives under patriarchy. It may be that treason in *Trifles* would be best understood and appreciated in a class that read it alongside *The Gulag Archipelago* and *Native Son*—texts in which, as in *Trifles,* dominance, submission, and subversion are thematized in ways that help to gloss the struggle in Glaspell's play. Gaining an understanding of how and why the oppressed characters in those texts engage in law-breaking, disruptive, subversive behavior may help to overcome some of the resistance to Mrs. Hale and Mrs. Peter's transgressions in *Trifles*. I have not yet experimented with this kind of intertextual interaction. But as Fetterley makes clear, it is probably the explicitly *gendered* nature of Mrs. Hale and Mrs. Peter's behavior that raises hackles. In my experience and practice (still in a highly experimental state), the best strategy for dealing with resistance to the gendered treason in *Trifles* is, simply, discussion of that resistance, in the hope that the process that Louise Rosenblatt describes in the passage quoted earlier will be one that continues beyond the classroom. The reader-response tools of situating oneself as a reader, of collective scrutiny and evaluation of responses, of ongoing revision of those responses are, I believe, what we need to "reinterpret our old sense of things in the light of this new literary experience, in the light of the new ways of thinking and feeling offered by the work of art" (Rosenblatt 107).

NOTES

1. A strategy I've found particularly useful in bringing students to a consciousness of how they read is the introduction on the first day of a literature class to Elizabeth A. Flynn's categories of the dominant, submissive, and interactive reading of a text. Briefly, the dominant is characterized by detachment that resists involvement, the submissive by involvement that resists detachment, and the interactive by a capacity for both involvement and detachment to produce a meaningful interaction with the text (267–71). These are accessible concepts for undergraduate college readers, not only to bring them to a consciousness of themselves as readers but also to show them the merits of trying to assess the kind of reading they are engaged in with particular texts.

REFERENCES

Fetterley, Judith. "Reading About Reading: 'A Jury of Her Peers,' 'The Murders in the Rue Morgue,' 'The Yellow Wallpaper.' " In *Gender and Reading: Essays on Readers, Texts, and Contexts*. Ed. Elizabeth A. Flynn and Patrocinia P. Schweikert. Baltimore: Johns Hopkins University Press, 1986. 147–164.

Flynn, Elizabeth A. "Gender and Reading." In *Gender and Reading: Essays on Readers, Texts, and Contexts*. Ed. Elizabeth A. Flynn and Patrocinia P. Scheikert. Baltimore: Johns Hopkins University Press, 1986. 267–288.

Glaspell, Susan. *Trifles*. In *Types of Drama*. Ed. Sylvan Barnet, Morton Berman and William Burto. Boston: Little, Brown and Company, 1985. 69–76.

Gilligan, Carol. *In a Different Voice: Psychological Theory and Women's Development*. Cambridge, MA: Harvard University Press, 1982.

Ibsen, Henrik. *A Doll's House*. In *Types of Drama*. Ed. Sylvan Barnet, Morton Bermann and William Burto. Boston: Little, Brown and Company, 1985. 31–65.

Petry, Ann. "Like a Winding Sheet." In *Black Writers of America*. Ed. Richard Barksdale and Keneth Kinnamon. New York: The Macmillan Company, 1972. 763–768.

Piercy, Marge. "For Inez Garcia." In *Living in the Open*. New York: Alfred Knopf Publisher, 1976. 90–92.

Rosenblatt, Louise M. *Literature as Exploration*. 3d ed. New York: Noble and Noble, 1976.

Shange, Ntozake. *For Colored Girls Who Have Considered Suicide When the Rainbow is Enuf*. New York: Bantam Books, 1980.

Solzhenitsyn, Aleksandr. *The Gulag Archipelago, 1918–1956*. Trans. Thomas P. Whitney. New York: Harper & Row, 1974–78.

Sophocles. *Antigone*. In *Oedipus the King and Antigone*. Trans. & Ed. Peter D. Arnott. New York: Appleton-Century-Crofts, 1960. 61–105.

Wright, Richard. *Native Son*. New York: Perennial Library, 1968.

Walker, Alice. *The Color Purple*. New York: Harcourt Brace Jovanovich, 1982.

CHAPTER 17

Reading and Teaching from the Outside:

Responding to Native American Literature

David W. Furniss

A number of years ago, I got a late-night panicky phone call from an acquaintance who was directing a weekend college program for adults at a local community college. She needed a "guest-lecturer" for that weekend's session on Alice Walker's *The Color Purple:* the speaker she had lined up had just cancelled. She recalled talking to me about the novel at a party one time, and thought I might be able to "come up with something." Partly out of sympathy for her predicament, and partly because I needed the money, I agreed to do it.

I immediately regretted it, and my anxiety increased almost by the hour as the weekend approached. Viewed from any angle, the situation seemed impossible. I was to deliver a lecture, a teaching technique I had never much liked as a student, and had certainly never used in my years as a high school English teacher or as a graduate assistant teaching freshman composition. Worse, I was to speak to a group of working people who were giving up their precious Saturdays, clearly not an audience likely to meekly accept captivity. Still worse, I was to lecture about a novel I had read once before, for enjoyment: I had no pithy notes in the margins, no cross-references, no underlined passages! Worst of all, I was to come before this group as a white male and pose as an authority ("lecturer" implied authority to me, anyway) on Walker's novel.

I decided to accept my limitations, in fact, to acknowledge them at the beginning of the session, and to further admit to the class that I was nervous about my role. Having done that, I asked myself a couple of opening questions, and asked them to respond as well: How is this novel different from others we've read? What do we expect when we read fiction, and to what extent does the novel fulfill those expectations?

To my surprise, that was as much structure as I needed that day. I had written several pages of notes, including other questions, answers to the questions, page numbers of important passages that I might read aloud, all prepared because I was afraid I'd get little or no response. I didn't need them. My memory of the session has faded quite a bit, but I do remember that we spent nearly ninety minutes on the opening questions. There was a wide range of reactions. Some were moved by Celie's coming of age and getting of wisdom, some were outraged at the explicitness of some of the language, some were bewildered by the jumps in time, or by the mix of fiction and history. But there was also this commonality: each of us was in some way an outsider approaching this novel. The novel held surprises for each of us, violated at least one expectation we brought to it. I can't speak for the others in that group, but this experience taught me the value of not only acknowledging but using the surprises and problems that arise from reading, that result from my experiences and preconceptions.

As I write this now, five-odd years after my "lecture" on *The Color Purple,* I find my teaching situation (to quote a common phrase in my students' essays) similar but different. At the University of Wisconsin-River Falls I teach a course titled Literature for Adolescents to juniors, seniors, and graduate students, many of them English majors, most of them preparing to teach in elementary or secondary schools. The course is designed to acquaint students with the various genres of young adult literature, with changes in the field, and with issues related to adolescence and teaching adolescents.

During the semester, we read a number of novels with African-American or Native American protagonists. This is an important feature of the course, first of all because young adult literature has provided a market much more accessible to minority writers than has adult, "mainstream" literature, and as such is more diverse. It is also important because, although most of my students are not members of ethnic or racial minority groups, their students may well be. Alternatively, if their students are outsiders like themselves, they should be prepared to give their students access to these texts. Finally, the university community is committed to increasing students' awareness of cultural diversity, and to designing courses that reflect that diversity.

On the reading list, I have included two Native American novels: Oliver LaFarge's *Laughing Boy* and Hal Borland's *When the Legends Die.* When I was drawing up the syllabus, these two seemed to make a good pair. Although they were written nearly forty years apart, both stories take place at roughly the same time, 1910–1920. Moreover, to simplify somewhat, both address the issue of assimilation.

There are also a number of interesting and important contrasts. Borland's novel is by and large an adventure story set in southwestern white society. Thomas Black Bull, after losing his parents, is forced to leave "the old way." After degrading attempts to "civilize" him at the agency school fail, Tom shows a talent for breaking horses that lands him in the care of a rodeo circuit gambler. He eventually becomes a famous rodeo rider, and nearly succeeds in destroying his past, and himself, before returning at the end of the novel to his old home in the mountains, determined to learn the "old ways" again.

Laughing Boy is a coming-of-age novel concerning a romance between the title character and Slim Girl, an orphaned girl forced, like Thomas Black Bull, to assimilate. Laughing Boy leaves his Navajo clan to live with Slim Girl. The novel's action focuses on the dilemmas each face: Laughing Boy risks ostracism from his clan if he stays with Slim Girl; she, fearing he will leave her, tries to bind him by creating a ritual involving alcohol. The novel is immersed in the Navajo culture of the period; its pace is much slower, almost meditative. Furthermore, as I said earlier, it is a romance, whereas *Legends* is an adventure full of rodeo-circuit action. Thus, the novels make very different demands on their readers, despite their similarities in terms of theme and time frame.

The course is concerned with preparing students to teach, and thus is not strictly a literature course, so I do ask the class eventually to talk about how young readers might react to the text, what sorts of readers might enjoy it, and what problems young readers might encounter in reading it. But I always begin by asking for personal responses from the class. My goal in approaching these minority novels is for us to acknowledge and put to use our "outsider" status, to identify problems and questions we face as readers in responding to experiences far removed from our own. After all, while most of the prospective teachers in my course are white and attended predominantly white secondary schools, there are many public school districts in the Upper Midwest with a very diverse student population. My students, therefore, should anticipate teaching in schools very different from their own.

Moreover, as I argued earlier, even if most or all of their students are white, they should try to find ways into these novels in order to help their outsider students enter them. In any case, they will need to learn how to read novels like these first, before they can discuss them with their students. Thus, it is important that the course work on two levels: students respond to the reading first, then they begin to project how young readers may respond.

My approach in class is to begin with the former, asking students to respond in personal terms, to identify where their problems were in reading, what surprised them, how they reacted to the protagonist and other characters, I have found the students quite willing, for the most part, to do this in class discussions. However, I have had more difficulty getting them to do this in writing. I will elaborate on this shortly.

Attempting to generate personal responses to use as grist for class discussion, I have tried three different kinds of writing assignments, one kind for each year I've taught the course. The first year, I required the class to keep reading journals, in which they recorded reactions of the sort described earlier, or drew comparisons to other novels. Although many of the journals were interesting, this approach didn't work well. For one thing, my teaching schedule made it impossible to look at the journals more than three times during the term, which made me feel rather hypocritical in asking students to write in them diligently. I think a number of the students, deliberately or otherwise, reacted to this contradiction: to my dismay, their entries became shorter and less thoughtful as the term progressed, rather than the reverse. In addition, I believe that most students who have taken many writing and education courses are "journaled out," to borrow a phrase used by one of my students in another class. So they tend to take a rather perfunctory, oh-this-again approach.

The next year, I dispensed with the journals, and returned to a type of writing assignment I'd used in introductory literature classes a number of times, asking students to write short (200–400-word) out-of-class responses to questions I raised during class, due the next class meeting. These are supposed to resemble journal entries: They're informal, personal, nonacademic. My role was to react to them on a similar level, to respond to them personally and informally. The only requirement was that they were to be turned in on time. I assigned one of these in connection with the two Native American novels. After we finished discussing *Laughing Boy,* I asked the class to read *When the Legends Die* and write a reaction to it in which they compared their responses to the two novels.

An odd thing happened when the students wrote their responses. Despite my repeated assurances to them that I wanted personal reactions, in their own voices, what I got was, for the most part, writing that sounded like the following two excerpts, taken from the opening paragraphs of two responses to the assignment I already described. Bear in mind, once again, that the great majority of the ten out-of-class responses I assigned read very much the same way.

> The novels *Laughing Boy* and *When the Legends Die* explore the problem of the confrontation of Native American culture and white American culture in the southwestern United States in the early years of the twentieth century. Both novels portray a conflict that is unresolvable, although the Navaho culture in *Laughing Boy* remains more viable than the Ute society in *Legends.* The Indian protagonists in each need to redefine themselves in light of their experiences in the white world.

> These novels portray Native Americans as complex, unstereotyped individuals, not as the "noble savage." The major themes are survival between conflicting cultures and personal identity. There is also a universality to the novels; we all have to make choices about how to live our lives. There is also the theme of male/female love and relationships. . . . In both books there is accuracy and detail about the culture and history of the Native American, and it's from their point of view, which allows the reader to see the reasons behind the state of the American Indian today, and the limited choices they have available.

A graduate student in English education wrote the first excerpt; the second came from a senior English major. Both of them, and especially the former, show the writers to be well-trained in constructing a literary analysis, learned through hours of composing dozens of five-page essays. Most intriguing, however, is not what's in these responses but what isn't. Both of these writers did indeed compare the two works, and their pieces are admirable studies in how to use that particular rhetorical strategy. But neither compared their own responses to the books, and in fact neither admitted to having a personal response of any sort, visceral, aesthetic, or otherwise. Particularly revealing is the phrase in the second piece, "allows the reader:" a familiar bit of prosaic distancing from the dreaded first-person singular pronoun.

For me the most poignant piece came from another graduate student, an excellent student and very willing to discuss her subjective responses to the readings orally. Her written response to *Laughing Boy* and *Legends,* like the first one presented earlier, is a near-perfect piece of academic architecture, including indented quotations to support generalizations about the novels' themes and styles. At the end there is this "p.s." about *Legends:* "My stomach hurt when I finished reading this book." When I read this student's response, I was torn between conflicting reactions of my own. On the one hand, I was impressed with her sophistication. For example, she was the only student in the class who noted the stylistic shift in *Legends* after Tom Black Bull is forced to join the white world. On the other, I was surprised and dismayed to see that something in the nature of the task or in this student's training had constrained this normally forthright person. She had an intense reaction to the novel, but felt obliged to relay it as a brief afterthought.

In the set of eighteen responses to this question, I found very few that included any personal reactions, and only three students elaborated on their feelings about the novels. Two of them were not English majors, and in fact were students who struggled throughout the term, especially with the longer essays required. Compare their opening statements with the two already quoted:

> I found that *When the Legends Die* caught my attention quicker and kept my attention. I think it tends to read easier because there is not a lot of Indian words or phrases present throughout as there is in *Laughing Boy*.
>
> I liked the novel *Laughing Boy* but at times it was hard to understand what was going on. For example: when the wives of one of the Navajo set his saddle outside the door it took me awhile to figure out that they had kicked him out of the house. I felt that the novel *When the Legends Die* was clearer than *Laughing Boy* in this aspect. Also the language of the Navajo is hard to follow in *Laughing Boy* and it wasn't presented as important in my estimate. When Laughing Boy was singing I skipped over the lyrics because of the language.

In addition to the sort of literary analysis/explication that the first two students wrote, the rest of the class tended to bring the terminology of the course to bear in their discussions, rather than expressing personal reactions. For example, many compared the novels in terms of genre, as in this student's comment that "*Laughing Boy* is more of a romance, and *Legends* is more of an adventure." Others talked about readability, how the novels differed in terms of natural readership. One student managed to cover *both* the question of genre and that of audience in his first paragraph: "*Legends* is what I would consider a minority adventure story written for a younger audience (ages twelve to fifteen), while I see *Laughing Boy* as a minority historical romance aimed at an older audience (ages fifteen plus)."

Obviously, this assignment did not produce the kinds of responses that might have led us to examine our preconceptions about Native Americans, to deal with our difficulties in approaching and processing the novels and the sources of those difficulties, with the three exceptions just quoted. In particular, I wanted to pursue the fact that those two less sophisticated students found *Laughing Boy* less engaging because of its language, slow pace, and detailed accounts of rituals. I wanted to ask why they thought LaFarge includes phonetically transcribed Navajo lyrics, why he gives so much space to the conversations between characters, to the rhythms of their speech. I wanted to hear if others in the class would agree that the novels "may be confusing or boring if some of these rituals are not known," as one of the three writers quoted earlier said later in her response, to see, possibly, whether their outsider status had affected their experience or assessment of the novel.

The class discussion on the two novels that followed tended to concentrate on questions of audience and genre, not on personal response. In fact, I had noticed that, although discussions were still lively, the class had tended more and more to *begin* with these sorts of analytical concerns. These novels are assigned more than halfway through the term, and no doubt this increases their tendency to develop a pattern of response echoing the course terminology.

When I read the two personal reactions to the class, without identifying the writers, I finally was able to get the rest of the class to begin to articulate how they responded to the novels, and how their responses were different. Many others remarked that *Laughing Boy* made them feel like true outsiders, made them feel somewhat excluded, and talked about how *that* unfamiliar status felt to them. Later, a number of students told me that their initial frustration with *Laughing Boy* had changed to real sadness, as a result of recognizing that the world LaFarge renders in such detail and so unapologetically was ending even as he wrote.

My experience with last year's class impelled me to change my approach yet again. I concluded that out-of-class writing for a group of experienced essay-crankers will produce writing that resembles a formal essay—thesis, supporting quotations, academic language—noting that two of the exceptions were *inexperienced* essay-crankers. Let me emphasize that I was pleased that so many of the students could analyze the literature in these sophisticated ways, and could write well-organized, detailed discussions of character, genre, theme, and so on. But I felt that their previous experience in literature classes, and in my own course, had the effect of distancing them from the material, or more likely, of distancing them from their own transactions with it. This was something I wanted to avoid, particularly in dealing with fiction by nonmainstream authors. Many of these students, in my experience, already see themselves as far removed from the feelings expressed by characters in these novels, and from the issues raised in them.

The class's reaction when I read personal responses to them suggested the direction I should take. Generally, I begin each seventy-five minute class session with a question, and the students write for ten minutes or so in response. Occasionally, I prepare them for these responses by asking them to "consider" some issue as they read, and then frame this consideration as a question the next time. The only sort of response I now assign them to write outside of class is one in which I ask them to stop in their reading and react to a particular section of the text immediately. Such a response, of course, would be difficult to write from memory in class.

These writings form a course journal consisting of some twenty-five entries. To begin the class discussions, I ask for volunteers to read or summarize their entries, although I encourage the former. I have found that nearly every student volunteers at least once in a while, and the rest will read if I call on them. I also write responses to my question, and read them every so often. At the end of the term, I ask that they choose five to seven of their "best" entries, give them titles, and turn them in unrevised as part of their class grade (25 percent of the term grade). They are free to define "best" however they please.

I assigned three responses for our discussions of *Laughing Boy* and *When the Legends Die* (which we read in that order). Two of these were at-home reactions to the opening pages, Chapter 1 in *Laughing Boy* and Part 1 of *Legends*. The only instructions for these writings were to stop at the specified point and react to what they had read so far. These reactions could take the form of questions, a list of problems, theories as to where the novels were headed, their feelings toward the novel or the character, what they understood or what confused them so far, or anything else. The third writing was a comparative response like the one I'd assigned the previous year, this time completed in class.

I collected all three sets of responses to these novels. In this case, I was fibbing a little to the class when I told them that they could choose which entries to hand in. I had intended all along to ask for their responses to the these two novels for the purposes of completing this article, although I didn't tell them this until the end of the term.

Concerning the responses to the opening sections, the students' responses to *Laughing Boy* most often revealed their outsider perspectives. I had expected this: LaFarge's novel makes few allowances for readers unfamiliar with Laughing Boy's world. As one

reader put it, "*Legends* explains more of the Indian tradition to me than *Laughing Boy*."
Several readers were perplexed at the outset of *Laughing Boy*. Here are some examples:

> I am confused. Where is the story going? . . . So much seems to have happened, yet the story
> has gone nowhere. . . . What year is this occurring in?
>
> So far, I'm having a little difficulty getting into the book. It is hard for me to relate to the
> Indian ways of life and values and there are things I cannot understand, such as some of the
> expressions and language.
>
> I had a hard time figuring out what was going on during the ceremony in the first chapter.
> I'm assuming there will be more of this confusion in the rest of the book.

Most of the responses echoed these questions, although some students were more in-
trigued than bothered by their uncertainty, as this one was:

> I was really drawn to the book by the first chapter. . . . I felt as if I was missing something,
> and I desperately wanted to figure it out. . . . My overall impression of *Laughing Boy* after
> reading the first chapter is one of curiosity. I can't wait to finish it.

In the discussion that followed, students debated their reactions to the novel as a
whole, comparing their first impressions with their feelings on completing the book. I
asked them to clarify their reasons for finding it "slow," as a number did, and why some
of them thought the book too "detailed" concerning customs and rituals. In fact, the class
was sharply divided between those who found this detail, and LaFarge's use of Navajo
language and speech rhythms beautiful, and those who found it boring. We spent some
time discussing why LaFarge might have chosen to write the book in this way, to avoid
explanations tailored for outsiders, and why some of us expect such explanations.

There was more disagreement when it came to the students' comparative responses.
Among the out-of-class responses I assigned the year before, I received very few in which
the writer stated a preference for one or the other books. This time, although the instructions were the same, almost all of the responses stated whether the reader liked *Laughing
Boy* or *Legends* better. The class was divided almost equally, with a few more students
preferring *Laughing Boy*. I was particularly interested to note that a number of those
students who had found the beginning of *Laughing Boy* confusing ended up preferring it to
Legends.

During class discussion, I was struck (as were the students) by how completely
opposite the reactions often were. The written responses reveal the same deep disagreements. Note the contrasts in the following groups of statements:

> — I enjoyed *Laughing Boy* because it is not as complex as *Legends*.
> — The conflict in *Legends* is more obvious than the conflicts in *Laughing Boy*.
>
> — *Legends* . . . was draggy and somewhat difficult to get through.
> — *Legends* was very adventurous while *Laughing Boy* seemed to be dull.
> — I found *Legends* harder to read than *Laughing Boy*. It seems to be moving slower, and is
>   occasionally hard to follow.
>
> — In *Laughing Boy*, the narrator got inside the minds of both Laughing Boy and Slim Girl,
>   which made it somewhat confusing.
> — There was . . . more access to the characters' thoughts in *Laughing Boy*, which helped to
>   understand why the characters did what they did.

Many of the differences between the students' responses focused on the question of detail, and how they define "detailed." In *Laughing Boy,* the issue concerns the language, the characters' meditations and stories, the accounts of the rituals. Some welcomed this, found it interesting, even beautiful. Others found LaFarge's approach made the novel dull, or hard to penetrate. In commenting that *Legends* is more "action-packed," for instance, one reader added that "the language is much simpler to understand, with no Indian language at all."

In *Legends,* there is a great deal of detail concerning the rodeo, with sometimes lengthy descriptions of Tom's bronco rides. For some readers, this was exciting; others found it tiresome. This student found *Legends* less engaging than *Laughing Boy* for this reason. Note how she defines "detail" in this case:

> The story progressed rapidly, and was less detailed than *Legends. Legends* went into detailed accounts of bucking patterns and other events that did not directly or in some cases indirectly have to do with the themes presented.

Apart from the wide divergence of opinion on the two novels, the other striking feature of the written responses is their utter contrast from those my students wrote the previous year. As I hope is evident from the excerpts given here, these reactions convey much more of the students' preliminary reactions, their first transactions with the texts. They aren't *crafted* statements resembling examination answers or critiques; they aren't written primarily for my eyes, as most of those earlier ones had been.

I don't mean to suggest here that all of the students who had troubles getting into the novels at first (recalling the first impressions quoted) arrived at a different view as a result of subsequent discussions. However, a number of the students did alter their thinking somewhat concerning *Laughing Boy.* As far as I can tell, Slim Girl became the protagonist in several class members' eyes. The second day of discussion, two or three stated as much: they felt Slim Girl's conflict is the central one, because it foreshadowed what would inevitably happen to Laughing Boy. They began to see that his view of the whites (the "Americans")—as buffoons easily snookered in trading—only serves to mask the threat they represent to his culture, a threat Slim Girl perceives clearly.

For some, particularly the female students, this became a way into the novel, and a way of accommodating to the difficulties of language and context they had experienced earlier. This was gratifying for me. LaFarge's novel is clearly more distancing than Borland's, which was certainly written to appeal to a mass audience. In fact, one of the things I have come to admire most about *Laughing Boy* is this sense of determined, iconoclastic resistance to popular appeal. (In spite of this, millions have read it since its publication in 1929.)

What was most gratifying was the passion with which many of the class members discussed the novels. In previous years, we had talked about the issues these books raise. Although my students are outsiders, they know enough or have heard enough to be able to talk about injustice, the tragic loss of culture and dignity forced by assimilation, the massacres and forced migrations. Their out-of-class responses reflected on these things at length, and most were able to identify examples of these themes during class discussions.

But I had the strong sense that, this time, the themes came through more clearly, in rawer form, perhaps, and the students were less likely to look at the novels (particularly *Laughing Boy*) as history books. This is not to say that students in earlier classes were not moved by the novels (recalling the student whose "stomach hurt"). However, I argue that this group of students, in general, got much closer to what the events in the history books really signify by getting closer to these characters and their world—close enough, I like to think, to be able to talk to other outsiders *and* insiders about them in a way they might not have been able to before.

I recognize that my conclusions must be provisional: I'm talking about a small number of students and tasks. Nonetheless, I would argue that the more spirited and complex discussions that followed were a result of students having the opportunity to describe and clarify their reactions in a setting that discouraged their impulse to externalize their responses. They had to cope, in the case of these two novels, with first impressions, with gut reactions stemming from their experiences and expectations. As one student confessed after reading the beginning of *Laughing Boy,* "I keep anticipating an act of violence, or for someone to steal his horse. I must have many stereotypes about Native Americans."

I *can* say that I intend to continue using short, in-class writing (or occasionally carefully limited out-of-class writing) in this class. The results were very consistent: nearly all of the responses the students turned in at the end of the term were honest, emotive, and in their own voices. I do recognize the value of other sorts of written responses and other types of journals. But my experience with this class tells me that as students progress through school, they become more and more inclined to believe that all writing assigned by a teacher must look and sound the same. After all, they are learning in most of their classes, either directly or implicitly, that they need to master academic prose in order to survive in an academic setting.

The best way to restrain their impulse to take an objective stance, to carefully present evidence, to choose just the right word, is to make sure they don't have enough time to do it. And if they realize that they need not reveal every response to their teacher or fellow students, they may be more willing to be honest. What they will have at the end of the term is a record of responses they can sift through and choose from, responses they wrote as they read, not the night before I was scheduled to look at them: a mirror of themselves as readers, then and now.

Let me close by emphasizing my own outsider status. I did not intend (nor could I) in talking about these novels to present myself as someone who "understands" Laughing Boy or Tom Black Bull. It would be hypocritical and absurd to imply to my students that I am somehow above making judgments according to stereotype, and that my role is to show them how wrong-headed and closed-minded they are. Rather, my goal is for them to locate what they respond to in their reading, what intrigues them, what makes them yawn, and then to articulate this at first to themselves. After this, we can exchange responses in hopes of coming to some understanding of what sort of readers we are, and what sort we want to be.

REFERENCES

Borland, Hal. *When the Legends Die*. New York: Bantam, 1964.

LaFarge, Oliver. *Laughing Boy*. Boston: Houghton Mifflin Company, 1929.

Walker, Alice. *The Color Purple*. New York: Washington Square Press, 1983.

CHAPTER 18

Empathizing with the African-American Experience:

Role Visualization through Composition

Ogle Burks Duff

As we prepare for the twenty-first century, inhumanity among fellow human beings remains a critical concern. Daily our newspapers catalog senseless violence, racism, ethnic wars, joblessness, environmental abuses, and homelessness. What is the role of educators in the preparation of students to live and work harmoniously with cultural, religious, ethnic, and/or racial differences? How can we as English educators, teachers, and supervisors challenge our students in the classroom to see and feel the diversity of the human condition?

Through literature we can provide experiences, explorations to enable students to think and feel life and to develop an understanding of what it means to be a human being. This opportunity to engage in making meaning of literary experiences helps the students to understand themselves. Through self-understanding, the students will be able to understand others. Of course, this conceptualization of self is not as simple as it sounds, and certainly not so simple to implement.

As English teachers we're always searching for ways to make literature come alive. We want our students to feel what the characters feel. We want them to know the joy and pain of living without suffering the consequences themselves. Exploring life through literature can provide these kinds of experiences. Rosenblatt argues for the role literature plays in providing broad experiences. "The infinite diversity of literature plus the complexity of human personality and background justify insistence on the special nature of the literary experience and on the need to prepare the student to engage in the highly personal process of evoking the literary work from the text" (*Literature* 31).

To facilitate the student's ability to evoke the literary work, we must devise strategies that create a confluence of the affective and cognitive domains, thus enabling our students to experience literature through involvement and to assess the meaning of that involvement through detachment. By using reader-response theory that provides a framework for

---

accomplishing these two purposes in the literary experience, "the range of potential responses and the gamut of degrees of intensity and articulateness are infinitely vast, since they depend not only on the character of the text but even more on the special character of the individual reader" (Rosenblatt, *Reader* 49).

SUMMARY OF THE STORY

The story selected as a referent for developing empathy through the application of reader-response theory is "On the Road" by Langston Hughes. The setting is the midwest during the Great Depression of the 1930s. Sargeant, an African-American hobo, arrives in town on a freight train. As he searches for shelter from a snowstorm, the hostility he encounters illuminates the problem of the homeless of the 1990s. The larger theme of people's inhumanity to their fellow human beings is projected through the series of incidents that develop.

It is a cold, snowy evening. Chilled and hungry, Sargeant knocks on the door of the parsonage, is rejected by the white minister, and is hastily directed to a relief shelter in another section of town. But Sargeant sees the church adjacent to the parsonage and knocks on the door. Receiving no response, he continues to knock. In a fit of desperation, he begins to pound on the door attracting the attention of passers-by and eventually the police who try to stop him.

The events that follow are illusory—a mixture of reality and fantasy. As the police pull him, he grabs one of the church pillars and holds it as the police are beating him over the head. In the scene, he pulls down the pillar, which causes the church and Christ on the cross on top of the church to fall in the snow. Christ comes to life and Sargeant walks down the street with him to the railroad yards where there are other homeless. Christ is planning to hop a freight to Kansas City that evening. They bid each other farewell as Sargeant finds refuge in the hobo jungle. The next morning Sargeant scrambles out of the jungle with other hobos to grab a freight. As he attempts to pull himself up into a moving coal car, he is rapped across the knuckles by one of the policeman in the coal car. Sargeant continues to cling to the pole and begins to holler. Reality returns when he discovers he is in jail and is actually clinging to the bars of his jail cell.

RATIONALE AND PROCEDURE

To "walk a mile in my shoes" is literally impossible, but through vicarious experiences in literature using reader-response theory, the student will have the opportunity to learn and feel what it is like to be an African American. This insight hopefully will enable the student to have a better understanding of human nature and human relationships in general and a deeper awareness of problems in black–white relationships in particular. This monologue writing exercise is designed to capture the students' feelings as they respond from Sargeant's point of view. What is required is not only their suspension of disbelief, but a visualization of themselves in the character of Sargeant. Their responses from this posture create a challenging experience that may lead to a level of empathy. The level of success in their achieving this task is dependent on their prior knowledge, which includes what they bring to the text and the immediate situation: mood, feelings, preoccupations, conditions.

To establish a frame of reference and stimulate interest in reading the story, and participation in the response activity on empathy, I opened with a series of questions: Why are there people sleeping under the bridges? Who are they? Where did they come from? Name some of the agencies that are providing shelter and food for these people. What do you think should be done to help them? How is our community helping? After discussing the problem of present-day homelessness, I introduced the story. The students were instructed to read the story silently. Without discussion as soon as they had finished reading, they were to begin writing a response-monologue. Their instructions were to write in the first person, using the characterization of Sargeant, revealing the internal dimensions of his feelings, attitudes, and beliefs as he reacts to his environment. What-ever they felt as they entered the character of Sargeant, they were to incorporate into the monologue. Furthermore, they were asked to portray the African-American experience as seen through Sargeant's eyes as he resolves or attempts to resolve the conflict. Specific points to consider include:

1. How does the character view and feel about his world?
2. How does the character view and feel about himself?
3. In what way is he affected by his environment?
4. What is his attitude toward his situation?
5. From the known to the unknown, what is universal about your character's experi-ence?
6. Try to illustrate these aspects as you develop your monologue.
7. In other words, how does your character think, act, and feel, as a result of being an African American as well as a human being? How do you suppose Sargeant feels about what is happening to him?

To allow the students the privacy of their individual thoughts and feeling, the writing assignment was completed without discussion because discussion in this setting often-times may be an intrusion, chilling the emotions. I wanted their responses to reflect their thoughts and feelings as the character. However, I did offer assistance to anyone who was unclear about the task.

In addition to the monologue, each student was to write a reaction to the experience and an assessment. Their reaction was to estimate their perception of the experience as African-American or universal and whether they thought Sargeant's being an African American lent a special or different aspect to the experience. As assessment they were to gauge their understanding of Sargeant as an African American (very good, good, fairly adequate, adequate) and their ability to reflect this understanding in their monologue.

Later when the task was completed, the students read their monologues aloud, sharing their feelings and uncertainties with their classmates. They also had an oppor-tunity to discuss their responses and their assessment of the activity.

DISCUSSION OF RESPONSES, REACTIONS ASSESSMENT

It is important for the instructor to be sensitive to the diversity of responses that may develop based on the experiential background of the students. Using the monologue as a response strategy necessitates teacher super sensitivity because some students, even those in a graduate program, have had limited experiences with other races and socioeconomic classes. To what extent can white middle-class students and African American middle-class students identify with the plight of a poor black man in a Depression setting? Will there be a perceptional difference reflected in the responses? Are the students emotionally capable of experiencing the literature through their imagination? What do they bring to the literature to enable them to evoke the "poem"? To what degree will they be able to experience vicariously the plight of Sargeant? (The race designation terms *blacks, African American,* and *Negro* are used interchangeably. The story uses the term *Negro.* Unless otherwise indicated, the respondents are white.)

The monologue of P. F., demonstrates an awareness of problems of the underclass and of racial discrimination.

> There ain't no justice in this world, that is what He's gonna git in Kansas City and anywhere else He goes. Better off up on that cross where He can at least let His head hang down and get some peace—even if He's gotta get himself nailed down to get it. No peace down here, not for a Negro what got no job in times like these. There's hobos that's white too, yeah, that's true. But a bum with Black skin got nowhere to hide, nowhere to sleep, 'cept in this jail. And that ain't no place to get warm or rest, that's for sure. Colder in here than it is outside and these cops are gonna make it colder for this Black bum. Wonder why Christ would want to come down here and walk around in the likes of this world? Couldn't be no worse up on that cross, even after 2000 years. He'll see it ain't no kind of life hoboing around from town to town, never knowing where to sleep or what He'll get to eat. Don't feel like rattlin' down no cell doors now. Naw, too tired and too cold to cause all that fuss. Let them cops alone for awhile as I buzz off.

P. F. seems to be into the character's thoughts with a feeling for his behavior and speculation. He has tried to illustrate with some veracity the mind set of Sargeant as the "Points to Consider" are incorporated into his monologue. There also appears to be a show of bravado in P. F.'s interpretation of Sargeant's reaction to the "cops." Drawing the line of discrimination experienced by hobos and the line as experienced by African-American hobos is realistic considering the period of the Depression. P. F. was also affected by the Christ imagery. In his assessment of the character, he states:

> I saw Sargeant as a bum or hobo first, and as a Black bum second. This story is a Depression story, with hard times evident for more people than Sargeant. His plight was aggravated by his Black skin, this is true; but I think his problems are essentially that he is a hobo during hard times. Being a Black hobo makes it harder, but any kind of hobo had it tough then. The religious images of the story are interesting. . . . that Christ seems to identify with the hobo element in this era, which is, I think, a valid point. Christ probably would feel more at home with the bums than with the prosperous today—he was back where he lived.

P. F.'s remarks and his monologue reflect a good understanding of Sargeant as an African-American human being who is frustrated by the system that continues to deny his humanity. The Christ imagery is supported as an acknowledgment of the range of discriminatory practice in the community.

L. A. also seems to have eased into empathizing with Sargeant as a suffering man who has numerous doors slammed in his face because he is black. Yet she states in her assessment that she "wasn't able to gain much information on his character—how he truly thought or felt." She minimizes her skill in drawing inferences from the images, but acknowledges that the assignment made her think about what Sargeant was experiencing. Consequently her monologue reveals an understanding and a feeling for the character:

> I feel that the world is full of doors—always being slammed in my face—as in the relief house, the reverend's house and the church—jail. Everyone is always slamming doors or they are always locked—to shut me out because I am Black in a world full of snow. I believe that I am a person too—who can take those doors and make them move. Christ and I are alike in the sense that we are both shunned from society and hung on a cross because of who we are. If I could have anything, I would not to have to worry about a place to sleep, eat, or to be out in the cold. Every place would be like the jungle where there are no doors. I think and act like I can do anything I want, since this is the only way I can get anything since no one will let me past their doors. I don't like or appreciate what is happening to me. I feel like no one really cares— I want to make them care to show them that I am human—that my knuckles hurt and bleed red blood just like theirs—those who are like the snow—cold, wet, and slippery who melt when the heat is too much for them.

> *Assessment*
> I personally liked this assignment. I thought it was a neat way to think about how a character feels. However, I wasn't able to gain much information on his character—how he truly thought or felt. I simply drew my statements from metaphors or at least what I felt were metaphors in the story. I have to admit though, I really liked the assignment, and it made me think about what he was saying in the assignment.

Although the monologue activity was a free response, the student must understand the story to portray how the character thinks and feels. Several of the students expressed uncertainty regarding their ability to speak in the character of Sargeant because they are not black.

H. S. sees Sargeant as vindictive in his pulling the church down, "I'll destroy this church since they won't help me."

> I feel that the world is unfair to me. I am only looking for a place to sleep and no one will help me. I see a church which is where there is always supposed to be a friend to help me. But the white people don't want me near their church. To get them back—I'll destroy their church since they won't help me. I just want a place to sleep. Don't they understand that there's nothing wrong with me. After I have destroyed their church, I have freed Christ since they have kept him away from me on the cross. He is my friend and companion. He also is looking for somewhere to go.

> *Assessment*
> I feel that I receive a good understanding of Sargeant. However, I found it a little difficult to speak in his character. I understood how he felt and could empathize with him, but since I have never found myself in an even similar situation, I could not "fill his shoes" completely.

H. S. responds as Sargeant, but the source of her inference of vindictiveness raises questions. Did she misread/misinterpret, or did she become overwhelmed with the tragedy of his suffering discrimination and impose her own attitude toward the incident to this situation? Free spontaneous response does not imply that she doesn't need to be true to the work; yet it does provide the freedom to draw inferences from behaviors and perceived attitudes, which may later be "modified, rejected or accepted" (Rosenblatt, *Literature* 76).

Understanding the motivation of Sargeant is important to understanding the story. Understanding him as a black man in America would suggest a need to understand "the problem of the color line" in America (Dubois). Most students, even those from the suburbs who have had limited direct contact, have some awareness of race relations in America. The degree to which this is true manifests itself in the ability of the student to move beyond Sargeant as a hobo to Sargeant as a black hobo.

P. M., a black female, felt the pain of Sargeant as a black man:

> My hands are numb from the cold, but I don't feel it. I don't feel anything anymore. I wasn't always this way. Once I had a dream. It was only a spark at first. (I was just a kid then.) But as I grew older and older that spark became a flame and burns deep inside me. It was a dream that was dying to become real. When I tried to bring that dream out into the open, it died. All of a sudden it just died. It was almost as if someone declared that African Americans are not supposed to have dreams; and if they do they must keep them to themselves, all pent up inside. That's how some African Americans die premature deaths—they're strangled by their own dreams. My dreams came to the surface and nearly destroyed me. The whole world pointed at me, Black and White alike as if to say: "You should have known better, Sargeant. You should have known your place." Somebody, please tell me. Where is my place cause it sure ain't here on earth? I should have gone with Christ to Kansas City.

> *Assessment*
> I feel that I received a very good understanding of Sargeant as a Black human being and was able to reflect this in my monologue.

L. T., a black female, expresses sarcasm toward the discriminatory institutional practice of the church in rejecting Sargeant because he is black. She makes the distinction between the church and God in her remarks:

> I am tired of being locked out with flimsy explanations and civilized barbarism. Tired of strange looks that never see me anyway. I used to believe that people just weren't thinking until I realized how much thought went into locking me out. Surely, a man of God would think about the cold; but that consideration is reserved for stray dogs. I know he knows the mission is closed to me. He doesn't care. Perhaps, he believes his God will be merciful. Perhaps, he thinks he can hide from God. This church is just a structure, a warm place. If it were more than that, the door would fling open, unlocked. I pray that it will fall in. I pray that God will hear me. He has heard me before. Well, do Jesus! The stone is rolled away! Judgement is upon us! This stone man need not enter by the back door, disguised as a beggar. This spirit in the stone need only walk among us, watch us. I will endure any hardship, absorb all pain because I know He is watching. I know judgement is near. I know I have done my best. God knows. God knows.

The universality of Sargeant affected R. L. in a more personal way, as noted in her assessment: "I chose not to focus completely on the Black issue because the feelings I got from the story and reflected on are similar to those I feel." As she indicates Sargeant's blackness served only as the catalyst for inciting her consciousness to the larger issue of a human being who is different from others not gaining acceptance. That sense of humanity is characterized in her monologue:

Your thoughts of me drench me from head to toe, cold and wet. Without you I have enough problems of my own—problems you will never have because you will never take them on. I cannot help it. Just because I am not like you, you turn me away, drench me in your cold hate, wet anger dripping and soaking me to the bone. You think you've got me then. I laugh back at you and in my own warmth I survive. I keep myself alive for I know I am not completely alone. You just fail to see your petty concerns keep us from being together. You force me out with no where to turn, thinking I have no one to turn to. It is you who will have no one to turn to in the end if you keep turning on people like me. My dark heat will enclose you, force you into the fires of hell, no door to break down there, while I, in turn, welcome that which comes from the sky.

Assessment

Sargeant feels his world has closed him out. Sargeant fights for himself, not letting himself be closed in by those who try. His environment pushes him forward unknowingly. I feel I understood Sargeant as a human being, Black, his reason for being different from others. In my monologue I reflected his difference as a human being; for me that was the heart of the situation, being Black was the instigator, the trigger. I chose not to focus completely on the Black issue because the feelings I got from the story and reflected on are similar to those I feel. Perhaps not so dramatically, but have strongly nonetheless. I could not discount that in my monologue and in my reaction. I feel for Sargeant, for his being put out, not for his being Black. We are all put out by others at times. Often by those who mean the most to us. In this sense I put myself in Sargeant's shoes.

Approximately half of the students in this class are seeking teaching English as a second career. They have been in the work force and are now changing careers. Usually they are more mature and less inhibited; as older students, they know who they are and their goals are more clearly defined. J. M. has lived in many places in the United States and has worked in various occupations from fisherman to construction boss. His ability to internalize the character from the perspective of a white man who has experienced poverty "then add to that . . . the burden of color" reflects the diversity of his life experiences. His response deals with every man's need for a home.

It's a good life! Lovely when you have something or someone to reach for, but it's darn lonely when you have nothing and no one. When I walk the streets and see lights in the houses, I know there are folks in there. They may be poor and they may be lonely, but they have a home. Something to hold on to, a place to hide from the cold, the cold of night and the cold of man's carelessness to other men. If only I could have one night of warmth—dry my clothes and warm my skin. But what good is one night? I will be here again tomorrow night. Tonight's the night I face the inevitable. I am poorer than poor. I have nothing but the awareness that I have nothing—I am the dogs in the alley, the cats in the garbage—no, I am less—I am an animal with reason—commanded by my own intellect to feel my worthlessness—humiliated by my humanness. When I was a child, I would go to the tents with my grandmother and she told me and I believed—that Jesus would save me, where have you gone sweet Jesus?

Assessment

I feel that I received a good understanding of Sargeant as a Black person and was able to reflect this in my monologue. I think this is an *outstanding* method for getting student to *think* how it *might* be. I can empathize with this as a poor white man then add to that what I realize to be the added burden of color. This exercise has great possibilities.

As J. M.'s response illustrates, what students bring to the literature, whether they are graduate students or adolescents will color their transaction with the work. "The past experiences and acquired attitudes that shape these perceptions need not be seen as contaminants, but simply as the characteristics of the individual and therefore unique reader (Probst 14).

The last response in this group is not a monologue. M. W. commented that she believed that "it is impossible to completely share the same experience with a person, but you can get pretty close." Her response is an analysis of Sargeant rather than an effort at empathy. What develops is intellectual distance rather than an effort at identifying with the character as a human being. What this student has brought to this literary moment is her own insecurity and inhibitions. There were no color or social class limitations on the level of empathy; yet M. W. rationalized that she could not have a good or very good understanding because she is not homeless nor is she black. Her comfort zone was at the intellectual level, hypothesizing and distancing the events of the story from herself. She does not internalize but maintains what Rosenblatt refers to as an efferent stance. "She is interested only in what the words point to—the objects, ideas, and actions designated. Her own response to these concepts or to the rhythm, sound, or associations of the words are of no importance to her, . . . the more she ignores them, the more she makes herself impersonal and transparent, the more efficiently she reads" (*Reader* 24).

The response of M. W. is shared to illustrate the efferent stance:

> Sargeant is a very frustrated person. I think that he feels that his world is a jail cell. Though he is homeless and unemployed, he cannot get shelter and food because he is Black. He realizes that there is a difference in society between the homeless, and that difference is skin color. Sargeant only wants help, but he cannot get it anywhere. I think that the story taking place, in winter is significant as the cold weather not only shows that the weather is bad, but it symbolizes how he views the world of the white man—and that is cold and bleak. I think his experience, to a degree, is universal with all homeless people, but it differs because he is Black, homeless and unemployed. He believes if he were white he would have had a place to stay that night, and he probably would have. I think that he would like to crush his world and return to something pure. By calling the hobo camp the jungle, I think that he wants to go somewhere warm and clear. When he shakes off the snow from his body he is trying to shake off the white man's world.

> *Assessment*
> I believe that I have a fairly adequate understanding of Sargeant as a Black person. I obviously cannot have a good or very good understanding because I am not homeless and I am not Black. I have achieved a higher degree of empathy than I had before. I believe that for someone to fully understand another person's situation, one must "walk a mile in their shoes." I understand that it is impossible to completely share the same experience with a person, but you can get pretty close. In this situation, the closest I could ever get would be to be a homeless person. I cannot change my skin color, but I could identify with the homeless if I were to become one.

REFLECTIONS AND BENEFITS

As stated earlier, there were no right or wrong responses and we can expect multiple transactions from a group of readers in response to the same text. The literary transaction may involve an interplay between different cultures or systems of ideas and values that may be applicable to the world evoked by the reader. "The reader draws from his own internalized culture in order to elicit from the text this world which may differ from his own in many respects." This tension is implicit in any literary transaction (Rosenblatt, *Reader* 56). "The reader's primary goal as he meets the text is to have as full an aesthetic experience as possible given his own capacities and the sensibilities, preoccupations and memories he brings to the transaction" (132).

The rationale focused on enabling the students to have a better understanding of, and feeling for, human nature and people's relationship to their fellow human beings in general and a deeper awareness of problems in black–white relations in particular by responding through a monologue.

The students shared these by reading them aloud in class and discussing their level of empathy as well as their perception of Sargeant. The class interaction was healthy and challenging as their later reflections reveal. The students had a week to mull over the value of the response activity and its implications for teaching literature. They wrote their reflections in class the week following their responses and discussion. Several students raised issues regarding the honesty and depth of the responses. There was also concern about what "if a response had revealed someone as a racist, what would have happened? How would a high school classroom continue the dialogue?" L. T. a very perceptive young African-American woman, stated:

> In my opinion, the "empathy activity" was enlightening. I would use it as an exercise before reading materials that concerned racial issues, or issues in which students needed to identify with an opposing point of view. I was very interested in the part of the activity that directed us to share our responses. If a response had revealed someone as being a racist, what would have happened? The activity opened many doors to dialogue, but then we didn't get the opportunity to delve into the issue. How would a teacher in a high school classroom continue the dialogue? In my research concerning the teaching of multicultural viewpoints, the need for teachers who had examined their racial perspectives was critical.

The open-ended responses did open many doors to dialogue; as we listened to the responses, we could conclude that there were students who had difficulty involving themselves with Sargeant. Questioning his own response as well as the response of other classmates, B. C. comments:

> Personally, it was engaging, but I wonder about the honesty of my response: and I have the same problem with the honesty or depth of a lot of the other responses I heard. I don't necessarily fault this, but I think that what people perceived as the "affective" goal of this lesson encouraged them to write something which reflected that goal. It was also interesting to hear how many monologues and responses sort of decentered the fact that the guy is Black. If I recall, one question specifically asked you to consider if this was a particular experience that reflected "being Black or Black-White relations."

B. C.'s insight suggests the dilemma of many of the students: They had difficulty internalizing Sargeant as a black man. But they did make a stab at it, and they did value the experience. This is a beginning.

A recurring theme in the assessments and reflections was "it is hard to know what a situation is really like unless you have experienced it." How can students grow if they do not allow themselves to be a flower, a lion, a Caesar, or a tree stump. We ask children to imagine, and yet we find adults who have difficulty role playing, not able to put themselves in the shoes of another. The inability or the unwillingness to shed the shackles of inhibitions, to differentiate between intellectualizing and empathizing is the difference in degrees between efferent reading and aesthetic reading.

M. W.'s reflections reveal an appreciation for the activity, but a reluctance or an inability to stretch her imagination and feeling to empathize.

> I found the activity to be a good tool to help teach empathy. However, as an educator, I could see a problem with responses in the monologue, in that the students in the activity could make generic responses. If I were teaching a creative writing class, I would employ this activity because it shows the students a different way of thinking and a different form of writing (or monologue) than they may have been exposed to. As a student, I developed some empathy for the character, but it is difficult to say I had a great deal of empathy, because it is hard to know what a situation is really like unless you have experienced it. As a teacher, I think that it is important to realize the former statement going into the activity.

The majority of the students were able to internalize some aspect of Sargeant's character by participating in the monologue:

> The approach to "On the Road," using the concept of empathy and first person monologue to engender empathy was a marvelous exercise. It permitted me, the writer, to "become," based on my own sense of identification of myself and experience, Sargeant. It was a cerebral role playing. Frankly it nearly brought me to tears. I suspect that what a person or student "brings to the text," will directly affect the "depth" of empathy in this type of exercise; however, I see this, at the very least, as a diagnostic approach that could enable the instructor to get a sense of the affective development of her students. Too, if you believe that the depth of personalization is directly related to the quality of the writing, then this is a good exercise for enjoying that sort of strength in writing.

> I thought it was valuable to put myself in the place of the homeless man. It gave me a stronger sense of what the main character was really feeling. The monologue I wrote forced me to readily feel what Sargeant felt in a way I hadn't through simply reading. Above all, it made me realize that I was only able to empathize up to a certain point. I know that what Sargeant experienced was more difficult than anything I have ever had to endure, so my degree of empathy was limited. That, in itself, was I believe, a very important point to realize.

Finally, L. A.'s comments sum up the meaning of the activity:

> This was a beneficial educational tool since I was able to learn more about my own responses and what they meant in comparison with other classmates' responses. Being able to write about how I would feel as that character brought me closer to the story and what it would mean to be Black or poor. This man suffered because the world was cruel to him. The implication of this type of activity for education illustrates to me that education is growing and exploring new realms of activities. These activities will help to perpetuate responsible reflections from the students. Once the literature is related to their lives, it becomes more important and meaningful for them.

Teachers must examine their own attitudes toward race, gender, and religious and cultural differences so that they are able to guide their students. Challenging the student's responses if they reflect racist or sexist attitudes does not solve the problem; it may only exacerbate it. Providing interaction strategies to address the revelation that unconsciously may have been exposed would be a more effective strategy for alleviating or modifying such an attitude. Infusing nonwhite literature into the literature curriculum and engaging students in creative dramatic activities would provide a diversity of literary experiences for such students. Role playing characters from these works or writing letters to these characters would be helpful for improving the quality of their responses. Students could be given other situations where they might be their own opposites in personality, sex, and race. Creating dialogue for their roles would necessitate their (a) internalizing the character and (b) analyzing their responses by reflection, their attempt to make meaning of this experience.

I have used this activity several times in different classroom settings with age groups from high school through college. On those occasions, the students read the story and taped their monologues extemporaneously. Thinking and feeling on their feet evoked a much more immediate response. Preparing adolescents for this type of engagement requires warm-up activities to stretch their imagination; that is, pretend you're very cold; lost in the mountains; a child abandoned in a snow storm; an elderly women in a house without heat in winter; a homeless man in search of shelter. For each of these situations the teacher might ask questions such as: How do you feel? What do you see? How are you going to get out of this predicament? When the teacher feels that the students have a sense of the characters and situations they have imagined, then the story should be introduced. This approach for getting into the story has worked for me. Adolescents, who often lack maturity, frequently have the sensitivity and awareness to empathize with others who may be different. This type of response does demand the student's intense involvement with a literary selection. It does provide for levels of involvement to allow for those who may be sensitive to other human beings but may have to struggle to stretch their emotional energies to identify with someone of a different race, especially one who is definitely marginal and of a long ago period.

The success of these kinds of activities depends on the willingness of the students, their trust in the teacher, the teacher's willingness to expand her comfort zone, and the classroom atmosphere. We cannot forget that the level of success will be influenced by what the student brings to the experience. It is important to remember that we can only hope that brief experiences we provide in our classrooms transfer in some way to the daily behavior that reflects positive living skills. But if one student was able to capture the essence of the experience, through this response activity, we have broken ground.

CONCLUSIONS

Some of the students' assessments are striking because when they discussed or reacted to the work for its historical value, the issue of race was repeatedly discussed. However, when the students related the text to the present day, the issue of race was conspicuous by its absence. In the present day the issue of race was never acknowledged. For example, the assessment of C. J. C. clearly shows an historical consciousness when she states: "His alienation was that much deeper in the 30's. Being a hobo was bad enough, but being a Black hobo was a bit worse." On the other hand, this awareness is lacking when she connects the text to the present only through its relevance to the issue of homelessness.

The same student states that in the suburbs of the 1990s "the kind of trouble Sargeant had is not usual." There is a lack of awareness that these issues still confront us.

The purpose of the lesson was to develop a level of empathy for a character in a short story through the application of reader-response theory in writing a monologue as Sargeant. What we have discovered about some of the students is a resistance or a total lack of attention to the issue of racism in contemporary society. Rosenblatt (*Reader* 42, 46) cites William James's concept of "selective attention" as distinctive of the literary experience, involving, first adoption of a focus of attention, or a stance, and second, selection of responses, relevant to the text. She further iterates that "aesthetic reading is characterized by the reader's turning his attention toward the full lived-through fusion with the text." Previous responses addressed the universal experience conveyed by the dilemma of Sargeant as a homeless man seeking shelter. Efforts to identify with his blackness ranged from no identification to pity to sympathy, any of which suggests feelings and attitudes of rejection or superiority. Sympathy for the downtrodden may be the extent to which some students at this point in their lives can emote in relating to the pain of someone so very different from anyone in their experiential background, imaginary or real. A few of the students were able to achieve empathy.

Yet these are graduates with undergraduate degrees in English—a requirement for admission. They have been educated to interpret, analyze, evaluate (all efferent concepts), but not to feel. Is there any wonder that many of our high school students see literature as something only to interpret and explicate?

If we want students to recognize the confluence of the cognitive and affective domains in the literary experience—to transact with the poem—our pedagogical approach must be modified. Humans not only think, they feel. The reader-response experience provides an opportunity for all of us to learn what it means to be a human being by providing us the opportunity to experience a range of encounters with life through the aesthetic stance.

What can we do? We can provide opportunities for our students to respond to various kinds of literature by writers from different ethnic and social backgrounds exploring a variety of concerns. Having students respond and analyze their responses will enable them to grow concomitantly in emotion and intellect. "The teaching of literature necessarily involves helping the student to handle social, psychological, and ethical concepts" (Rosenblatt, *Literature* 109). An essential element in any meaningful reading of literature is the personal contribution of the reader. To assure the success of this initial step, the teacher must be responsible for creating an environment that makes possible a spontaneous response from the student (Rosenblatt, *Literature* 108).

The second step is the students' clarification of their response to enable them more fully to understand the literary work and their own attitudes and feelings toward it.

REFERENCES

Dubois, W. E. B. *The Souls of Black Folk*. New York: Fawcett, 1967.

Hughes, Langston. "On the Road." In *Dark Symphony: Negro Literature in America*. Ed. James Emanuel and Theodore L. Gross. New York: Free Press, 1968.

Probst, Robert E. *Response and Analysis: Teaching Literature in Junior and Senior High School.* Portsmouth, NH: Boynton/Cook, 1988.

Rosenblatt, Louise M. *Literature as Exploration.* 4th ed. New York: Modern Language Association, 1983.

————. *The Reader, the Text, the Poem: The Transactional Theory of the Literary Work.* Carbondale, IL: Southern Illinois University Press, 1978.

CHAPTER 19

Reader Response to Roethke's "My Papa's Waltz":
Exploring Different Perspectives

Jean E. Brown and Louise Garcia Harrison

> *The poem, then, must be thought of as an event in time. It is not an object or an ideal*
> *entity. It happens during a coming-together, a compenetration, of a reader and a text.*
> *The reader brings to the text his [her] past experience and present personality.*
> *(Rosenblatt,* Reader *12)*

The notion that reading a poem is an interactive event between the reader and the text provides a unique set of challenges for teachers in providing opportunities for students to be actively engaged in their experiences with literature. As Rosenblatt reminds us, "The personal nature of the learning process places a decided responsibility upon the teacher" (*Literature* 247). This responsibility demands that teachers aid their students to become active in their transactions with literature. This becomes especially challenging because many students have experienced literature as a "guided" exercise in which they are directed to accept an interpretation of the work. These students then have difficulty accepting the freedom to respond and interact with the text. They are frequently conditioned to seek the "correct" response as it is determined by some distant literary authority or by the more immediate classroom authority, the teacher. By providing students with opportunities to interact with the text, teachers are able to help lift the "screen" that traditionally occurs between students and their reading.

In order to help students begin to become more responsive to their reading, teachers need to provide literature that will offer students the opportunity to be able to identify with their experiences in reading. "My Papa's Waltz" by Theodore Roethke has proved to be a selection that always elicits adamant responses from students because it allows for the meeting of readers, armed with their range of experiences, and the text.

In this chapter, we explore the responses that our students, at all levels from high school—grades nine through twelve—through graduate school, have had in experiencing the poem. In addition to examining the student responses, we also explore the impact that the social context has on student responses. Although the poem appears to be a simple remembrance of a childhood experience, it has a powerful effect on readers of all ages. The experience with "My Papa's Waltz" does become "an event" for readers.

MY PAPA'S WALTZ

The whiskey on your breath
Could make a small boy dizzy;
But I held on like death:
Such waltzing was not easy.

We romped until the pans
Slid from the kitchen shelf;
My mother's countenance
Could not unfrown itself.

The hand that held my wrist
Was battered on one knuckle;
At every step I missed
My right ear scraped a buckle.

You beat time on my head
With a palm caked hard by dirt,
Then waltzed me off to bed
Still clinging to your shirt.
                    —*Theodore Roethke*

METHODS FOR INVOLVING STUDENTS

In teaching "My Papa's Waltz" to our students we have used two primary teaching methods: the first is a brainstorming approach; the second is a written response or journal approach, which leads to both whole-group or small-group discussion. While both of these approaches involves students in a different way, their responses to the poem are consistent regardless of the approach. Most of this chapter focuses on student responses obtained by using the second approach of written responses and discussion; however, brainstorming is also examined.

The brainstorming activity involves teachers using an overhead projector with a transparency of the poem. The process involves showing one line of the poem at a time, beginning with the title. Teachers then engage students in speculation about each line, generating many possible interpretations. Initially, students often speculate that the title means "a dance the father does," or "the waltz may stand for his life." As possible meanings are generated, a student recorder writes all of the responses in list form on the chalkboard. Periodically, the class stops to review the responses in order to decide which responses are no longer valid as they have seen more of the text. In a poem with stanzas, the end of each stanza is an appropriate place to review and eliminate responses unsupported by the text. If the students come to consensus that any response is no longer appropriate, it is eliminated from the listing. In using this approach with "My Papa's Waltz," inevitably, the students' responses fall into two broad areas: first, are those that support the notion that the poem is a happy recollection of childhood and second, there are those that support a negative response to the poem.

After the whole poem is revealed, all responses are examined and the process of eliminating inappropriate responses is continued. The nature of responses to this poem creates an opportunity to have students acknowledge, if not accept, different interpretations of the poem. The method we use is to consolidate them into lists, categorizing the responses of students. Each list is examined along with the text of the poem, demonstrating that students are able to accept the responses of others while supporting their own.

The other classroom strategy that we have used with this poem is the less directive. Students are given the opportunity to write about their responses to the poem. We have students who have had limited experience responding to literature, so we begin by modeling with the whole class exploring another poem. Roethke's "Child on Top of a Greenhouse" provides an appropriate springboard. After this introductory experience, we both use a similar approach in presenting "My Papa's Waltz." First, after distributing copies of the poem, we read the poem to the class (either once or twice, depending on their experiences with responding to poetry). In this way students have the opportunity to hear the language and to begin to create images in their minds. Then we ask that students become active readers as they read it to themselves and to determine, in their view, what was happening in the poem. We also ask students if the poem recounts either a pleasant or an unpleasant experience, stressing that there are no "right" answers. In most cases, the students are asked to write their responses.

Following the writing experience, students are given the opportunity to share their reactions by reading their responses either in small-group discussion or during whole-class discussion. Some students will choose to talk about their reactions rather than read their papers. Regardless, their responses then become a springboard for class discussion. All responses are welcomed in the discussion. Students are encouraged to relate their responses to the text as a means of helping others recognize differing views. Inherent in the process is that students recognize perspectives that are different from their own.

Writing about "My Papa's Waltz" provides students with a valuable experience. It helps them to articulate the transaction they have experienced while reading. They then realize that experiencing literature is more than an analytical dissection. As a result, their responses mirror a wide range of human emotions from joyous memory, to fond recollection, to leery anticipation, to sad remembrance, to painful identification, or to poignant and painful awareness. The range of emotions that the poem elicits confirms Boyer's argument for greater attention to be given to literature in the secondary school curriculum: "Literature addresses the emotional part of the human experience. Literature transmits from generation to generation enduring spiritual and ethical values. As great literature speaks to all people, it must be available to all students" (97).

Most students have had a personal identification with the situation in the poem and with the young boy who is waltzed around the kitchen by his father. For those students who empathize with the boy, they react in two primary ways. For many of them, it evokes a positive remembrance of childhood play with their fathers; for a number of others the poem is evocative of unpleasant or, on occasion, painful experiences. In these types of personal responses readers relate the poem to their own lives, making a subjective connection with the young boy and his waltz. One ninth-grader exemplified, poignantly, how powerful the connection can be when she wrote:

> I remember when I was about six years old, my father had been drinking some and he pretended like I was a (sic) airplane and flow (sic) me to my bedroom to go to bed. Then he tugged (sic) me in, give (sic) me a kiss good-night and then after that night I never-ever seen (sic) him again.

> And this isn't a very good memory though. But when I read this poem thats (sic) what I started to remember from the past.

Other students are either unable or unwilling to empathize with the boy. These students react from a third-person perspective, being sympathetic to the situation that they generally perceive to be a difficult one. They respond to the small boy, but they either do not or cannot relate his experience to their own lives and experiences.

STAGES OF DEVELOPMENT AND READER RESPONSE

By examining student responses at various stages of their development, a number of differences in the type and perspective becomes obvious. Although the examples of the responses from the graduate students and undergraduate students differ greatly in syntax and linguistic sophistication from those of the high school students, it is the range and depth of their experiences that make the greatest difference in how they respond. These differences reflect the fact that the high school students are closer in age to the boy in the poem, and they are still involved in the family structure as dependents, whereas even the traditional-aged college undergraduate has, most often, left home and has gained a degree of independence and autonomy. The secondary students view the poem from a more limited point of reference, their own experiences:

> The man I pictured was my father. He has a blue collar job, as Roethke describes so well. When I decided to go to bed, he would not waltz me, but carry me piggyback up the stairs to my room, read me a story, and wish me goodnight. Although my mother would say we made too much noise in a playful way, I still had fun.

For this reader, the poem provides the event in which he is able to think back on a pleasant memory, and the description of the mother's reaction added authenticity to the response because his mother, too, had commented about the rough-housing, though in a "playful way." Such a response by younger students seems to be directly influenced by their current, ongoing relationship with their fathers. For older students, their perspective of the family has expanded and changed; distance has an impact on their view of the poem. This difference becomes even more pronounced for nontraditional undergraduate students or graduate students who have families of their own. The following response from a secondary English teacher who was working on a master of arts in teaching degree, illustrates the contrasting impact that experiences have on her response to the poem.

> We danced a lot for years. Even today, I feel that only men over sixty are worth dancing with. We were so silly that Mother did her adult frown at us kids and (at) Dad, with a youngster on each shoe. We'd giggle and laugh and fall into a heap—but always to very good music. Later, ages 10–16, he'd teach me (to) foxtrot and waltz and polka and I would teach him American Bandstand dances—it was magic, and I still remember, and I always will. Now Oedipus is dead and I "understand" Dad—but the memory is still golden.

The perspective of time has helped the second reader to view her experience and her whole relationship with her father from a more objective perspective. Implicit in this response is the recognition that while she and her father have had difficulties over the years, there is still that special memory of time shared and differences put aside. Interesting in the passage is also the ongoing and changing nature of the dancing ritual that she experienced with her father.

Experience also leads readers to understand reactions that may be based on biases. One undergraduate who is also a grandmother realized that her first reading of the poem led her to make assumptions about the degree of "drunkenness" of the father.

> As I reread the poem, I realized that it didn't say that the father was intoxicated, only that his breath smelled of whiskey. When we read, we often assume things that relate to our own biases. This poem portrays the sense of a healthy, loving relationship between father and son. Unfortunately, my past experience with drunken fathers and stepfathers has negatively influenced my opinions of fathers in general and drunken fathers in particular.

The level of development of this student allowed her to look beyond her obvious negative experiences, respond to the text itself and acknowledge the merit of the relationship that she recognized in the poem.

PERSONAL AND NONPERSONAL STUDENT RESPONSES

Students who view the poem from a positive perspective seem to respond to the poem holistically. They are influenced by their total impression of the experience they have with the text. The following response from a tenth-grader illustrates this type of response:

> I find the "Waltz" to be an exciting and pleasant memory from a young child's life and one that I can relate to. I believe that most children have such experiences as these. With me, my father would give us what he called, "the Treatment." Though it sounds bad, he would simply tickle us. We would usually laugh until we cried, but as small children we were always doing whatever possible to dare my father to tickle us.

This student and others see the waltz as a happy remembrance because they are able to respond to the poem through positive experiences with their fathers. The romping between the boy in the poem and his father triggered a parallel experience that the students had with their fathers. For some older students it sometimes reminds them of experiences that their children are having:

> I can picture the romping and identify with it. We do the same at our house (minus the whiskey). It reminds me of how my husband and I will either pick up one of our children and do a fast dance around the room or have them stand on our feet and frolic around. I guess it goes even further back to when I danced on my father's feet. Like the boy in the poem, you get a feeling for timing and rhythm that way.

This undergraduate student describes the continuity of a happy family tradition filled with warmth and love. She has chosen to relate to her children as her father related to her.

One ninth-grader compares the boy's experience with his own, demonstrating that "each reader brings to the transaction not only a specific past life and literary history, not only a repertory of internalized 'codes,' but also a very active present, with all its preoccupations, anxieties, questions, and aspirations" (Rosenblatt, *Reader* 144).

> This poem does not remind me of anything or does not bring me to a memory of me (sic) and my father. Me (sic) and my father enjoy watching funny movies on TV or HBO, and we get along very well. The poem is about a boy who probably has a great relationship with his father and who would show his emotions, give a lot of affection to his father.

Although this student seems to have a positive relationship with his own father, he recognizes that something is missing. For him the poem provides a vicarious recognition that there is a warmth and affection between the boy in the poem and his father that the reader longs to have. His response to the poem accomplishes what Aleksandr Solzhenitsyn in his 1972 Nobel Acceptance Speech discusses as the inherent value of literature: "can overcome man's unfortunate trait of learning only through his own experience . . . recreating in the flesh what another has experienced, and allowing it to be acquired as one's own" (93).

While these students are able to respond from a positive viewpoint, the poem is an unpleasant or even frightening experience for many students. Most of them cite specific experiences from their own childhoods as indicative of how the boy must have felt about the waltz. These students use an analytical approach. They usually cite specific language from the poem to support their negative responses, such as:

whiskey

dizzy

held on like death

waltzing was not easy

countenance could not unfrown itself

battered

scraped a buckle

beat time

still clinging to your shirt

Certainly, in isolation these words and phrases do have negative connotations. For these students, the words and phrases fit together to paint a picture of an unhappy experience in which the young boy is subjected to the whims of his inebriated father.

> Most of the feelings were negative ones associated with alcoholism in my immediate family. I felt a sadness for the boy because I can relate very well to the "whiskey on your breath" and the mother's frown.

For one undergraduate student, a woman in her late thirties, a mother of three who had returned to school after being divorced, the poem evoked a specific unhappy memory:

> The poem made me mad. It was just like when my former husband would come home and roughhouse with the kids and get them so riled up that they couldn't get to sleep. He was only

there for the fun and I had to do all the dirty work. The kids thought he was the big hero and I was the villain. I could really relate to the mother in the poem.

Her experiences provided her with the insight to recognize and to empathize with the forgotten person in the poem, the mother. From her account, she also felt that she was reduced to the role of the enemy while she tried to maintain order in the family. Another student expressed the impact of the language when he said: "I couldn't get into the poem. The first line, talking about the whiskey, reminded me so much of my dad that I couldn't read any more of it." This type of response or overreaction to the poem appears to be the result of the process Rosenblatt describes as when a reader "projected on the text elements of his past experience not relevant to it, and which are not susceptible of coherent incorporation into it" (*Reader* 11). For this student the past experience was so unpleasant that the student was unable to entertain any possible involvement with the poem.

Many students, who have studied literature as an academic exercise in which they seek the correct interpretation have a difficult time establishing a transactional relationship with their reading. The following response by a ninth-grader sees the poem positively; however, he does not interact on a personal level. Although his insights are perceptive, he does not engage directly with the poem:

> I liked this poem because it presented closeness of a boy and his father. The poem hints that the man is a hard worker and spends time with the boy whenever he can. At least, that was my first reaction.
>
> The poem was constructed neatly and the rhyme gave it an added emotion of innocence or joy.
>
> And it shows how secure the boy feels in his father's arms, which may have been why the author chose to write the poem in a rhyming fashion.

His response is a good example of this type of reaction, more likely to be sympathetic rather than empathetic to the text. He made the assumption that the boy had a good relationship with his father and that interpretation colored his whole reaction to the poem.

SOCIAL CONTEXT

Over the years, students have responded to the boy remembering the smell of whiskey on his father's breath, but recently the attitudes of college and graduate students more often assume that he is drunk during the waltz and his "drunkenness" is the product of alcoholism rather than a singular experience. Certainly, the public awareness of alcoholism has increased in recent years. Public service announcements in the media, organizations like Mothers Against Drunk Driving (MADD), and cautions from the medical establishment have all led to a heightened awareness of the potential problems of drinking. The only reference to drinking is in the poem's first line. The text does not support nor does it deny the assumptions of alcoholism or even drunkenness. Interestingly, whereas today's secondary students are more conscious of the "whiskey on your breath" than students were when we first used the poem seventeen years ago, they are also less judgmental and less likely to assume a drinking problem than the older students. There is a matter-of-fact acceptance by these students, even if they assume that the father was drunk during the waltz. One ninth-grader expressed this attitude:

> I think that the father was probably drunk, and that is why they're dancing. I know my father wouldn't have danced with me unless he was drunk (which didn't happen very often).

His attitude of acceptance is typical of many of the younger readers. The drinking is a reality to be recognized but not necessarily judged. The extreme example of the acceptance of drinking among the secondary students was illustrated by the ninth-grader whose response to the poem was beyond the text as he related an experience he had drinking at a party and returning home drunk himself and getting grounded by his stepmother. Again this example is of an irrelevant experience stifling a student's ability to interact with the text.

The impact of social change—family structure—is evident as an influence on how some secondary students respond to the poem. The number of students from single-parent homes is significantly different now than it was when even the undergraduate students were growing up. Some students whose parents are divorced were unable to interact with the poem from their own personal experiences because they had never "frolicked" with their fathers. Several of the students translated the experience to an uncle who danced with them, whereas another was reminded of experiences with a friend's father. An additional implication of the single-parent home was described by one of the undergraduate students:

> Poems like this make me really sad because they remind of what I missed when I was a kid. My dad was killed in Viet Nam when I was only two, so I never knew him. I would have been glad even if he did smell of whiskey once in a while. Just to have known him. . . .

The influence of current social concerns manifests itself in another significant way in the interpretation of the poem. Although some students have traditionally viewed the poem as an unpleasant experience, the interpretation of abuse is a recent development. The attention to abuse evokes powerful emotional responses; there are words that have special connotations when they are used in this context ("battered," "scraped a buckle," and "beat time"). The word *battered* has gained a whole new meaning than it had when Roethke wrote the poem. But readers respond from the perspective of their times and to those expressions that are familiar. For today's reader, the term *battered* has a strong emotional impact. It is interesting that a frequently used expression such as "beat time" in this context evokes a negative response from some readers.

Additionally, the spectre of violence in society is identified by several students who assumed that the "battered knuckle" indicated that the father was involved in a fight when he stopped for the drink. Others made an even more startling assumption: the knuckles were battered when Papa hit the boy or his mother. Several students even expressed concern that the boy was endangered while dancing.

On the other hand, other students from families where the father is a blue-collar worker frequently assumed that he hurt his hand because he is a laborer. A tenth-grader said: "I think that the boy's father was a hard working man that is involved in some sort of manual labor because of his battered knuckle and palm caked with dirt."

DIVERSITY OF OPINION

> I love this poem, have always loved it, because of its technical excellence—its rhythm, its imagery, its mingling of pleasure and pain. Will I condemn the father because he is drunk and hurts the son unknowingly? No—and Roethke didn't either. Papa just was.

The evidence that the poem evokes a range of student responses is well documented by the examples that we have examined. They reflect the reader's experiences, life situation, and culture in relation to the text. As teachers recognize the potential that a text provides for diverse reactions, they will view the diversity of student responses as an indication that the process of making the connection between the reader and the text is coming to fruition. In this process one of the central areas of discussion is on the differences in interpretation among the students. The teacher's role is not to attempt to find ways to reconcile differing opinions, but rather to help students to accept and to honor attitudes different from theirs. These responses are broadly either personal or nonpersonal and those students who have personal responses react either positively or negatively to their experience reading the poem. The discussion then moves to an exploration of *how* and *why* there have been these variations.

By using both the brainstorming and the written response and discussion approaches, students are encouraged to express their reactions in a supportive, accepting environment. In this process students freely exchange their responses. Students are neither expected to come to a common attitude nor to adapt their transactions to conform to any other responses. The sharing of student reactions either as they read their responses or through the class discussion is conducive to building a sense of community within the classroom. In this environment, students are willing to disclose very personal reactions. It is the nature of this poem and the type of intense transactions that the students have with it that helps to establish this supportive classroom climate. This feeling of community, in turn, provides for students' willingness to hear differing attitudes and to acknowledge another perspective. The honesty, candor, and openness of this experience serves to make students more respectful of their peers, the diversity of their lives, and of the differences of their opinions.

Rosenblatt explains that the reader "may learn indirectly about others' experiences with the text; he [she] may come to see that his [her] own was confused or impoverished, and he [she] may then be stimulated to call forth from the text a better poem. But this he [she] must do him[her]self, and only what he [she] him[her]self experiences in relation to text is—again let us underline—*for him* [her], the work" (*Reader* 105). Therefore, through class discussion we can provide enriched opportunities for students to explore their experiences with the text so they may choose to reexamine their responses.

The experiences that we, as teachers, have had in using "My Papa's Waltz" with students at all levels, affirm that responding to literature can be an "event" that speaks, often poignantly, to their lives and perspectives rather than an academic exercise in which they seek correct interpretations. This type of personal connection with literature provides readers of all ages with opportunities to be active participants in their relationship with the text.

REFERENCES

Boyer, Ernest L. *High School: A Report on Secondary Education in America*. New York: Harper & Row, 1983.

Roethke, Theodore. "My Papa's Waltz." In *The Pocket Book of Modern Verse*. Ed. Oscar Williams. New York: Pocket Books, 1972. 433.

Rosenblatt, Louise M. *Literature as Exploration*. 4th ed. New York: Modern Language Association, 1983.

———. *The Reader, the Text, the Poem: The Transactional Theory of the Literary Work*. Carbondale, IL: Southern Illinois University Press, 1978.

Solzhenitsyn, Aleksandr. *Nobel Lecture*. New York: Farrar, Straus and Giroux, 1972.

Glossary: Key Concepts and Strategies

Aesthetic stance. The approach of a reader toward a text that focuses attention on her or his senses and feelings in the experiencing of the text; that is, what is being lived through *during* the reading event. Aesthetic responses are personal and unique since private language nuances come into play along with personal associations, attitudes, and values. Refer to *Efferent stance; Stance.* (See Chapters 2, 5, 15, 17, and 18.)

Biographical criticism. Based on the view that the literary work is primarily a reflection of the author's life, personality, and times, this critical approach assumes the text can be interpreted in terms of the author's intention. (See Chapters 2 and 6.)

Biopoem. A structured autobiographical poem with a designated number of lines which can be varied to suit individual purpose. Each line has a lead and a specified number of words to indicate how it is to be completed. (See Chapter 15.)

Dialogue journal. Refer to *Journal; Response.* (See Chapter 5.)

Efferent stance. The approach of a reader toward a text that focuses attention on the denotative definition of words, on their public meanings. The reading is impersonal, removed from emotional involvement. The purpose of efferent reading is the ideas, the information or instruction to be learned or acted upon after the reading event. Refer to *Aesthetic stance; Stance.* (See Chapters 2 and 18.)

Expressive writing. Personal writing that expresses the feelings or examines the ideas of the writer. Often the writer explores or discovers aspects of the self or clarifies the relationship of self to the world. Expressive writing may take various forms, but it tends toward the informal. (See Chapter 10.)

Feminist criticism. An approach to literature that takes into account the image of women characters in texts, the place of women writers in the literary canon, and the unique responses of female readers to texts as contrasted to those of male readers. In the assumption that the reader (i.e. gender) is significant in establishing meaning, feminist criticism falls within the reader-response context. (See Chapters 2, 6, 11, and 16.)

Gendered reading. Terminology used to suggest the impact of the gender of a reader on her or his response to and interpretation of a text. Refer to *Feminist criticism*. (See Chapter 16.)

Historical criticism. The critical approach involving the study of historical materials; that is, the history of literary periods, movements, and culture, in order to understand the literary document. (See Chapters 2 and 6.)

Imaginative writing. Writing that creates or recreates experience, rather than explains it, that uses language to evoke emotions and experiences in others. Imaginative writing includes drama and narratives—fables, tales, short stories, novels, poetry, and others. (See Chapter 10.)

Intentional fallacy. The assertion that negates references to evidence outside a text to establish the interpretation of that text. Such evidence might include statements by the author which express her or his intentions—purpose, meaning—or information about the author's life, beliefs, and times. In the first instance, the author's intentions may not be borne out in the text. Further, the text must speak for itself to its audience. (See Chapter 2.)

Journal, response. When used with literature, the purpose of this writing activity is to engage or elicit the reader's personal response to a text. It is intended as a process response, a reflection of spontaneous feelings and attitudes. There are several names and formats for such journals, including reading journal, learning log, and dialogue journal. The last involves a written dialogue between two readers responding to a text, perhaps two students or a student and a teacher. (See Chapters 2, 7–10, and 12–18.)

Learning log. Refer to *Journal, response*.

Marxist criticism. An approach to literary criticism that is based on the economic and cultural theory of Karl Marx. Such critics examine the ideological background of the authors and the expression of social realism in the text. To the extent that the reader is significant in establishing meaning, Marxist criticism falls within the reader-response context. (See Chapter 6.)

New criticism. Literary criticism that is based on the primacy of the text. The literary work is perceived as an object, autonomous from the world. The text is examined objectively with close analysis of the internal interrelationships, such linguistic relationships as word interactions, figures of speech and symbols, and the central theme. The author—intentions and biography—and social factors are rejected; the reader is depersonalized. (See Chapters 2, 3, 5, 6, 10, and 14.)

Plausibility. Comparable to the term *validity*, this suggests the probability of an interpretation reflecting elements of a text, being coherent and inclusive of its various features and language subtleties. *Implausibility* suggests the opposite; that is, a response that is or tends to be outside the text. Refer to *Validity*. (See Chapters 8 and 11.)

Prereading. An activity conducted before a text is read or before it is discussed to prepare the readers for the text or the discussion. Such exercises tend to help students/readers to connect their personal experiences with those of the text or help them to activate and begin to shape their experiential response to the text. (See Chapters 1, 6–9, 11, 12, and 19.)

Psychological criticism. In this approach, the focus of critical attention is on the analysis of psychological aspects of the author so as to explain and interpret elements of the literary work, such as character and symbol. A reverse focus analyzes the writings of an author so as to establish her or his personality, feeling states, and development. (See Chapters 2 and 6.)

Reader response approach. The application of reader response criticism. Teachers establish a classroom climate using appropriate language, stance, processes, and procedures to encourage the active role of the reader with the text; readers use the concepts embodied by the theory as they process their reading. Refer to *Reader response criticism; stance.* (See Chapters 1–3, 5–9, 11–13, 15–17, and 19.)

Reader response criticism. That body of criticism that focuses on the reader in relation to the text as differentiated from other critical theories which ignore or reject the reader. There is an array of critical positions referred to by this terminology which are generally differentiated by their orientation toward the reader, toward the text, or toward the reader-and-text. By invoking the role of the reader as active recreater of the text, reader response criticism recognizes the validity of more than one interpretation, thus rejecting the notion of a single determinate meaning of a text. Refer to *Subjective criticism; Transactional theory.* (See Chapters 2, 6, and 8.)

Reader response diagram. An exercise designed to help students reflect on their transaction with the text. Each reader is asked to identify characteristics, attitudes or ideas of herself or himself along with aspects of the text that might have affected the transaction. (See Chapter 8.)

Reader's theatre. An activity using a script that involves rendering a literary work orally with some—usually minimal—movement and character interaction. The presentation may be staged but without props. (See Chapter 7.)

Reading event. A reading occasion; that is, an act of reading which occurs at a particular moment to an individual reader in the context of a particular situation or environment. (See Chapter 2.)

Selective attention. In a reading context, this term refers to the reader's process of selecting certain features of the text to relate to, certain subtleties of language and relationships to focus on or minimize. Consciously or unconsciously, the reader processes the text according to her or his dominant reader stance and interest, and is influenced by individual language and life experiences. The process is dynamic in the sense of response to individual elements and in the evolving of responses—the shifting and changing, the building and restructuring that occurs as the reader proceeds through the text. Refer to *Stance; Transactional theory.* (See Chapters 2 and 18.)

Simulation exercise or game. A type of role play in which readers are asked to take on the persona of a character (or in some way relate or respond to a character), enacting a "frame" of the character's life situation within or extending from the text. This activity might be oral, written, or a combination (e.g., creating a monologue, dialogue, or conversation; writing a diary, log entry, letter, or advertisement). (See Chapters 2, 7, and 18.)

Stance. The approach that a reader adopts toward the reading of a text, that is, to what the reader consciously or unconsciously directs her or his attention. A continuum of response possibilities (stances) exist from the predominantly aesthetic to the predominantly efferent and in between. The same text may be read in either direction, toward the efferent or toward the aesthetic, by different readers or by the same reader at different times. Refer to *Aesthetic stance; Efferent stance.* (See Chapters 2 and 10.)

Structural criticism. The focus of structural critics is on the operative structure of a literary work. This approach identifies and analyzes the conventions that characterize and differentiate the different forms (e.g., genre and sub-genre) as well as the elements of the text, such as narrative structure and characterization. (See Chapters 2 and 6.)

Subjective criticism. Primacy is given to the reader in this reader response position. Meaning emerges from the readers; they create texts as expressions of their individual "identity themes" or to produce self understanding. The focus is on the reader's response experience and its interpretation. The concept of the objective text is rejected. (See Chapter 2.)

Transaction. This term as it is applied in a reading context establishes the dynamic relationship of reader and text in which they go beyond merely affecting one another; each conditions and is conditioned by the other. The term *transaction* is differentiated from *interaction* which suggests two discrete elements acting on each other. Refer to *Transactional theory.* (See Chapters 2, 3, 5, 6, 8, 11, 13, 14, and 19.)

Transactional theory. The theoretical approach within the reader-response spectrum which insists that the reader and the text are mutually essential elements of a reading event. The text acts as a catalyst or stimulus for the reader, activating aspects of her or his personality and experience, as well as a guide or constraint during the reading process. The reader responds to the text as influenced by these aspects and the immediate situation, selecting features and nuances of language and relationships according to these internal/external factors. Refer to *Selective attention.* (See Chapters 1, 2, 4–6, 8, 15, and 16.)

Unsent letter. Refer to *Simulation exercise.* (See Chapter 15.)

Validity. A term denoting the appropriateness of a reading—interpretation—as measured against the constraints of the text. An out-of-context response or a strongly skewed response may be said to be an invalid or a less valid transaction with the text. This is not intended to suggest that there is a single correct interpretation or meaning of a literary work. Refer to *Plausibility.* (See Chapters 1, 2, and 5.)

Writing to learn. The use of writing as a tool for learning rather than for learning to write. It places emphasis on the writing process rather than on completion of a product. Frequently, it uses the short writing activities often associated with prewriting and prereading. (See Chapter 15.)

Bibliography

Representative selections of the following bibliography are annotated. In addition to books expressing reader-response theory and pedagogy, several recent titles expressing alternative theories are included for purposes of comparison.

Books

Beach, Richard, and James Marshall. *Teaching Literature in the Secondary School*. San Diego: Harcourt Brace Jovanovich, 1990.

Bettelheim, Bruno. *The Uses of Enchantment: The Meaning and Importance of Fairy Tales*. New York: Knopf, 1976.

Bleich, David. *Readings and Feelings: An Introduction to Subjective Criticism*. Urbana, IL: National Council of Teachers of English, 1975.

Bleich's stated aim is "to demonstrate that literature exists altogether on the basis of the subjective re-creation of the reader." He illustrates and analyzes levels of response to texts—perception, the affective and the associative. Further, Bleich discusses subjective interpretation as a communal act and provides suggestions for applying his ideas in the classroom.

———. *Subjective Criticism*. Baltimore: Johns Hopkins University Press, 1978.

Bleich asserts the power of individual readers to create and control interpretation of texts. He projects a three-stage reading process: subjective response; resymbolization, that is, the reader's desire and thrust toward explanation (interpretation); and negotiation with a community of readers to develop new knowledge. By stating that having an interpretation is not possible in "isolation from a community," Bleich seems to undermine his basic premise.

Burke, Kenneth. *The Philosophy of Literary Form*. New York: Vintage, 1957.

Cain, William E. *The Crisis in Criticism: Theory, Literature, and Reform in English Studies*. Baltimore: The Johns Hopkins University Press, 1984.

An extended discussion of New Criticism, followed by a review of the "state of criticism" in the twentieth century.

Clifford, John, ed. *The Experience of Reading: Louise Rosenblatt and Reader Response Theory.* Portsmouth, NH: Boynton/Cook, 1991.

Rosenblatt's Transactional (Reader Response) Theory is explored in the context of both criticism and pedagogy. Essay topics include: promoting the values of democracy, feminism, teacher-student relationships, bridging pedagogy and theory, and modes of reading.

Cooper, Charles C., ed. *Researching Response to Literature and the Teaching of Literature: Points of Departure.* Norwood, NJ: Ablex, 1984.

Corcoran, Bill, and Emrys Evans, eds. *Readers, Texts, Teachers.* Upper Montclair, NJ: Boynton/Cook, 1987.

Revising the basis for teaching literature and encouraging the experience of literature are the foci of this anthology. The chapters, after two on theoretical and historical background, provide classroom, reader-response practices. Four of these are concerned with writing, others with types of mental activity and methods of developing responses.

Culler, Jonathan. *Structural Poetics: Structuralism, Linguistics, and the Study of Literature.* Ithaca; Cornell University Press, 1975.

Eagleton, Terry. *Literary Theory: An Introduction.* Minneapolis: University of Minnesota Press, 1983.

Literary theories of the twentieth century—with some prefatory historical background—are defined and discussed. Eagleton, further, expresses the limitations of these theories from a social-political (Marxist Criticism) perspective.

Eco, Umberto. *The Limits of Interpretation.* Bloomington: Indiana University Press, 1990.

In this collection, Eco discusses aspects of interpretive theory and applies his thinking to a variety of materials. He proposes a "moderate" position: while acknowledging the concept of multiple readings of a text, he asserts that some reader-response critics overdominate the text, that "it is possible to reach an agreement, if not about meanings that a text encourages, at least about those that a text discourages" (45).

————. *The Role of the Reader: Explorations in the Semiotics of Texts.* Bloomington: Indiana University Press, 1979.

Farrell, Edmund J., and James R. Squire, eds. *Transactions with Literature: A Fifty-Year Perspective.* Urbana, IL: National Council of Teachers of English, 1990.

These essays, commemorating the 50th anniversary of the publication of *Literature as Exploration,* explore books for young people over that time span, the classroom tradition, and the research tradition. A retrospective essay by Rosenblatt and an extended bibliography round out the book.

Fetterly, Judith. *The Resisting Reader: A Feminist Approach to American Fiction.* Bloomington: Indiana University Press, 1978.

Fish, Stanley. *Is There a Text in This Class?* Cambridge: Harvard University Press, 1980.

In the early essays of this collection, the reader is identified as "the self-sufficient repository of meaning" in opposition to the text. Later, Fish advances the concept of the interpretive community, which supersedes both the reader and the text. A reader, as a "product" of a community, interprets meaning from a text as enabled by that community; interpretations will vary accordingly. Communities are defined by such aspects as culture, situation, context, perspective, and interpretive strategies.

Flynn, Elizabeth A., and Patrocinio P. Schweikart, eds. *Gender and Reading: Essays on Reader Texts and Contexts.* Baltimore: Johns Hopkins University Press, 1986.

Freund, Elizabeth. *The Return of the Reader: Reader Response Criticism.* New York: Methuen, 1987.

Greene, Gayle, and Coppelia Kahn. *Making a Difference: Feminist Literary Criticism.* New York: Methuen, 1986.

Hernadi, Paul, ed. *What is Criticism?* Bloomington: Indiana University Press, 1981.

Holland, Norman. *The Dynamics of Literary Response.* New York: Oxford University Press, 1968.

———. *Five Readers Reading.* New Haven: Yale University Press, 1975.

Identified as subjective/psychological criticism. This study of the detailed responses of five readers to the same texts reveals, according to Holland, that ". . . the way one puts a story together derives from the structures in the mind one brings to the story" (39). While acknowledging that readers "draw on" textual features, Holland focuses on their "identity themes" as the source of meaning.

———. *Poems in Persons: An Introduction to the Psychoanalysis of Literature.* New York: Norton, 1973.

Iser, Wolfgang. *The Act of Reading: A Theory of Aesthetic Response.* Baltimore: The Johns Hopkins University Press, 1978.

Identified as a "reception" theorist, Iser acknowledges the active role of the reader—the reader is present in the text" (118)—and the potential for more than one interpretation of a text. His discussion relates how the strategies of the text guide or direct the reader who fills in gaps, textual indeterminacies. It seems that the features of the text control the meaning, giving it, ultimately, greater prominence.

———. *The Implied Reader: Patterns of Communication in Prose Fiction from Bunyan to Beckett.* Baltimore: Johns Hopkins University Press, 1974.

Kintgen, E. R. *The Perception of Poetry.* Bloomington, IN: Indiana University Press, 1983.

Loban, Walter, Margaret Ryan, and James R. Squire. *Teaching Language and Literature,* 2nd ed. New York, Harcourt, Brace and World, 1969.

Mailloux, Steven. *Interpretive Conventions: The Reader in the Study of American Fiction.* Ithaca, NY: Cornell University Press, 1982.

Mailloux compares and analyzes five theories of reader-response criticism: the subjectivism (psychological), phenomenology (intersubjective), and structuralism (social). He proceeds to develop a social reading model that is "temporal and convention-based." Interpretive conventions are defined as "shared ways of making sense of reality . . . communal procedures for making intelligible the world, behavior, communication and literary texts" (149).

Moran, Charles, and Elizabeth F. Penfield, eds. *Conversations: Contemporary Critical Theory and the Teaching of English.* Urbana, IL: National Council of Teachers of English, 1990.

Milner, Joseph O., and Lucy F. Milner, eds. *Passages to Literature: Essays on Teaching in Australia, Canada, England, the United States, and Wales.* Urbana, IL: National Council of Teachers of English, 1989.

Nelms, Ben F., ed. *Literature in the Classroom: Readers, Texts, and Contexts.* Urbana, IL: National Council of Teachers of English, 1988.

The three sections of this collection of essays echo the subtitle: I—expresses response and reading theory, both theoretically and in practice; II—illustrates several approaches: response, historical, structural, sociological, and feminist; III—provides discussion of "social dimensions," such as multiethnic and international.

Ong, Walter J. *Orality and Literacy*. London: Methuen, 1982.

Probst, Robert E. *Response and Analysis: Teaching Literature in Junior and Senior High School*. Portsmouth, NH: Boynton/Cook, 1988.

Teaching literature through the transactional model of reader-response criticism is the center of this text. Its concepts inform discussions of, for example, classroom strategies, text selection, the literature curriculum, and evaluation.

Purves, Alan, Theresa Rogers, and Anna O. Soter. *How Porcupines Make Love: Notes on a Response-Centered Curriculum*. 2nd ed. New York: Longman, 1990.

Literature instruction and curriculum development are the two foci of this text. Discussions of the response-centered curriculum and the role of the teacher are followed by explanation-illustration of teaching strategies: discussion, use of visuals, oral, and written activities. Concluding chapters are concerned with assignments and examinations.

Purves, Alan C., and Richard Beach. *Literature and the Reader: Research in Response to Literature, Reading Interests and the Teaching of Literature*. Urbana, IL: National Council of Teachers of English, 1972.

Rosenblatt, Louise M. *Literature as Exploration*. 4th ed. New York: Modern Language Association, 1983.

Identified as the first to establish the importance of the reader in creating meaning, Rosenblatt discusses the nature of the literary experience, asserting the relationship of reader and text in evoking a "poem." The influence of personal, social, and cultural aspects is expressed. Significant implications for teaching are drawn, underlying themes being the development of humanistic concerns and democratic values and practices.

————. *The Reader, the Text, the Poem: The Transactional Theory of the Literary Work*. Carbondale: Southern Illinois University Press, 1978. 2nd ed. 1992, forthcoming.

The focus of this work is theoretical. Rosenblatt enunciates fully the transactional nature of the reading process, exploring in detail the "poem as event" and the "evoking of a poem." She expresses the efferent-aesthetic continuum and the "openness and constraint" of the text; that is, the factor of validity. The text concludes with a discussion of response and interpretation for all readers in relation to criticism.

Scholes, Robert. *Textual Power: Literary Theory and the Teaching of English*. New Haven: Yale University Press, 1985.

Scholes acknowledges the role of the reader, eschewing the New Critical approach. However, he concentrates on the power of the text. Establishing three related skills—reading, interpretation, and criticism—he illustrates their teaching and argues for a curriculum of textual studies; that is, textual knowledge and skill. In his final chapter, he contests Stanley Fish's concept of interpretive communities.

Slatoff, Walter J. *With Respect to Readers: Dimensions of Literary Response*. Ithaca, NY: Cornell University Press, 1970.

The varieties of involvement as shaped by individual differences among readers are explored, and divergent responses in relation to the guidance and limitation of the text are detailed. Slatoff expresses the need to go beyond the seeking of commonalities among responses; that is, to reflect on and discuss the differences as well. A general discussion of pedagogical implications concludes the book.

Suleiman, Susan R., and Inge Crosman, eds. *The Reader in the Text: Essays on Audience and Interpretation*. Princeton: Princeton University Press, 1980.

This anthology focuses on reading and the reader, its primary aim being "to explore fundamental questions about the status—be it semiotic, sociological, hermeneutic, subjective—of audience in relation to the artistic text" (vii). The introductory essay discusses six varieties of audience-oriented criticism. An extensive bibliography is included.

Squire, James R., ed. *Response to Literature*. Champaign, IL: National Council of Teachers of English, 1968.

Thompson, Jack. *Understanding Teenagers' Reading: Reading Processes and the Teaching of Literature*. Melbourne: Methuen Australia Pty, Ltd. (New York: Nichols Publishing Company), 1987.

Tompkins, Jane P., ed. *Reader Response Criticism: From Formalism to Post-Structuralism*. Baltimore: Johns Hopkins University Press, 1980.

A clear overview of the major theoretical positions within the body of reader-response criticism. The collected essays are arranged logically to show relationships among the positions but also to pattern the focus on text orientation through reader-plus-text to reader domination. The closing chapter provides a historical "shape of literary response."

Articles

Anderson, Philip M. "The Past *Is* Now: Approaches to the Secondary School Literature Curriculum." *English Journal* 75.8 (Dec. 1986): 19–22.

Athanases, Steven. "Developing a Classroom Community of Interpreters." *English Journal* 77.1 (Jan. 1988): 45–48.

Black, Stephen A. "On Reading Psychoanalytically." *College English* 39.3 (Nov. 1977): 267–274.

Blake, Robert W., and Anna Lunn. "Responding to Poetry: High School Students Read Poetry." *English Journal* 75.2 (Feb. 1986): 68–73.

Report of a study of what five untrained high school students do as they process a new poem.

Beach, Richard, and Linda Wendler. "Developmental Differences in Response to a Story." *Research in the Teaching of English* 21 (1987): 286–297.

This study compared the inferences of readers from four class levels (secondary and college) about characters' acts, perceptions, and goals. Readers' cognitive development, social cognition, and self-concepts significantly affected their focus.

Beehler, Sharon A. "Close vs. Closed Reading: Interpreting the Clues." *English Journal* 77.6 (Oct. 1988): 39–43.

Bleich, David. "The Subjective Character of Critical Interpretation." *College English* 36.7 (Mar. 1975): 739–755.

Projects the dynamics of the subjective response, denying the objective text. Bleich contrasts his position with that of Holland.

Carey, Robert F. "The Reader, the Text, the Response: Literary Theory and Reading Research." *English Quarterly* 18.3 (Fall 1985): 17–23.

Carlsen, G. Robert. "Literature IS." *English Journal* 63.2 (Feb. 1974): 23–27.

Chase, Nancy D., and Cynthia R. Hynd. "Reader Response: An Alternative Way to Teach Students to Think about the Text." *Journal of Reading* 30 (1987): 530–540.

Clifford, John. "A Response Pedagogy for Noncanonical Literature." *Reader* 15 (Spring 1986): 48–61.

———. "Transactional Teaching and the Literary Experience." *English Journal* 68.9 (Dec. 1979): 36–39.

Presents a philosophy of teaching literature founded on Rosenblatt's transactional theory.

Connor, John W., and Irene Chalmers-Neubauer. "Mrs. Schuster Adopts Discussion: A Four-Week Experiment in an English Classroom." *English Education* 21.1 (Feb. 1989): 30–38.

Corcoran, Bill. "Spiders, Surgeons, and Anxious Aliens: Three Classroom Allies." *English Journal* 77.1 (Jan. 1988): 39–44.

Three clusters of classroom strategies are presented, responding to three features: readers, texts, and cultural contexts.

Culp, Mary Beth. "Literature's Influence on Young Adult Attitudes, Values, and Behavior, 1975–1984." *English Journal* 74.8 (Dec. 1985): 31–35.

Report of a study to ascertain the influence of literature based upon the responses of the readers themselves.

DeMott, Benjamin. "Learning How to Imagine a Poem." *English Education* 22.2 (May 1988): 71–87.

Dilworth, Collett B. "The Reader as Poet: A Strategy for Creative Reading." *English Journal* 66.2 (Feb. 1977): 43–47.

Dionisio, Marie. "Responding to Literary Elements through Mini-lessons and Dialogue Journals." *English Journal* 80.1 (Jan. 1991): 40–44.

Duke, Charles R. "The Case of the Divorced Reader." *English Journal* 66.2 (Feb. 1977): 33–36.

The negative effect on readers of distancing the text is contrasted to personal response experiences.

———. "Tapping the Power of Personal Response to Poetry." *Journal of Reading* 33 (1990): 442–447.

Eeds, Maryann and Deborah Wells. "Grand Conversations: An Exploration of Meaning Construction in Literature Study Groups." *Research in the Teaching of English* 23 (1989): 4–29.

The way readers and teachers build meaning together is expressed and illustrated in this study. Teacher behavior as it influences these "conversations" is described.

Fillion, Bryant. "Reading as Inquiry: An Approach to Literature Learning." *English Journal* 70.1 (Jan. 1981): 39–45.

Flood, James, and Diane Lapp. "A Reader-Response Approach to the Teaching of Literature." *Reading Research and Instruction* 27.4 (Summer 1988): 61–66.

Proposes a design for an instructional process for response-based teaching.

Flynn, Elizabeth A. "Composing Responses to Literary Texts: A Process Approach." *College Composition and Communication* 34 (1983): 342–348.

Flynn illustrates the process of responding to a literary text, moving from "expressive" or "writer-based writing"—relating texts to their own experience to "reader-based writing"—that is, *about* literary texts, reflecting analysis. Journal writing is used in the initial stage.

———. "Gender and Reading." *College English* 45 (1983): 236–253.

A comparison of the attitudes, strategies, and interpretations of men and women to the same stories.

Fowler, Lois Josephs, and Kathleen McCormick. "The Expectant Reader in Theory and Practice." *English Journal* 75.6 (Oct. 1986): 45–47.

Galda, Lee. "A Longitudinal Study of the Spectator Stance as a Function of Age and Genre." *Research in the Teaching of English* 24 (1990): 261–278.

The movement of students toward a spectator stance, that is "to evaluate more broadly, to savor feelings, and to contemplate forms," is documented according to grade level. Also revealed is the impact of genre upon the response process.

Gilles, Carol. "Reading, Writing, and Talking: Using Literature Study Groups." *English Journal* 78.1 (Jan. 1989): 39–41.

Graham, Joan, and Robert E. Probst. "Eliciting Responses to Literature." *Kentucky English Journal* 32.1 (Fall 1982): 30–46.

Greco, Norma. "Recreating the Literary Text: Practice and Theory." *English Journal* 79.6 (Nov. 1990): 41–46.

Hesse, Douglas. "Canon and Critical Thinking: An Inductive Teaching Strategy." *English Journal* 66.2 (Feb. 1977): 37–42.

Howell, Suzanne. "Unlocking the Box: An Experiment in Literary Response." *English Journal* 66.2 (Feb. 1977): 37–42.

Hunt, Russell, A. "Toward a Process-Intervention Model in Literature Teaching." *College English* 44 (1982): 345–357.

Hynds, Susan. "Bringing Life to Literature and Literature to Life: Social Constructs and Contexts of Four Adolescent Readers." *Research in the Teaching of Literature* 23 (1987): 30–61.

Two questions are explored in this study: How students bring social-cognitive processes to reading and what contextual factors in and outside the classroom appear to influence readers' connections between literature and life.

————. "Interpersonal Cognitive Complexity and the Literary Processes of Adolescent Readers." *Research in the Teaching of English* 19 (1985): 386–402.

This study examines the degree to which interpersonal cognitive complexity affects readers in their perceptions of characters as well as to story comprehension, response preferences, and literary attitudes.

Jacobsen, Mary. "Looking for Literary Space: The Willing Suspension of Disbelief Revisited." *Research in the Teaching of English* 16 (1982): 21–38.

The author's students describe their experiences while reading a short story. What they contribute to the reading and what might block their responses are discussed.

Langer, Judith A. "The Process of Understanding: Reading for Literary and Informative Purposes." *Research in the Teaching of English* 24 (1990): 229–260.

The meaning-making processes of middle and senior high school students are described. Four stances that are taken toward texts are explored, revealing that the focus of readers' concerns in each stance differs. Characteristics of readers' approaches to reading for literary and information purposes are differentiated.

Leitch, Vincent B. "A Primer of Recent Critical Theories." *College English* 39 (1977): 138–152.

Lindberg, Barbara. "Teaching Literature: The Process Approach" *Journal of Reading* 31 (1988): 732–735.

Mandel, Barrett J. "Text and Context in the Teaching of English." *English Journal* 68.9 (Dec. 1979): 40–44.

Expresses the limitations of teacher dominated "contexts" and offers an alternative approach.

McAnulty, Sara J. "Breaking the Barriers: Teaching Martin Jamison's 'Rivers'." *English Journal* 78.2 (Feb. 1989): 75–78.

McCormick, Kathleen. "Theory in the Reader: Bleich, Holland, and Beyond." *College English* 47 (1985): 836–850.

Alternatives to the purely spontaneous response statements within a reader-centered course are offered and discussed.

Muldoon, Phyllis A. "Challenging Students to Think: Shaping Questions, Building Community." *English Journal* 79.4 (Apr. 1990): 34–40.

Myers, Kris. "Twenty (Better) Questions." *English Journal* 77.1 (Jan. 1988): 64–65.

Peterson, Bruce T. "Writing about Responses: A Unified Model of Reading, Interpretation, and Composition." *College English* 44 (1982): 459–468.

Petrosky, Anthony R. "From Story to Essay: Reading and Writing." *College Composition and Communication* 33 (1982): 19–36.

Petrosky draws the connections between reading, responses to literature, and composing. They share similar processes, "rooted in the individual's knowledge and feelings and characterized by the fundamental act of making meaning." The reading-response journal is used to generate responses.

Pradl, Gordon M. "Close Encounters of the First Kind: Teaching the Poem at the Point of Utterance." *English Journal* 76.2 (Feb. 1987): 66–69.

Probst, Robert E. "Adolescent Literature and the Curriculum." *English Journal* 76.3 (Mar. 1987): 26–30.

———. "Dialogue with a Text." *English Journal* 77.1 (Jan. 1988): 32–38.

Projects criteria for successful dialogue with a text along with sample questions for various foci.

———. "Mom, Wolfgang, and Me: Adolescent Literature, Critical Theory, and the English Classroom." *English Journal* 75.6 (Oct. 1986): 33–39.

The assumptions of New Critical literature instruction are questioned; reader-response concepts are promoted as is the appropriateness of adolescent literature.

———. "Response-Based Teaching of Literature." *English Journal* 70.7 (Nov. 1981): 43–47.

———. "Three Relationships in the Teaching of Literature." *English Journal* 75.1 (Jan. 1986): 60–68.

The three relationships—reader and text, among readers, and between texts—are examined as to their assumptions and classroom implications.

———. "Transactional Theory in the Teaching of Literature." *Journal of Reading* 31 (1988): 378–381.

Purves, Alan C. "Putting Readers in Their Places: Some Alternatives to Cloning Stanley Fish." *College English* 42 (1980): 228–236.

Rabin, Sydell. "Literature Study Groups: Teachers, Texts, and Readers." *English Journal* 79.6 (Nov. 1990): 47–51.

Reed, Susan D. "Logs: Keeping an Open Mind." *English Journal* 77.2 (Feb. 1988): 52–56.

Roemer, Marjorie G. "Which Reader's Response?" *College English* 49 (1987): 911–921.

A classroom situation in which contrasting responses emerge, serves as a vehicle for exploring the effects to such openness in the classroom and the attitudes and behaviors of teachers.

Rogers, Theresa. "Exploring a Socio-Cognitive Perspective on the Interpretive Processes of Junior High School Students." *English Quarterly* 20.3 (Fall 1987): 218–230.

Compares the effect of social context on interpretation in two types of discussion: question-answer and response centered.

Rosenblatt, Louise M. "The Acid Test in Teaching Literature." *English Journal* 45.2 (Feb. 1956): 66–74.

———. "The Aesthetic Transaction." *The Journal of Aesthetic Education* 20.4 (Winter 1986): 122–128.

The aesthetic stance is discussed as it may be adopted by a reader but also as it applies to other arts. Implications for curricula and classroom methods are suggested.

———. "The Literary Transaction: Evocation and Response." *Theory Into Practice* 21.4 (Autumn 1982): 268–277.

———. "A Performing Art." *English Journal* 55 (1966): 999–1005.

———. "The Poem as Event." *College English* 26 (1964): 123–128.

Rosenblatt counterposes her sense of the reader's role in "making" the poem against that of New Critics.

———. "Toward a Transactional Theory of Reading." *Journal of Reading Behavior.* 1.1 (Winter 1969): 31–49.

———. "Viewpoints: Transaction Versus Interaction—A Terminological Rescue Operation." *Research in the Teaching of English* 19 (1985): 96–107.

The distinction between the usages of *transaction* and *interaction* in defining or describing the reading act or reading event is clarified. Aspects of Rosenblatt's theoretical position are incorporated.

———. "What Facts Does This Poem Teach You?" *Language Arts* 57 (1980): 386–394.

The reader's activities in making meaning from texts are differentiated according to the focus of attention, the reader's adopted stance. The efferent and aesthetic modes are described.

———. "Writing and Reading: The Transactional Theory." *Reader* 20 (Fall 1988): 7–31.

Compares the reading transaction with the writing transaction, expressing parallelisms and differences. Aspects of theory are incorporated as well as discussion of the writer as reader.

Rouse, John. "An Erotics of Teaching." *College English* 45 (1983): 535–548.

In the context of exploring the factor of personal relationships between students and teacher, Rouse contrasts the assumptions and learnings of the theoretical approaches of Holland, Bleich, and Rosenblatt as well as the potential differences in personal relations.

Sampson, Gloria P., and Nancy Carlman. "A Hierarchy of Student Responses to Literature." *English Journal* 71.1 (Jan. 1982): 54–57.

Schaars, Mary Jo. "Teaching *My Antonia* with Guidance from Rosenblatt." *English Journal* 77.1 (Jan. 1988): 54–58.

Schuman, R. Baird. "Keeping Current in Critical Theory." *English Journal* 73.6 (Oct. 1984): 59–63.

Senger, Heinz, and B. M. Lynn Archer. "Exploring *Sounder:* The Novel, the Screenplay, and the Film." *English Journal* 78.8 (Dec. 1989): 48–52.

Schull, Ellen. "The Reader, the Text, the Poem—and the Film." *English Journal* 78.8 (Dec. 1989): 53–57.

Squire, James R. "The Current Crisis in Literary Education." *English Journal* 74.8 (Dec. 1985): 18–21.

Tanenbaum, Miles. "*1984:* A Confessional Reading and Teaching Approach." *English Journal* 78.4 (Apr. 1989): 31–34.

Tanner, Stephen L. "Education by Criticism." *English Journal* 75.6 (Oct. 1986): 22–26.

Tanner presents an exercise in which critically opposing views are discussed, promoting both awareness of multiple views and the recognition of the student's own voice.

Weaver, Constance. "Parallels Between New Paradigms in Science and in Reading and Literary Theories: An Essay Review." *Research in the Teaching of English* 19 (1985): 298–316.

Key concepts from scientific disciplines and current reading and literary theory are compared, illustrating that they share an emphasis on "organicism and process, specifically the process of transaction between interdependent entities."

Webb, Agnes J. "Transactions with Literary Texts: Conversations in Classrooms." *English Journal* 71.3 (Mar. 1982): 56–60.

Wyman, Linda. "Faking Out the Darkness: Trudell's 'The Jump Shooter'." *English Journal* 76.6 (Oct. 1987): 89–91.

Illustrates a class's aesthetic experience with a poem.

Zaharias, Jane A. "The Effects of Genre and Tone on Undergraduate Students' Preferred Patterns of Response to Two Short Stories and Two Poems." *Research in the Teaching of Literature* 20 (1986): 56–68.

———. "Literature Anthologies in the U.S.: Impediments to Good Teaching Practice." *English Journal* 78.6 (Oct. 1989): 22–27.

Discusses the tasks that textbooks assign in relation to general principles based on current theory. Exemplary activities are presented.

Zancanella, Don. "Teachers Reading/Readers Teaching: Five Teachers' Personal Approaches to Literature and Their Teaching of Literature." *Research in the Teaching of English* 25 (1991): 5–32.

Index

Note: Page numbers in *italics* refer to glossary entries. Page numbers with an "n" refer to end-of-chapter notes. Literary works discussed are listed under "Literature" and "Poetry." Authors of the literary works discussed are listed under "Authors of literary works" and under their own names as main headings.

and reading, 22–23
selection of, 156–157
shared responses to, 28
stance toward, 26–27, 214, *231*, *233*
teachers' own reading of, 51–52
validity of responses to, 27–28, 72–74, *234*
when writing "from" literature, 118–121
Thoreau, Henry David, 144–154
Transaction, *233–234*
Transactional theory of literature, 21–32, 64,
    76, 164–165, 218, *234*. *See also*
    Response-based instruction
and classroom practice, 28–32
and readers' responses, 23–24
    shared responses, 28
    validity of, 27–28, 72–74, *234*
reading in, 22–23
stance in, 26–27
text in, 25–26

Unsent letters, 180–181, *234*

Validity of responses, 27–28, 72–74, *234*
Vande Kieft, Ruth, 129, 135–136

Walker, Alice, 198–199
Welty, Eudora, 128–142
Women. *See also* Gender and reader responses
in "The Chrysanthemums," by John
    Steinbeck, 21–22
in "The Lament," by Anton Chekhov, 76
in "Petrified Man," by Eudora Welty, 129,
    130, 134–137

in *Trifles,* by Judith Glaspell, 187–196
Writers of literary works. *See* Authors of
    literary works
Writing. *See also* Journal writing; Writing-to-
    learn strategies
"about" literature, 124–125
as aid to discussion, 190
expressive writing, *231*
forms of, in response to literature, 117–118
"from" literature, 118–121
imaginative writing, *232*
of monologues, as role visualization,
    208–214
"of" literature, 121–124
"of" poetry, 122–123
of preliminary responses, 131
of scripts for response-based instruction,
    106–108
—*in response to specific works*
    "My Papa's Waltz," by Theodore
        Roethke, 222–227
    Native American literature, 200–206
    "On the Road," by Langston Hughes,
        208–218
    Ordinary People, by Judith Guest, 97
    Walden, by Henry David Thoreau,
        147–148, 149, 151–154
Writing-to-learn strategies, 176–183, *234*
biopoems, 177–180
journal/learning log writings, 181–182
topics for classroom discussion and critical
    essays, 182
unsent letters, 180–181